T0301300

Varieties of Capitalism

Varieties of Capitalism

Second-Generation Perspectives

Edited by

Thomas Palley

Founding Editor, *Review of Keynesian Economics* and Principal, Economics for Democratic and Open Societies, USA

Esteban Pérez Caldentey

Editor, *Review of Keynesian Economics*, Economic Commission for Latin America and the Caribbean (CEPAL), Chile

Matías Vernengo

Founding Editor, *Review of Keynesian Economics*, Professor, Bucknell University, USA

A SPECIAL ISSUE OF THE REVIEW OF KEYNESIAN ECONOMICS

Edward Elgar

Cheltenham, UK • Northampton, MA, USA

Published by
Edward Elgar Publishing Limited
The Lypiatts
15 Lansdown Road
Cheltenham
Glos GL50 2JA
UK

Edward Elgar Publishing, Inc.
William Pratt House
9 Dewey Court
Northampton
Massachusetts 01060
USA

For further information on the *Review of Keynesian Economics* see
www.elgaronline/roke

A catalogue record for this book is available from the British Library

Library of Congress Control Number: 2022950005

This book is available electronically in the **Elgar**online
Economics subject collection
http://dx.doi.org/10.4337/9781035312757

MIX
Paper from
responsible sources
FSC
www.fsc.org   FSC® C013056

ISBN 978 1 0353 1274 0 (cased)
ISBN 978 1 0353 1275 7 (eBook)

Printed and bound in Great Britain by TJ Books Limited, Padstow, Cornwall

Contents

Review of Keynesian Economics, Vol. 10 No. 2, Summer 2022, pp. 1–38

Theorizing Varieties of Capitalism: economics and the fallacy that 'there is no alternative (TINA)'

Thomas Palley*
Principal, Economics for Democratic and Open Societies, Washington, DC, USA

The Varieties of Capitalism (VoCs) approach has the potential to transform economics. It implicitly emphasizes the plasticity of economies, whereby their character and outcomes are significantly a matter of choice. This paper augments VoCs theory to include a distinction between varieties and varietals of capitalism. Drawing on biology, varieties correspond to species and varietals correspond to sub-species. The paper proposes an analytical framework that unifies VoCs theory. It adds a mesoeconomics that links macroeconomics and microeconomics. That mesoeconomics concerns the institutions, behavioral norms, rules and regulations, and policies that characterize the economy and influence its performance. The mesoeconomic structure is described using the metaphor of a box, the six sides of which correspond to the major dimensions of capitalist economies. The design of the box is the product of societal and political choices, which places politics at the center of VoCs analysis. Policy space and policy lock-in are important concerns as they impact the choice set. The fact that economies inevitably involve choice means there is an inescapable normative question regarding what type of capitalism society will have.

Keywords: *varieties of capitalism, varietals of capitalism, mesoeconomics, globalization, policy space, policy lock-in*

JEL codes: *P0, P1, D2*

1 INTRODUCTION: TINA VERSUS VARIETIES OF CAPITALISM

Margaret Thatcher often used the phrase 'there is no alternative' to justify her agenda to remake the British economy in a Neoliberal image.[1] That phrase has become known as TINA and the thinking behind it has seeped into public understanding. The result has been a tacit straitjacket which has restrained economic policy for 40 years. According to its logic there is not just no alternative to capitalism, there is no alternative to Neoliberal capitalism.[2]

---

* Email: mail@thomaspalley.com.
1. The phrase was first used in a speech to the Conservative Women's Conference, 21 May 1980, as: 'There is no real alternative.'
2. Neoliberalism is a political economic philosophy that consists of two claims, one political and the other economic. The political claim is that a free-market *laissez-faire* economy is necessary for the promotion and protection of individual liberty. The economic claim is that a free-market *laissez-faire* economy is the best way of delivering economic prosperity since it ensures economically efficient outcomes. Palley (2012, ch. 2) provides a fuller discussion of the history of Neoliberalism and critiques thereof.

Journal compilation © 2022 Edward Elgar Publishing Ltd
The Lypiatts, 15 Lansdown Road, Cheltenham, Glos GL50 2JA, UK
and The William Pratt House, 9 Dewey Court, Northampton MA 01060-3815, USA

Over the last twenty years there has emerged a compelling new discourse under the banner of Varieties of Capitalism (VoCs).[3] That terminology was introduced by Hall and Soskice (2001) and its appealing common sense opens the possibility of breaking free of the TINA delusion. This paper critically explores the new discourse. It argues that the VoCs framing has achieved what four decades of heterodox economics research has been unable to accomplish: a magical combination of words that effortlessly lifts the spell of TINA.

The terminology has kicked open the door, but the advantage needs to be pressed. That advantage will fail absent a theoretically coherent and comprehensive analytical framework. This paper argues the existing VoCs discourse is still under-theorized. First, there is the need to distinguish between 'economic theory' and the 'theory of VoCs.' Second, the theory of VoCs needs to distinguish between 'varieties of capitalism' and 'varietals of capitalism.' The latter are variations within a particular variety.

The paper proposes an alternative analytical framework rooted in the view that the economy is a socially constructed organization. That lens on the economy moves 'choice' to the front and center of the VoCs discussion. In sharp contradiction of TINA, societies have a choice regarding the VoC they want. That choice is subject to constraints, and an interesting feature is that past choices can constrain the current and future choice set via a process of policy lock-in and lock-out (Palley 2017/2018). That said, some space for choice will always be present. TINA does a double injury. First, it blinds society to the existence of choice. Second, it smuggles in thinking and policies that lock-in the Neoliberal VoC.

2   TINA AND MAINSTREAM ECONOMICS

The TINA construction of the economy draws importantly on mainstream economics. Absent that support, it is doubtful TINA would have managed to gain and sustain the traction it has. The connection to mainstream economics is evident in multiple ways. First, it is reflected in the Washington Consensus doctrine of the 1990s, which still prevails even if its repeated failures have compelled proponents to tone down their advocacy. The Consensus was defined by Williamson (1990), and it constitutes the basis for the standard economic reform package for troubled economies advocated by the IMF, the World Bank, and the US Treasury Department.[4] The doctrine tacitly claims to provide an economic model for economies of all stripes, be they developed or developing economies.

Second, TINA thinking draws on core economic theory as described by the competitive general equilibrium (CGE) model (Arrow and Debreu 1954). That theory posits an 'ideal' economy which is used to benchmark economic analysis. Real world economies are interpreted via that ideal, but they are marked by 'market imperfections' and 'government policy failures.'[5] The important point is the ideal is viewed

---

3.   In the rest of the essay VoCs refers to the plural (varieties) and VoC refers to the singular (a variety).

4.   The Consensus consists of ten policies: fiscal discipline, elimination of subsidies, market-determined positive real interest rates, tax reform that broadens the base with moderate marginal tax rates, competitive exchange rates, trade liberalization, liberalized inward foreign direct investment (FDI), privatization, deregulation, and legal secure property rights. Liberalized inward FDI has often been interpreted as capital account liberalization. Williamson disagreed with the latter.

5.   Market imperfections include imperfect competition, monopoly and oligopoly, natural monopoly, information asymmetries, externalities, and failures in the provision of public goods. Government policy failures include bureaucratic failure, regulatory capture and rent seeking, and policy implementation failure.

as universal and applying to all economies. Given that frame, mainstream economics explains VoCs in terms of pathologies which induce deviations from the ideal, combined with differences in natural endowments and differences in stage of development as measured by the extent of accumulated capital and technological know-how.[6]

Third, TINA thinking draws on orthodox economics' meta-identification with nineteenth century forcefield physics (Mirowski 1988). That meta-identification is visible in the constructs of indifference curves in utility theory, isoquants in production theory, and the notion of market equilibrium as a gravitation point. The natural world of physics is given and there is no choice. Modeling economics on physics has inclined mainstream economics to view the economic system through a similar 'no choice' lens, though market failure and government failure introduce a wedge in which human action matters.

Analytically, the notion of an ideal economy promotes cookie-cutter TINA policy thinking, exemplified by the Washington Consensus. It also promotes the notion of convergence among economies. Above all, it promotes mechanistic thinking that is eloquently captured by Solow:

> The best and the brightest in the profession proceed as if economics is the physics of society. There is a single universally valid model. It only needs to be applied. You could drop a modern economist from a time machine – a helicopter, maybe, like the one that drops the money – at any time, in any place, along with his or her personal computer; he or she could set up in business without even bothering to ask what time and which place. (Solow 1985, p. 330)

3   A BRIEF LITERATURE REVIEW OF VoCs THEORY

In Molière's play *Le Bourgeois Gentilhomme*, Monsieur Jourdain learns to his surprise and pleasure that he has been speaking 'prose' all along. Monsieur Jourdain's experience has lessons for many economists who may be unaware that they have been talking about VoCs all along.

This section provides a brief literature review that helps frame the subsequent argument. Unfortunately, the literature is fragmented as it comes from different disciplines that are significantly siloed owing to the character of academia.[7] Figure 1 provides a taxonomy of the existing approaches to VoCs analysis. The figure shows that analysis has principally developed within the political science sub-discipline of Comparative Political Economy (CPE) and economics. Reflecting differences in disciplinary focus, the two sides of Figure 1 tend to emphasize different features. Political science emphasizes the role of the state as an economic actor, and it also views the economy through the lens of 'governance.' Economics focuses on the mechanics of the economy and economic policy. That said, there are obviously significant overlaps as the state and policy go hand in hand.

6.   The attraction to the notion of an ideal economy has deep roots in the history of economic thought, going back to the late nineteenth century *Methodenstreit* controversy between the German historical and Anglo-Saxon schools which was won by the latter. The German historical school emphasized the economic importance of local institutions, laws, customs, norms, and context (that is, a form of VoCs analysis). The Anglo-Saxon school emphasized axiomatic reasoning which has led to the construct of an ideal economy rooted in its axioms.

7.   Given the scale of the literature and the fact that it is significantly outside my own discipline of economics, I engage this endeavor with trepidation. The justification is that 'outside' eyes can sometimes yield new insights. I apologize in advance for omissions.

                                   Journal compilation © 2022 Edward Elgar Publishing Ltd

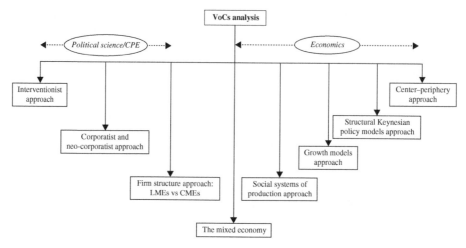

Figure 1   A taxonomy of prior contributions to VoCs analysis

3.1   The interventionist approach

Borrowing from Hall and Soskice (2001), the first column in Figure 1 is labeled the 'interventionist approach,' which is associated with the work of Shonfield (1965). The success of post-World War II (WWII) capitalism, referred to as 'modern capitalism,' is attributed to a new interventionist state. Part of that intervention is Keynesian demand management policy, but it is also much more. Planning and an array of supply management interventions that shape the composition of output, the investment share, and the distribution of income are argued to be critical.

France is identified as the poster child of success, while the UK is a disappointment. In diagnosing that difference in outcomes Shonfield (1965) emphasizes the role of the French statist tradition which provided a bureaucracy and a culture enabling the interventionist state. That is contrasted with the British political tradition which lacked those features and even inclined against them. That perspective and line of argument is absent in economics, and it opens the door to CPE. Shonfield's analysis focused on post-WWII Western Europe and identified the state as a key actor for modernizing laggard economies. That reasoning carries over to developing economies in which the state is a key actor for helping late industrializers catch up (Amsden 1989; Wade 1990).[8]

3.2   The corporatist and neo-corporatist approach

The second column in Figure 1 is labeled the 'corporatist and neo-corporatist approach.' Corporatism is an economic governance paradigm that was widespread in the 50 years

---

8.   An open question is the relationship between Shonfield's (1965) 'interventionist state' and the 'developmental state.' Is the latter just an amplification of the former with application to developing economies? Or is it a qualitatively different phenomenon requiring separate classification? One possible way of thinking about that is the interventionist state operates in the center, whereas the developmental state operates in the periphery.

                    Journal compilation © 2022 Edward Elgar Publishing Ltd

from 1920 to 1970.[9] It views the economy as consisting of three major actors: government, business, and labor. It advocates an economic governance structure in which business and labor form organized blocs, and then collaborate with government to shape economic outcomes. It is a form of centralized market governance and contrasts with decentralized market governance.

In the Neoliberal era (1980–today) corporatism has been on the retreat politically and intellectually. However, corporatism still provides a theoretical pole that is relevant for traditional CPE VoCs discourse which emphasizes economic governance. Additionally, it can be argued corporatist residues survive. For instance, it can be argued corporatism is relevant to Esping-Andersen's (1990) trichotomization of welfare state capitalism consisting of liberal (Anglo-Saxon), social democratic (Nordic), and conservative (Continental Europe) regimes. The last tend to be associated with countries that have a corporatist political history. A connection can also be drawn to Hall and Soskice's (2001) framework of liberal market economies versus coordinated market economies which is discussed next. Some CME countries have a corporatist political history.

The neo-corporatist approach (see Berger 1982) emerged in the late 1970s and 1980s. It was spurred by the relative macroeconomic success of Germany and other Northern European economies, both in maintaining growth and containing inflation during the difficult stagflation decade of the 1970s. In the neo-corporatist model economic success is explained through the lens of 'coordination,' which is an analytical refinement of the original corporatist argument. With the assistance and blessing of government, business and labor coordinate to deliver superior macroeconomic outcomes. Neo-corporatist coordination is argued to have been particularly successful regarding wage-setting (see Calmfors and Driffill 1988). The argument is that coordinated wage bargaining avoids the prisoner's dilemma problem whereby individual unions have an incentive to leapfrog each other with excessive wage demands, thereby generating macroeconomically sub-optimal outcomes. An essential feature of the neo-corporatist approach is a strong dense union movement that can speak on behalf of labor.

The neo-corporatist approach was fashionable in the 1970s and 1980s, when inflation was a dominant concern. However, with the political and intellectual triumph of Neoliberalism and the fading of inflation concerns, political advocacy of and analytical interest in neo-corporatism has also faded.

3.3   The firm structure approach: LMEs versus CMEs

The third column in Figure 1 is labeled the 'firm structure approach' and it represents the approach of Hall and Soskice (2001), who coined the term VoCs. They make the firm and its employment relations the fulcrum of VoCs analysis:

> We want to bring firms back into the center of the analysis of comparative capitalism and, without neglecting trade unions, highlight the role of business associations as key collective actors in the political economy. (Ibid., p. 4)

---

9.   It is often pejoratively associated with fascism, but it is better understood as being apolitical (Schmitter 1974). Thus, there is social democratic corporatism which emphasizes worker-centered tripartism. There is also Christian Democratic corporatism that emerges out of Catholic teaching on the economy (Schasching 1998). The latter advocates government, business, and labor come together to deliver a 'just' economy that delivers work which is consistent with 'human dignity.'

The central analytic construct is a distinction between liberal market economies (LMEs) and coordinated market economies (CMEs), which are distinguished by the way in which firms coordinate with and relate to each other and other economic actors.

> Broadly speaking, liberal market economies are distinguishable from coordinated market econo-mies by the extent to which firms rely on market mechanisms to coordinate their endeavors as opposed to forms of strategic interaction supported by non-market institutions. (Ibid., p. 33)

LMEs engage via arm's length market transactions, with firms being hierarchically organized and having the goal of shareholder value maximization. CMEs engage with other actors more in the spirit of partnership and via implicit long-term con-tracts.[10] The two modes of coordination are supported by different regulatory regimes, and they co-exist because the two modes have different comparative advantages rooted in the types of goods and services produced. Consequently, the modes produce differ-ent patterns of specialization of production.

The firm structure approach represents a major change of direction in CPE theory. It moves away from a focus on the state to a focus on the firm, though the state remains visibly present through its influence on the legal system and labor market policy. The approach also rests on microeconomic logic rather than macroeconomic logic, though the goal is still to explain macroeconomic performance differences.

The firm is identified as the central institution of capitalism, and Hall and Soskice use the Coase (1937)–Williamson (1975; 1985) theoretical paradigm to explain the existence and organization of firms. Their approach to employment relations is tacitly informed by the implicit contracts/handshake approach pioneered by Baily (1974) and Azariadis (1975). Within the firm, the focus is on firm governance, control, and deci-sion-making. That focus connects with the debate over the shareholder value maximi-zation (SVM) paradigm which has been argued to undermine economic performance (see Lazonick and O'Sullivan 2000). LME firms attend exclusively to shareholder interests and are dismissive of other stakeholders' interests, whereas CMEs are more attentive to the latter.

Hall and Soskice's (2001) firm structure approach is seminal in VoCs analysis, but it is subject to critique which helps identify where the analysis needs to go. A first set of critiques constitutes an internal critique that examines specific claims. For instance, Akkermans et al. (2009) question the claim that LMEs are radically more innovative than CMEs. Another internal critique focuses on the adequacy of the distinction and whether it can encompass all country capitalisms. That has led to a proliferation of VoCs types.[11] The big question is whether Hall and Soskice are too parsimonious with their two types, or whether their analysis is too one-dimensional (that is, the firm), thereby compelling a proliferation of types to handle the multi-dimensional nat-ure of capitalism? The latter is this author's view.

A second critique is silence on capital–labor conflict and exploitation. That silence stems from the adoption of a Neoclassical theoretical framework. The Neoclassical theory of the firm derives from the Neoclassical exchange paradigm. The starting

---

10.   Hall and Soskice (2001) focus on four dimensions in which LMEs and CMEs are distinct: industrial relations, education and vocational training, corporate governance, and inter-firm relations.
11.   For instance, Molina and Rhodes (2007) introduce the notion of 'mixed market economies (MMEs)' to explain Italy and Spain, so the framework does not even work for Western Europe. Similarly, King (2007) introduces the notion of 'liberal dependent post-communist capitalism (LDPC)' to characterize Central and Eastern European economies.

                    Journal compilation © 2022 Edward Elgar Publishing Ltd

point is the assumption that economic activity is motivated by the possibility of mutually beneficial exchange. The Coase (1937)–Williamson (1975; 1985) approach to theorizing the firm identifies impediments to market exchange which the firm solves. The result is an economy of markets and firms in which the addition of hierarchically organized firms helps reap more of the potential benefits of exchange. However, that is just one theoretical perspective. The Marxist theory of the firm (Marglin 1974; Bowles and Gintis 1990) views the firm as an instrument of exploitation so that the economic process is about both mutually beneficial exchange and conflictive exploitation.[12] The co-existence of exchange and conflictive exploitation renders the economic process one of bargaining, which is inevitably characterized by power. That, too, is absent in Hall and Soskice's (2001) approach, despite power and its distribution being essential considerations in capitalism.

A third critique is the narrow microeconomic focus. The 'LMEs versus CMEs' headline is broad and encompassing. However, upon excavation, the approach is purely microeconomic and centered on the firm, its employment relations, and its relations with supplier firms. That is insufficient to characterize capitalism. It is akin to looking at capitalism through a keyhole.

A fourth critique concerns the issue of destiny or choice. The general tenor of the argument is that CME VoCs are found rather than made, in that they cannot be readily constructed by policy (though the analysis is sufficiently ambiguous to leave the door ajar). That said, the CME VoC can be undermined by policy. CMEs seem to exist because of choices made long ago for unknown reasons. The two forms can co-exist because the CME form confers benefits on certain types of industries, giving them an institutional comparative advantage that enables survival. However, TINA lurks in the shadows, as the LME form seems to be the natural order that competition inclines the economy toward. That is a consequence of Hall and Soskice's (2021) underlying Neoclassical theoretical perspective which renders LMEs the benchmark natural order.

That leads to a fifth and fundamental critique regarding taxonomy. Hall and Soskice argue that the LME versus CME distinction is primitive, yet CMEs appear to be eroding. In this author's view, that erosion is due to the Neoliberal economic system, as has also been argued by Baccaro and Howell (2017) regarding European industrial relations. In that case Neoliberalism should be identified as a variety of capitalism, which is the argument developed in Section 4 below.

3.4   The mixed economy approach

Column four in Figure 1 transitions from political science's contribution to VoCs analysis to that of economics, with the latter's contribution largely coming from heterodox economics. That is likely because of the TINA inclination of contemporary mainstream economics which impedes engagement with VoCs analysis.[13]

---

12.   Palley (1998a; 2018) provides a simple model showing how the logic of exploitation can generate productive inefficiency. Firms may choose methods of production and organization that yield a smaller economic product but a larger profit share, yielding a higher level of profit.

13.   Mainstream economics does recognize varieties of economic systems, which has the letter P in the JEL classification system. However, that field is substantially a historical leftover from the Cold War era when economists studied central planning and there was also interest in collectivist economic organizations.

     Journal compilation © 2022 Edward Elgar Publishing Ltd

Column four is labeled 'the mixed economy,' which was an analytical approach that was popular in the Keynesian era (1945–1980), especially in British discourse. Figure 2 illustrates how the mixed economy perspective can be fit into a VoCs perspective. Economies take the form of mixed economies or centrally planned economies. A mixed economy consists of a mix of privately owned and state-owned enterprises. Hall and Soskice's (2001) firm structure approach can then be inserted below that, reflecting alternative ways of organizing privately owned enterprises. The state-owned sector can be divided into nationalized industries and publicly provided goods and services. The latter includes such things as defense services, transportation networks, and welfare state services.

Figure 2 illuminates several features. First, the mixed economy construct was very much a product of the Cold War, being juxtaposed with centrally planned economies. Second, since the end of the Cold War, the mixed economy concept has been discarded by mainstream economics in favor of the terminology of private enterprise or the free market economy. That is a mistake since government continues to provide significant services and be a large part of all economies. Third, the big issue surfaced by the mixed economy approach is the relative size of the privately owned and state-owned sectors, plus the composition of the activities within the latter.

Fourth, Figure 2 surfaces an important distinction between 'ownership' and 'governance.' The mixed economy approach was concerned with ownership. The focus was on the private versus state-owned distinction which was central to the issue of nationalization. Hall and Soskice (2001) are concerned with governance and organization of firms, which has become the focus of the modern theory of the firm.

Fifth, the mixed economy approach foreshadows critique of Hall and Soskice's (2001) framing of VoCs. Even if one accepts their LME/CME analytic distinction, it only applies to a portion of the economic system and is insufficient to fully characterize the economic system. Capitalism is a multi-dimensional system, which suggests VoCs need a multi-dimensional characterization. That critique also applies to the growth models approach which is discussed below.

Sixth, the mixed economy frame tacitly blesses government intervention. Nationalization was justified for industries with natural monopoly characteristics, strategically important industries, and as a tool for the modernization of capital-intensive industries. Public sector provisioning was driven by the rise of the post-WWII welfare state, and it was justified on grounds that the private sector underprovided public and merit goods

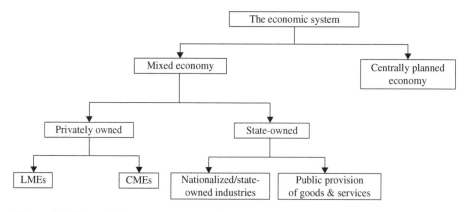

Figure 2   The mixed economy approach to VoCs

                    Journal compilation © 2022 Edward Elgar Publishing Ltd

(for example, health and education). The Neoliberal era has challenged that blessing. Nationalized industries have been largely privatized on grounds that they are politically contaminated in ways that promote productive inefficiency, and it is claimed problems such as natural monopoly can be better dealt with via regulation. The welfare state has also been under political attack and that attack has been supported by mainstream economic reasoning (Palley 2020).

Seventh, the state-owned portion of the mixed economy consists of nationalized industries and services produced by the welfare state (for example, health and education). Nationalization was one of the tools in the interventionist approach of Shonfield (1965), showing the two approaches are complementary.

Eighth, though not surfaced, politics lurks behind the mixed economy approach. It is relevant as it affects the relative sizes of the privately owned and state-owned sectors. As shown by Esping-Andersen (1990), politics is also relevant to the size of the welfare state.[14]

In sum, the mixed economy approach provides a useful angle for beginning the process of theorizing VoCs. Its replacement by the concept of a free market economy has been a step back in understanding as the state sector remains a large and critical component of every capitalist economy. Unpacking the logic of a mixed economy reveals the multi-dimensional nature of capitalism. However, the mixed economy approach is still only partial as there are other critical dimensions it misses. The challenge of theorizing VoCs is to construct a framework that can capture all those dimensions, rather than just some. Such a framework is proposed in Sections 6 and 7 below.

3.5   The social systems of production approach

The fifth column in Figure 1 is labeled the 'social systems of production approach' and refers to the French Regulation School and the Social Structure of Accumulation (SSA) School.[15] The former was pioneered by French economists Michel Aglietta (1979) and Robert Boyer (1990). The latter was pioneered by David Gordon, Richard Edwards, and Michael Reich (1982), who can be described as belonging to the US Neo-Marxist School. The two approaches share considerable elements in common, reflected by much co-authored work (for example, Bowles and Boyer 1989). For that reason, they are treated as a unified approach in Figure 1.[16]

The Regulation and SSA approaches shift the focus of analysis to long-run macroeconomics, reflecting their Marxist roots. Two fundamental components of Marxist thought are that the core problematic of capitalism is capital accumulation, and that

---

14.   Esping-Andersen (1990) distinguishes between liberal, conservative, and social democratic welfare state regimes. Palley (2018) argues that economic analysis of the welfare state should distinguish between mode of financing and mode of production of welfare state services. Welfare state regimes systematically differ regarding the size and scope of the welfare state, and those regimes also differ in how they finance and organize the production of welfare state services. Different political regimes choose different combinations of mode of financing and mode of production of welfare state services.

15.   The label 'social systems of production' is borrowed from Hall and Soskice (2001), but they only refer to the French Regulation School. The absence of reference to the SSA School likely reflects the siloed nature of the academy which impedes dissemination of ideas. It also likely reflects the fact that SSA theory is part of heterodox economics, which is ignored by mainstream economists and institutionally suppressed, thereby limiting its exposure.

16.   See McDonough et al. (2010) for an excellent succinct summary of these two schools.

process takes place in the economy, which is a system of social relations. The problematic is enduring, but the systems of social relations vary and change. Hence, the relevance for VoCs theory, but it is also a very different rationale compared to those that have come out of political science/CPE.

The SSA approach views capitalism as being organized through socially negotiated regimes of accumulation which generate long-wave growth cycles that end with crisis and a proclivity to stagnation. Crisis may then trigger the creation of a new accumulation regime. The Regulation School shares that broad perspective, but it is analytically finer. It distinguishes between the 'regime of accumulation' and the 'mode of regulation,' which together constitute the 'mode of development' (Boyer 1990). The regime of accumulation refers to the organization of production, including the determination of functional income distribution. The mode of regulation refers to the governance and disciplining of the system via policy and competition, both domestic and international. It parallels SSA analysis in that modes of development are prone to crises which can catalyse the creation of a new mode of development.

Several features are worthy of note. First, capital accumulation is central, and accumulation is prone to crisis via the Marxist mechanism of a falling rate of profit owing to rising capital intensity. Second, the organization of production and technology are central aspects of the analysis. Third, capital–labor conflict is also central. Fourth, technology and conflict converge in the labor exploitation process. Firms are organized and technology is endogenously developed by capitalists to discipline labor and increase capital's share.[17]

Fifth, the approach's Marxist inclination initially imposed a supply-side focus that was anti-Keynesian and had difficulty applying to the short run. That has been resolved by embracing the Kaleckian formulation of aggregate demand (AD), in which functional income distribution matters. That embrace has contributed to convergence with Post-Keynesian economics which has long advocated Kaleckian macroeconomics with its notion of demand regimes (wage-led versus profit-led). A key contribution to this convergence was the Neo-Kaleckian growth models of Rowthorn (1981) and Dutt (1984), which are the foundation of the growth models approach discussed next.

Lastly, the Regulation/SSA approach initially tended to ignore financial considerations, but that has been remedied by embrace of the construct of financialization (see Tabb 2010). That provides another source of convergence with Post-Keynesian economics, which has also engaged the construct of financialization (Stockhammer 2004; Palley 2007; 2021a; Hein and van Treeck 2010; Hein 2015; Kohler et al. 2019).

3.6   The growth models approach

The sixth column in Figure 1 refers to the growth models (GM) approach proposed by Baccaro and Pontusson (2016). They are political scientists, so it might be placed on the left-hand side of Figure 1. Instead, it is placed on the right-hand side for two reasons. First, that placement fits better with the flow of the narrative in Figure 1. Second, it rests on the Neo-Kaleckian approach to growth developed by Post-Keynesian economists, who have long worked extensively along similar lines, albeit not characterizing their research as VoCs analysis.

17.   This approach to firms was articulated by Marglin (1974), while the approach to technology was articulated by the historian David Noble (1977). In economic models, those features are captured through the effort extraction process (Bowles and Gintis 1990).

The GM approach adopts a macroeconomic perspective that focuses on the different components of AD and shows how different patterns of AD growth are associated with different demand drivers, particularly functional income distribution. Those different patterns of demand growth twist the structure of the economy, giving rise to economic and political consequences.

As mentioned above, the GM approach is theoretically grounded in the Neo-Kaleckian growth models of Rowthorn (1981) and Dutt (1984), which give a prominent role to the wage share. The growth model of Bhaduri and Marglin (1990) is also important as it introduced the distinction between wage-led versus profit-led growth.[18] Initially, much empirical research was directed at identifying whether country growth was wage- or profit-led (see Stockhammer and Onaran 2013 for a survey of findings).

In part, spurred by Baccaro and Pontusson's (2016) GM formulation, that empirical work has been elaborated to include additional influences on demand growth via debt-led and export-led growth (Hein and Martschin 2021). The former aims to incorporate effects of financialization on growth, while the latter incorporates long-standing Keynesian arguments often associated with development economics. Now, the framework is being further expanded to incorporate welfare state characteristics as determinants of demand growth (Hein et al. 2021). That expands the set of possible demand growth regimes.

The GM approach has become popular owing to its emphasis on wage-led growth which speaks to major contemporary political concerns. However, it too is subject to critique. First, according to Neo-Kaleckian growth theory, if an economy is wage-led, a lower wage share and increased personal income inequality (Carvalho and Rezai 2016; Palley 2017) will slow growth and lower economic activity. However, that underlying theory of growth is contested within Post-Keynesian economics, though the technical arguments have not crossed the divide into political science/CPE. One critical technical issue is whether the long-run equilibrium rate of capacity utilization is variable and subject to influence by AD. If it is not, the claim of wage-led growth fails.

Second, the GM approach has a narrow macroeconomic focus on growth. However, growth is just one facet of capitalism, albeit a critical one. In a sense, the GM approach is the twin of Hall and Soskice's firm structure approach. The latter looks at capitalism through the keyhole of microeconomics, while the former looks at capitalism through the larger keyhole of macroeconomics.

Third, the GM approach characterizes different patterns of demand growth as corresponding to Varieties of Capitalism, but there is a danger of defining Varieties of Capitalism in too shallow a way such that it loses significance by becoming just a list. For instance, export-led growth is widely viewed as being dependent on an undervalued real exchange rate. That might be better interpreted as a policy strategy rather than a variety of capitalism. That conceptual problematic is addressed in Section 5 below.

Fourth, and most importantly, the pattern and rate of growth of demand is a manifestation of underlying structures. That calls for a deeper theoretical dig that explains those structures: what are they, how do they affect the pattern of demand and demand growth, how did they come about, and what determines their evolution? Those issues are tackled in Sections 6 and 7 below.

---

18.   Kaleckian macroeconomics distinguishes wage-led versus profit-led demand. Neo-Kaleckian growth theory disguishes wage-led versus profit-led growth.

                  Journal compilation © 2022 Edward Elgar Publishing Ltd

3.7   The Structural Keynesian policy models approach

The seventh column in Figure 1 is labeled the 'Structural Keynesian policy models approach.' It is the approach this author advocates, and it is further elaborated in Section 6 below, which argues that many of the variety of approaches to VoCs analysis can be synthesized within it. The essence of the approach is that economies are constituted by rules:

> Structural Keynesianism views the notion of a natural market as a fiction, and instead maintains that markets are governed by rules and cannot exist without them. Some rules work better than others in promoting economic stability and social good, and the challenge is to establish those rules that do these things best. (Palley 1998b, p. xviii)

The Keynesian part of structural Keynesianism reflects the role of AD in determining output and growth, and AD is significantly influenced by income distribution. The structural component reflects economic policies, regulations, and institutions which are the matrix constituting the economy's rules. That matrix affects the distribution of power, which in turn affects income distribution.

Figure 3, drawn from Palley (1998c, p. 349), illustrates how the structural Keynesian policy models approach can be applied to explain the different macroeconomic outcomes in the US and Europe in the period 1980–2008. The US pursued a policy model (box B) that undercut the wage floor but generated expansionary macroeconomic conditions. The result was relatively full employment with rising income inequality. Europe pursued a policy model (box C) that maintained the wage floor but generated contractionary macroeconomic conditions. The result was relatively high unemployment, but the increase in income inequality was less. A policy model of expansionary macro policy plus maintained wage floor (box A) would have generated greater shared prosperity. A policy model of contractionary macro policy plus lowered wage floor (box D) would have generated depressed conditions characterized by higher unemployment and higher income inequality.

That approach is now being independently adopted by political science/CPE. Thus, Blyth and Matthijs (2017) call for recalibrating international political economy to incorporate macroeconomic policy regimes. However, the connection is not made to the Structural Keynesian policy models approach, reflecting the siloed nature of academia.

| | | Wage floor maintained | |
		Yes	No
Expansionary macro policy	Yes	A.	B. US
	No	C. Europe	D.

Source: Palley (1998b, p. 349).

Figure 3   Taxonomy of policy configurations

                                          Journal compilation © 2022 Edward Elgar Publishing Ltd

3.8   The center–periphery approach

The eighth column in Figure 1 is labeled the 'center–periphery approach.' That approach originated out of the Latin American Structuralist School of economic development (Prebisch 1950).[19]

Mainstream economics distinguishes between high-income, middle-income, and low-income economies. Economies are distinguished by their capital–labor ratios and their state of technological advance, with the development challenge being capital deepening and technological upgrading. The center–periphery approach maintains that the global economy is organized on systematically structured lines that privilege the center (developed economies) over the periphery (developing economies).

For Prebisch (1950), the global financial system constituted an important source of disadvantage as trade patterns generated financial flows to the center, thereby lessening financial constraints on its growth. In contrast, the periphery was subject to underlying financial outflows that impeded development and created proclivities to financial vulnerability and boom–bust cycles.[20] Furtado (1963) argued colonial development meant the periphery's pattern of development was outwardly focused, reflecting its role as supplier of primary commodities to the center. He also saw the periphery elite's cultural identification with the center and its imitative consumption behavior as problematic.

The center–periphery approach was taken a step further by Marxist dependency theory (Frank 1966), which characterized the structure in terms of exploitation whereby the center expropriated surplus and ensured a subordinated pattern of development. Appealing to Marxist labor value theory, Amin (1976) characterized the pattern of international trade as one of unequal exchange between center and periphery. That resonated with the findings of Prebisch (1950) and Singer (1950) which showed the periphery was subject to secularly declining terms of trade, with the price of its exports (primary commodities) falling relative to the price of its imports (manufactured goods) – a pattern that is now being repeated with periphery-manufactured goods exports. Both dependency theory and center–periphery theory resonate with the Braudel (1979)–Wallerstein (1974) world systems approach, which argues the global economy should be understood as a systemic whole rather than just a collection of national economies.

It is dangerously easy to view the center–periphery relationship as a one-way street with the periphery subordinate to the hegemonic center.[21] However, the periphery also impacts the center, as illustrated by contemporary globalization (see Section 6.3 below) – even if it has been designed by the center. The center–periphery approach also significantly changes the interpretation of globalization. The conventional view is that globalization promotes convergence via the combination of capital mobility and wage and profit rate equalization (Stolper and Samuelson 1941). However, a center–periphery perspective suggests 'hierarchy' is the destination, with periphery economies occupying a lower standing in the order. Rather than convergence there is diversity, but it is not diversity of choice. It is diversity imposed by the global economic system. From the standpoint of VoCs analysis, the center–periphery approach implies economies need to be indexed by their position in the global economy.[22]

19.   See Fischer (2015) for an excellent survey.
20.   See Pérez Caldentey and Vernengo (2016) for a full economic analysis of this phenomenon.
21.   That pitfall is encouraged by the fact that the center–periphery construct was developed by economists from periphery countries.
22.   An interesting question posed by developments over the past 40 years is whether China is part of the periphery or a new center (Fischer 2010; 2015).

                    Journal compilation © 2022 Edward Elgar Publishing Ltd

Lastly, another quasi-related approach is Gerschenkron's (1952) late industrializer framework. That framework is less pessimistic as it adds the twist that in some circumstances there can be benefits to being a late industrializer as countries can leapfrog the development process. They do so by adopting the technology and know-how of early industrializers, thereby avoiding the costs of innovation and learning which go with being first.[23] From the standpoint of VoCs analysis, it requires indexing countries according to whether they are early or late industrializers. If the issue of late industrialization fades with time, the relevance of such indexing would also fade with time.

4   HISTORICIZING VoCs ANALYSIS

Section 3 provided an overview of the theoretical terrain of VoCs analysis. There are two striking features. First, the discourse appears quite fractured. Second, it exhibits a tendency to focus on the present, giving little attention to history. An exception to that is the SSA approach, but even there the attention is modest. This section argues that a focus on history is important and has major theoretical implications.

Figure 4 provides a stylized history of VoCs in the North Atlantic region. It begins with eighteenth century mercantile capitalism followed by Victorian factory capitalism, Victorian globalized capitalism, managerial mass consumption capitalism, social democratic Keynesian capitalism, through to the current moment of Neoliberal capitalism.

The figure has multiple implications. First, it uses a taxonomy that is very different from that in Figure 1 describing the existing VoCs discourse. The taxonomy is constructed in terms of a historical characterization of capitalism rather than in terms of current technical characteristics. Second, the figure refers to just the North Atlantic region. The implication is that capitalism may vary by geographic region, reflecting

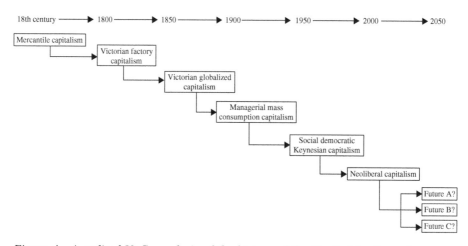

Figure 4   A stylized VoCs analysis of the history of the North Atlantic region

23.   Institutionally, late industrialization manifests itself in the financial structure, via reliance on investment banks to channel capital rather than decentralized financial markets. That reflects the fact that markets may not yet exist, and banks may also have superior analytical insight that enables better allocation of scarce capital.

                          Journal compilation © 2022 Edward Elgar Publishing Ltd

differences in both natural resource endowments and history (that is, economic, political, and social history). If capitalism varies by region, an essential question is: what is the relationship between those regions? To what extent is there a single world capitalist system versus a system of interacting capitalisms, and what is the dynamic between the pieces and the whole?[24] Those questions resonate with the issues raised by Latin American Structuralist theory, dependency theory, and world systems theory.

Third, today's capitalism is characterized as Neoliberal (Palley 2021b), but the capitalism of the future is an open question. Capitalism is a socially constructed system which, though not free to be anything, has space to take on a range of possible forms. That is the central argument of this paper. There is choice, contrary to the TINA doctrine. One of the challenges of VoCs analysis is to identify the margins and scope for choice. Moreover, those margins and scope are affected by past choices via the logic of lock-in (Palley 2017/2018).

Fourth, Figure 4 shows how capitalism is a sedimented system. Victorian capitalism is still present via the institution of the factory and via globalization. So too are the late nineteenth and early twentieth century business innovations of mass market consumption and the managerially controlled firm.[25] Keynesian social democratic capitalism is also still very present through the welfare state and counter-cyclical macroeconomic policy. The innovations of earlier capitalisms endure, reflecting the sedimentary process.

Fifth, capitalism should be understood as a dynamic self-transforming process, which connects with the logic of the Austrian School of economics as represented in Schumpeter's (1942) theory of creative destruction. The changing nature of capitalism calls for a theory of transformation, which is currently a lacuna within VoCs analysis. Figure 4 is suggestive of the type of factors that are important for such a theory: (i) Technology is important, be it engineering or intellectual technology. Victorian factory capitalism was spurred by the steam engine and its provision of a powerful reliable centralized source of power. Victorian globalized capitalism was spurred by the railroad, the steamship, the telegraph, and refrigeration technology, all of which facilitated increased long-distance trade – especially of perishable commodities. Mass market consumption capitalism was spurred by intellectual innovation regarding product marketing (for example, advertising and brands). Managerial capitalism was driven by organizational change within business. (ii) Events matter. Thus, the rise of social democratic Keynesianism was spurred by the Great Depression and WWII. The former served to discredit capitalism, while the latter created a decisive political opening for reform. The turn to Neoliberal capitalism was spurred by the stagflation dislocations of the 1970s. (iii) Ideas matter. Keynes's formulation of Keynesian economics explained the Great Depression and full employment in WWII, and Keynesian counter-cyclical stabilization policy was an important underpinning of post-war social democratic Keynesian capitalism. Likewise, the ideas of the Chicago School of economics were important in the turn to Neoliberal capitalism. (iv) Politics matter. Victorian globalized

---

24.   As regards interaction, one might distinguish between static and transformational interaction. For instance, Keynesian macroeconomics identifies a form of static interaction in the form of cross-country AD spillovers which change the level of activity within the existing system. Technological spread and competition constitute transformational interactions which change the structure of the pieces and/or the system.
25.   Identifying mass market consumption and the managerially controlled firm as a VoC shows how VoCs analysis connects intimately with business history, as exemplified by the work of Chandler (1977).

 Journal compilation © 2022 Edward Elgar Publishing Ltd

capitalism was significantly informed by Britain's adoption of free trade, symbolized by the 1846 repeal of the Corn Laws. Changing the political consensus was critical in both the turn to social democratic Keynesian capitalism and the turn to Neoliberal capitalism. In both instances policy has been critical, and policy turns on politics.

Sixth, Figure 4 is suggestive of a wave theory of VoCs akin to Kondratieff long-wave theory. The taxonomy in Figure 4 shows VoCs as being long-lived and the factors driving change (discussed above) have a resemblance to those in Kondratieff theory. The latter emphasizes major technological breakthroughs which spawn accelerated growth that then crests and dies back as opportunities for application are exhausted. A long-wave VoCs theory embraces a wider construction of technology defined as scientific and engineering ideas, business practice and organization, and policy ideas.

Seventh, the turn to social democratic Keynesian capitalism and Neoliberal capitalism were both driven by 'crisis' events. For the former it was the Great Depression and WWII. For the latter it was the stagflation of the 1970s. That suggests crisis theory has a role to play in VoCs analysis, with crisis sometimes being the handmaiden of the death and birth of VoCs. That connects with the SSA Marxist approach in which regimes of accumulation exhaust themselves, thereby eventually calling forth a new regime. However, the Marxist formulation of crisis is specifically constructed in terms of the falling rate of profit, whereas a VoCs perspective would permit a wider set of causes of crisis such as changed social expectations or economic dislocation from causes other than a falling rate of profit.

Looking to the future, multiple potential crises lurk over the horizon. Those include catastrophic climate change, employment dislocations caused by robotics and artificial intelligence, societal dissatisfaction with economic inequality and economic insecurity, and economic stagnation caused by Keynesian demand failure. Interestingly, those potential crises could set up a VoCs reversal that brings back a modified form of social democratic Keynesian capitalism. Indeed, the Neoliberal era can be interpreted in such terms, with Neoliberal capitalism being an attempt to bring back a modified form of pre-Keynesian capitalism. The implication is that capitalism circles back as well as moving on.

5   THEORIZING VoCs

Figures 1 and 4 provide two alternative taxonomies of VoCs analysis. Figure 1 taxonomizes VoCs in terms of theoretical approaches. Figure 4 taxonomizes VoCs in terms of historical experience. At first blush, the two figures appear orthogonal, which speaks to deficiencies in existing VoCs theory. The analytical challenge is to construct a theoretical framework which can piece the two together consistently. The balance of the paper is directed to that end.

5.1   The inescapable choice: which economic theory?

The starting point is recognition that capitalism is an economic system, which means explaining it (and its varieties) inevitably calls upon economic theory. Consequently, VoCs analysis confronts the inescapable issue of which economic theory to use in theorizing capitalism. The challenge of theorizing VoCs is illustrated in Figure 5 and involves four stages. The first stage begins with acceptance of the legitimacy of the concept of VoCs. The second stage concerns selecting an economic theory with which to analyse VoCs. The third stage involves applying that economic theory in

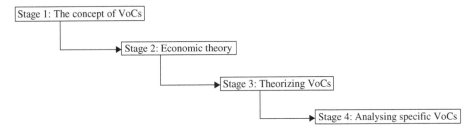

Figure 5   The four stages of theorizing VoCs

the analysis of VoCs. The fourth stage involves dissecting VoCs theory to accommodate 'varietals' of capitalism.

The first stage issue regarding the legitimacy of the VoCs concept was addressed in Section 2's critique of TINA. The VoCs concept rests on the view that the economy is a socially constructed system. That view rejects the notion of a fictional ideal economy against which existing arrangements can be benchmarked. This sub-section addresses the issue of selecting an economic theory with which to analyse VoCs.

Existing proponents of VoCs analysis are significantly Keynesian in inclination. The main features of Keynesianism are: (i) the notion of demand-determined output; (ii) the inability of economies to rapidly self-adjust and restore full employment via price level, nominal wage, interest rate, and exchange rate adjustment; (iii) belief in the real effectiveness of monetary policy (that is, fully expected monetary policy has real effects), which is usually viewed as implying a belief in a long-run trade-off between inflation and unemployment;[26] and (iv) belief in the effectiveness of fiscal policy, which implies the fiscal multiplier is always positive (though its size may be counter-cyclical) and bond-financed fiscal policy is effective.[27] That belief inclines VoCs practitioners to be against fiscal austerity, as exemplified by Blyth (2014).

The Keynesian disposition of existing VoCs theory puts it at loggerheads with mainstream economics which either rejects or substantially qualifies all four of the above Keynesian propositions. That observation illustrates the significance of economic theory which is an issue that has not been adequately confronted. The economic theory adopted in stage 2 will shape subsequent stage 3 theorizing regarding the institutions and functioning of VoCs. That is because the chosen theory will impact the interpretation of institutions and policy choices.

VoCs theory has originated out of the political science sub-field of CPE. That origin has enabled it to escape the strict confines of contemporary mainstream economics. Hence the prevalence of traditional Keynesian thinking. It is doubtful such analysis would have been able to emerge from within economics. In a sense, VoCs theory has flown under the radar.[28]

26.   Contemporary mainstream macroeconomics also believes in the effectiveness of monetary policy, but its role is to stabilize employment around the natural rate of unemployment. Keynesians make a stronger claim whereby monetary policy can shift the equilibrium unemployment rate.
27.   The potential ineffectiveness of bond-financed fiscal policy rests on the Neo-Ricardian hypothesis (Barro 1974) which is a pillar of modern mainstream macroeconomics.
28.   On a personal note, I have long envied political scientists who feel confident and capable of engaging in discussion of capitalism without going through the misery of economics training.

(footnote continues overleaf)

That is the good side of the story. The downside is VoCs discourse has been insufficiently attentive to theoretical controversy over how the economy works. As VoCs analysis gains standing it can expect to confront critique on those grounds. The danger is it will confront pressure from mainstream economics. That may take the form of being dismissed on grounds that it is theoretically unsound. Alternatively, it may be captured by mainstream economics and redirected back into the TINA mold.

There are some signs that this issue is already surfacing, as evidenced by emerging debate regarding the macroeconomic frame for VoCs analysis. The incipient debate is captured by comparing papers by Stockhammer (2021) and Hope and Soskice (2016). Stockhammer (2021) advocates the GM approach and proposes a Neo-Kaleckian growth model supplemented by the inclusion of inside debt, the presence of which impacts AD and can be the cause of financially induced cycles and instability. In contrast, Hope and Soskice (2016) advocate using a New Keynesian-styled macroeconomic framework.

In its most sophisticated form, New Keynesian macroeconomics is referred to as dynamic stochastic general equilibrium (DSGE) theory. It draws its inspiration from Arrow–Debreu (1954) theory but modifies the CGE model to incorporate nominal rigidities and market failures. That approach has been substantively criticized (see Dullien 2009; Podkamminer 2021; Storm 2021).

From the standpoint of the current paper, the critique is that New Keynesian macroeconomics tacitly adheres to TINA thinking because it retains the Arrow–Debreu CGE pedigree, albeit camouflaged by nominal rigidities and market failures. In effect, it retains the notion of an ideal economy that benchmarks economic analysis for all economies. Variety is implicitly deemed a product of economic pathology and the imagined ideal provides a blueprint of what society should aim for. Consequently, it also implicitly pushes a normative agenda aimed at a creating a CGE economy.[29]

An even deeper critique of the Neoclassical CGE ideal is its ontological impossibility. The fact that the theory is still embraced speaks to its ideological character. Moreover, intellectual engagement is treacherous as engagement tacitly legitimizes CGE theory, and engagement also risks trapping the critic in an unwinnable debate with a fiction.[30] In sum, CGE-based theory (which includes New Keynesian DSGE theory) constitutes a misleading basis for theorizing VoCs.

All theory imposes abstraction, and all theory also aspires to be universal. That is true of both Keynesian and Marxist theory. Keynesian theory asserts the universality of the principle of aggregate effective demand-determined output. Marxist theory asserts the universality of the problematic of capital accumulation and a falling rate of profit. However, unlike Neoclassical CGE theory (on which New Keynesian

---

Capitalism was always my motivating interest, but I felt I had to study economics first. To my deep disappointment, I found that not only does economics dismiss the notion of VoCs, it also dismisses the notion of capitalism. Economists talk of capital, but not of capitalism.

29.   Neoclassical economics emphasizes market failures. Those failures are realistic, and it sometimes appears as if they are interpreted as justifying the paradigm. However, those failures are fully consistent with Keynesian and Marxist theory, and there is nothing exclusive to Neoclassical theory about them. For instance, Adam Smith (1776 [2004], pp. 102–124) was aware of the adverse effects of collusion and restriction of trade and movement in *The Wealth of Nations*. Keynesian and Marxist theory accept those failures but reject interpreting them as the cause of departure from an ideal economy that would otherwise exist.

30.   Arrow–Debreu (1954) theory is a logically tight construction. The only way to disprove it is to engage with its assumptions, but that is what mainstream economics does its utmost to prevent.

DSGE theory rests), neither Keynesian nor Marxist theory assert an ontologically impossible ideal economy for purposes of understanding capitalism.[31] Instead, both are open process theories that deliver different economic outcomes under different institutional settings and contexts. Those settings are influenced by history and political choice, but there is no ideal. That makes them a superior basis for theorizing VoCs.

The analytic openness and enduring relevance of Keynesian and Marxist theory is illustrated by consideration of Neoliberalism. Palley (2012; 2021b) argues that Neoliberalism constitutes a VoC which replaced the prior social democratic Keynesian VoC. However, Keynesian economic logic continues to apply, as does Marxist logic. Neoliberalism has not undone the logic of either. It has just placed them in a new institutional and political context. Thus, from a Keynesian perspective one might argue we now have military-industrial plutocratic Keynesianism which aims to implement demand management policy by tax cuts benefitting corporations and the wealthy, and monetary policy that aims to underwrite and inflate asset-prices capitalism (Palley 2021a, pp. 484–486). Galbraith (2008) provides an alternative characterization labeled 'predator state' capitalism, whereby the state is controlled by Big Business which preys on the state.

Putting the pieces together, the existing VoCs discourse leans toward Keynesian and Marxist frames. There is good analytical reason for that. However, it also means the existing discourse leans away from mainstream economics and tacitly threatens it. Consequently, if mainstream economics engages VoCs theory, it will seek to impose a New Keynesian DSGE theoretical frame. Were that to happen, it would be a step back and the promise of VoCs discourse would be diminished.

5.2   Varieties versus varietals of capitalism

Stage 3 concerns the challenge of identifying and theorizing specific VoCs. Taxonomy is a key tool whereby biologists organize their understanding of the world, and it is a useful starting place for theorizing VoCs. Borrowing terminology from biology, there are four ranked categories: family, genus, species, and sub-species. Figure 6 applies that borrowed terminology to VoCs theory. The family is economic systems. The genus consists of mixed economies and centrally planned economies. All capitalist economies are mixed economies, with each having a large state sector. However, they differ in the scale and composition of that sector. The species is VoCs. At the bottom comes the sub-species which refers to varietals of VoCs, which are varieties within a specific VoC.

Varietals of capitalism (sub-species) are the most difficult category as they are easily misclassified as varieties of capitalism (species). Sub-species/varietals share major characteristics with species/varieties, but they also have different facets. Classification mistakes occur when facets are misinterpreted as major characteristics.

---

31.   Marxist theory also has a teleological idealistic dimension when viewed as a theory of history. Thus, Marx argued capitalism was a long and necessary stage through which society passed on its way to socialism. The logic of that teleological dynamic was capitalism is inherently beset by contradictions in the capital accumulation process and socialism resolves those contradictions. Removing that historical prediction strips away the teleological ideological dimension. In that case, Marxist theory reduces to one of proclivity to economic crisis. Capitalist accumulation is beset by contradictions that generate recurrent crises, each of which requires a system reset. However, the system can remain capitalist.

                              Journal compilation © 2022 Edward Elgar Publishing Ltd

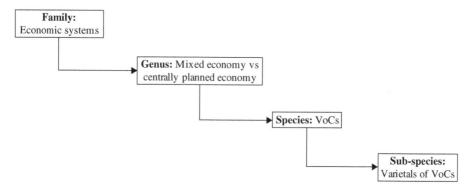

Figure 6   A taxonomy for VoCs theory

Social democratic Keynesian capitalism illustrates the sub-species/varietal problematic. Western Europe exhibited the paradigmatic form of social democratic Keynesianism. It had large government-organized welfare states that provided the full array of welfare state services (housing, healthcare, education, public pensions, and unemployment income support), and its Keynesian macroeconomic stabilization policy emphasized fiscal policy fine-tuning. In contrast, US social democratic Keynesianism was a varietal that can be described as New Deal military-industrial Keynesianism. It had a smaller welfare state, preferring to provide social protection via tax subsidies (Garfinkel and Smeeding 2015; Palley 2020). It also had far larger military spending. The New Deal aspect reflects openness to infrastructure spending and agricultural price supports. US Keynesian stabilization policy also emphasized counter-cyclical monetary policy. Western Europe was also more friendly to labor unions and tripartism. That shows how neo-corporatism is consistent with social democratic Keynesian capitalism, and it is better understood as a facet rather than a VoC. The important point is the US and Western Europe both had social democratic Keynesian capitalism, yet there were significant differences reflecting the fact that they were varietals (sub-species) drawn from a shared variety (species).

Neoliberal capitalism also exhibits different varietals. Palley (2012, pp. 21–31) distinguishes between 'hardcore' and 'softcore' Neoliberalism, with hardcore Neoliberalism corresponding to the paradigmatic form advocated by the Chicago School of economics. Softcore Neoliberalism is associated with the MIT School of economics and advocates some cushioning of the harsh effects of a deregulated internationally open economy. Using that frame, the US corresponds to hardcore Neoliberal capitalism, whereas Western Europe corresponds to softcore Neoliberal capitalism. Note that Hall and Soskice's (2001) firm structure approach is consistent with Neoliberal capitalism, with the LME versus CME distinction being a varietal marker. Baccaro and Pontusson's (2016) GM approach is also consistent with Neoliberal capitalism, with different growth regimes corresponding to varietal markers rather than different VoCs.

The variety vs varietals distinction is a critical part of the proposed approach to VoCs theory. It helps reconcile the existing literature described in Figure 1 with the historical framework in Figure 4. According to the logic of Figure 4, the existing VoCs discourse described in Figure 1 has a proclivity to characterize 'varietals' as 'varieties.' That said, the challenge of identifying and explaining varietals may be more difficult and much more rewarding than that of identifying varieties. VoCs tend to be long-lived so that in any era the principal challenge is one of identifying

                                   Journal compilation © 2022 Edward Elgar Publishing Ltd

varietals. Consequently, choice between varietals of capitalism is the principal margin of choice at any moment.

Lastly, CPE truly comes into its own regarding the question of varietals. Brief reflection suggests history and sociopolitical factors may be decisive for understanding and explaining why countries choose one varietal over another. That makes sense for explaining differences between the US and Western Europe in the eras of both social democratic Keynesian capitalism (1945–1980) and Neoliberal capitalism (1980–today).

6   BOX ECONOMICS: AN ALTERNATIVE THEORETICAL FRAMEWORK

The previous section argued that the analytical challenge is to construct a theory of VoCs that is rich enough to account for both different VoCs and multiple varietals within a particular VoC. This section presents an analytical framework that does that.

The current CPE approach to VoCs theory is dominated by the Hall and Soskice's (2001) firm structure approach and Baccaro and Pontusson's (2016) GM approach. Those two approaches represent dramatically different perspectives. The former is microeconomic and focuses on firms' governance, employment relations, and inter-firm relations. The latter is macroeconomic and focuses on different demand growth regimes. The two tend to be presented as competing approaches. However, rather than being at odds, this section suggests they are consistent. The problem is something is missing so that the theory is incomplete.

The framework presented below argues there is a missing middle 'mesoeconomics,' which can be understood in terms of the Structural Keynesian approach discussed earlier. As shown below, not only does that framework help reconcile the firm structure and GM approaches, it also provides a general framework for considering varietals of capitalism. It does that by surfacing the different economic margins that serve to define varietals.

Figure 7 shows a more generalized formulation of the Structural Keynesian policy models approach presented in Figure 3 in Section 3. The structural characteristics of the economy are now described as a demand regime (macroeconomic) and a supply regime (microeconomic).[32] The demand regime can be Keynesian or Neoliberal,

			Supply regime (microeconomic)	
			Social democratic	Neoliberal
Demand regime (macroeconomic)		Keynesian	A. 1945–1980	B. US post-2008?
		Neoliberal	C. Western Europe 1980–2008?	D. US 1980–2008

Figure 7   The reformulated Structural Keynesian economic policy model

32. 'Demand regime' replaces 'expansionary macro policy,' and 'supply regime' replaces 'wage floor maintained.'

while the supply regime can be social democratic or Neoliberal. A Keynesian demand regime corresponds to the virtuous circle growth model described in Palley (2012, ch. 9), in which investment drives productivity growth, which drives wage growth, thereby driving demand growth that spurs investment. The Neoliberal demand regime breaks the circle by severing the productivity–wage growth link. Instead, demand growth is driven by credit and asset-price inflation. The social democratic supply regime corresponds to an economy which is regulated (especially the labor market) to the benefit of labor. The Neoliberal supply regime corresponds to a deregulated economy.

The social democratic/Keynesian combination (box A) corresponds to the social democratic Keynesian VoC that ruled from 1945 to 1980. The Neoliberal supply/ demand combination (box D) corresponds to the VoC that has increasingly prevailed since 1980. However, regime combinations can be hybrids. Thus, prior to the 2008 global financial crisis Western Europe might be described as a combination of a weakening social democratic supply regime plus a strengthening Neoliberal demand regime (box C) marked by fiscal austerity and tight monetary policy. In the US there was more of a shift to a pure (hardcore) Neoliberal regime (box D), but it too preserved some of the Keynesian demand regime via large counter-cyclical budget deficits. That said, as noted above, contemporary US Keynesianism might be better described as military-industrial plutocratic Keynesianism as budget deficits were significantly due to tax cuts for corporations and upper income households. Additionally, the New Deal dimension fell away as infrastructure spending declined as a share of GDP. Those observations reaffirm the relevance of the 'varietal' construct discussed earlier.

6.1   Mesoeconomics and box economics

Mesoeconomics is key to filling in the economic details of regimes. As shown in Section 7 below, it is also what connects the economics of VoCs with the politics of VoCs, thereby providing a unified theory.

The demand regime concerns macroeconomics. The supply regime concerns micro-economics. Figure 8a shows mesoeconomics as being the piece that links the two, and it can be described in terms of box economics (Palley 2011; 2012, ch. 9.) Mesoeconomics concerns the government sector, the rules and regulations governing markets and firms, and economic policy. Using a computer metaphor, the mesoeconomic component describes the economic software that governs the economic hardware. That mesoeconomic programming affects both microeconomic behaviors and macroeconomic outcomes, and that influence is captured by the directional arrows in Figure 8a.

The mesoeconomic software governing the economy can be described via the metaphor of a box. A box is a six-sided three-dimensional object, but in Figures 8b and 8c it is reduced to two dimensions.[33] The economic logic of the box is as follows. Capitalism is a social system, with organized production and transacting that involves social relations. The core social relation is that between capital and labor, and that relation has an inescapable conflictual character. Power is central to the relationship and its effects ramify through the political economic system. It is especially relevant for the

---

33.   The metaphor of a box is attributable to the late Ron Blackwell to whom I am intellectually indebted. My original framing of the problematic was four-dimensional (a square). Ron viewed both corporate governance and finance as stand-alone factors related to power, whereas I initially viewed finance exclusively through the lens of AD and was inattentive to the importance of corporate governance.

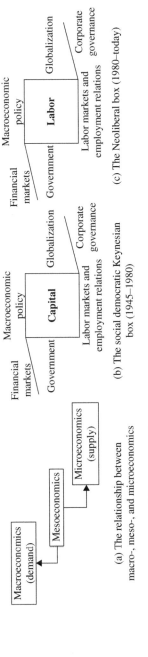

Figure 8   Mesoeconomics and box economics

functional distribution of income (that is, the wage–profit share split), which in turn affects AD, the rate of capital accumulation, the character of technological innovation, and political influence.

The balance of power is affected by the institutions, customary behavioral norms, rules and regulations, and laws governing the economy. It is also affected by macroeconomic conditions (for example, the unemployment rate). The box represents that matrix of influences. It identifies six critical margins where those influences come into play and affect the balance of power. Those margins are: (i) labor markets and employment relations; (ii) the government sector, which concerns public sector employment, the scale and scope of welfare state services, and the scale and scope of economic and social regulation; (iii) macroeconomic policy, which affects the unemployment rate and rate of growth; (iv) globalization, which impacts how the international economy affects the national economy; (v) corporate governance, which influences the goals and behaviors of firms; and (vi) the financial sector, which exerts control over corporations and affects the macroeconomy via provision of credit and asset prices.

The box is at the core of the proposed approach to VoCs analysis.[34] First, the box is central to the functioning of the economy and the determination of economic outcomes. Second, its design reflects both history and ongoing political choices, as well as being influenced by technology and the organization of production. The role of choice means capitalism is not a natural order characterized by singularity. Instead, capitalism is a socially constructed system. History and choice also explain why capitalism has a national or regional character.

The box is central to the capital–labor relationship as its design impacts the balance of power. In each era the box has a dominant tendency regarding that relationship, favoring either capital or labor. Figure 8b represents post-WWII social democratic Keynesian capitalism which favored labor, so that capital is 'in the box.' Figure 8c represents Neoliberal capitalism which favors capital and boxes in labor. Thus, earlier restraints on capital have been removed, as have supports for labor, and capital has also been given new supports and new options via Neoliberal globalization, which is fundamentally different from post-WWII globalization (Palley 2018).[35]

6.2   Some further refinements

Capital and labor are labeled above in monolithic terms, but the reality is they are fractured. For instance, Epstein (1992) distinguishes between industrial and financial capital. Additionally, industrial capital can be split into domestic and multinational capital, while labor can be split into manufacturing and service sector workers. Those subgroups have slightly different interests, which affects how they are impacted by the box and how they would like the box to be designed.

Recalling the distinction between varieties and varietals, a key challenge is how to decide when differences in the design of the box warrant classification as a different

---

34.   Recently, Hassel et al. (2020) have proposed a framework that has similarities with the box model. They link aggregate demand and supply via socioeconomic institutions, and those institutions can be interpreted as analogous to the sides of the box.
35.   For a fuller analysis of the six sides of the box as it applies to the US economy and how it has changed in the Neoliberal era, see Palley (2012, ch. 4, pp. 37–40 and ch. 9). Eisner (2011) provides a history of US political economy which can be read through the lens of the box framework.

VoC. Earlier, it was noted that VoCs are sedimented with innovations of the past carrying through to new VoCs. Figure 7, describing the Structural Keynesian approach, shows there can be hybrid models that are part social democratic Keynesian and part Neoliberal. Analytically, those complications mean it will be a judgement call as to when changes are sufficient to warrant reclassification of variety.

Lastly, the box is a dynamic structure that is constantly in flux. It is subject to marginal changes owing to changes in policy, changes in ideas and understandings, changes in behavioral norms, and changes in technology and business organization. That puts the process of change at the center of VoCs analysis. If the box is constantly being reconfigured, the factors driving reconfiguration are the ultimate determinants of the box's character. That requires consideration of political and societal forces, which are addressed below in Section 7.

6.3   Connecting the existing literature to the box

Figure 1 provided a taxonomy of the major strands of existing VoCs literature. That literature dovetails with the box. Shonfield's (1965) interventionist approach can be identified with the macroeconomic policy and government sides of the box. Tax incentives are used to stimulate and direct private sector investment and R&D spending, and government uses its bureaucratic capacity to plan economic growth and coordinate public and private investment.

The neo-corporatist approach can be identified with the labor market and employment relations side of the box, with government encouraging coordinated sector wage bargaining between business and organized labor.

The firm structure approach (Hall and Soskice 2001) also integrates neatly with the box. The approach takes a microeconomic angle on VoCs, and that angle intersects with the 'labor markets and employment relations' and 'corporate governance' edges of the box. It also illustrates the narrowness of the firm structure approach which neglects the many other dimensions of capitalism.

Baccaro and Pontusson's (2016) GM approach is macroeconomically focused. That explicitly connects it to the 'macroeconomic policy' edge of the box, but the approach also connects with the box in its entirety. The functional distribution of income is critical in Neo-Kaleckian growth theory which underlies their GM approach, and the box is intrinsically connected to determination of the functional distribution of income via its impact on the capital–labor balance of power. The mesoeconomic logic of the box therefore reinforces the GM approach, but growth is still only one facet of a VoC.

The SSA and Regulation Schools also have significant complementarity. The box can be interpreted as akin to a social structure of accumulation. However, SSA theory has historically concentrated on labor relations, exemplified by the 1950 Treaty of Detroit in which the United Auto Workers negotiated a five-year contract with General Motors that became the standard for the US auto industry. That contract is interpreted as symbolizing the cementing of a new post-war SSA between Big Business and Big Labor. In contrast, the box spotlights the many other dimensions that go into defining a VoC. The box can also be interpreted as akin to a comprehensive regime of regulation. The box surfaces the critical issues of capital–labor conflict and power, with its multiple margins influencing power and economic outcomes in a capitalist economy.

Lastly, the box framework connects with the social justice law and economics perspective on capitalism (Pistor 2019). Corporate law is critical for corporate governance and the behavior of the firm. Contract law is essential for all markets, labor law is essential for labor markets, and securities and bankruptcy law are critical for financial markets. Thus, law plays a critical role on multiple margins of the box, thereby influencing the balance of power between capital and labor.

6.4 More on globalization and the box

Globalization has been a key margin of Neoliberal capitalism, and the box diagram helps us to understand that issue as it relates to VoCs theory. Figure 9 shows how globalization fits into the box framework. The left-hand box denotes the center (Northern economies), while the right-hand box denotes the periphery (Southern economies). Globalization links the two.

Figure 9 yields several immediate insights. First, it shows how globalization serves to integrate national economies. Globalization is driven by a combination of private sector innovation (for example, technological and organizational innovation) and policy (for example, tariff removal and establishment of global intellectual property rights). Private sector innovations reduce the costs of internationally organizing economic activity. Policy changes also reduce those costs and may also make other jurisdictions economically more attractive.

Second, globalization is intrinsically relational and transformative. It is relational because it brings different economies together. It is transformative because doing so changes economies. The impact will depend on the character of the economies being joined and how they are joined. Joining together creates new conditions of competition and margins of competition, which change economic behaviors and choices. Figure 9 illustrates how Neoliberal globalization has increased contact between Northern (center) and Southern (periphery) economies. That has taken a high toll on Northern manufacturing employment and wages, which have been impacted by increased integration of Southern economies. In contrast, post-WWII globalization increased integration between Northern economies, and the effect was beneficial for Northern manufacturing and wages (Palley 2018). That shows how the economic character of globalization can vary.

Third, globalization raises issues about the relation between individual economies, their respective positions in the world economy, and the workings of the world economy. Figure 9 highlights that countries occupy different positions in the global economy, which is germane to the VoC characterization of country economies. That is captured by the classic 'center' versus 'periphery' distinction. It also shows countries are impacted by other countries, so that the evolution of national VoCs stands to be impacted by developments elsewhere. Those impacts work via such mechanisms as interdependency (for example, AD spillover effects), competition, and demonstration effects. The character of cross-country impacts will also depend on the character of the global economic system, which will affect the performance and viability of VoCs. That reasoning is behind activist demands for an 'alternative globalization' to replace Neoliberal globalization. Analytically, it is reflected in Rodrik's (2011) construct of the globalization trilemma and the debate over globalization's impact on national policy space (Palley 2021c). Globalization impacts policy space, and policy space impacts the viability of policy interventions associated with Shonfield's (1965) interventionist state.

In sum, globalization is a special side of the box because of its relational transformative character. Once globalization is recognized, national VoCs analysis is compelled to take account of both other country economies and the economic architecture of the global economy that governs relations between country economies.

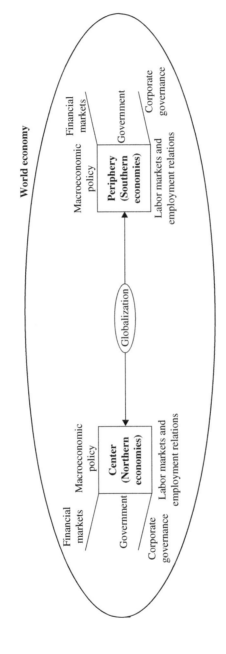

Figure 9   Neoliberal globalization and box economics

Journal compilation © 2022 Edward Elgar Publishing Ltd

7   MIND THE ECONOMICS BUT DON'T FORGET THE POLITICS

The primary goal of this paper has been to surface how capitalism involves meaningful choice. Contrary to Mrs Thatcher, there are alternatives. The analytics of the box is the terrain of economics. At this stage, I want to close the paper by venturing into the question of how countries choose the design of the box. That is the terrain of political science since the design is essentially an issue of collective choice.[36]

7.1   A stylized political–economic framework

The task of explaining the design of the box is massively complicated. The starting point is a simple stylized model illustrating the interface between economics and politics, which helps frame the discussion. That model is illustrated in Figure 10, which provides a topographical mapping of the political economic nexus.

The outer oval refers to the world economy, reflecting the fact that every national economy is part of the world economy. That means it is subject to the workings of the world economic system, is impacted by other economies in that system, and is impacted by the place it occupies in the world economy. Those factors constrain and restrict the available choice space, thereby influencing the ultimate design of each country's box. As noted above, the center versus periphery distinction is key for characterizing the place economies occupy. Periphery economies face constraints that are not in play with center economies.

The inner oval is labeled 'economic, social, and political endowment.' Every economy has a history and an endowment that it brings into the present. The economic endowment refers to its state of economic development, institutions, laws, business organization and practices, capital–labor ratio, level of technological development, accumulated wealth, distribution of wealth, etc. The social and political endowment refers to cultural and ethical values, behavioral norms, the complex of social relations, and beliefs. Those beliefs include ideas about how the economy works. Cultural and

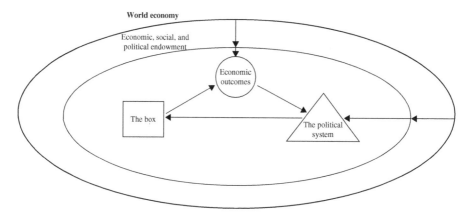

Figure 10   Design of the box: the interaction of economics and politics

36.   I venture across the boundary with trepidation, but if political scientists can engage in economics, it seems only fair that economists be allowed to engage in political science.

ethical values will influence the type of economy the country wants (that is, what might loosely be termed social preferences). Beliefs about how the economy works will influence what arrangements society thinks are viable (that is, the perceived choice set), and they may also influence beliefs about what is desirable. The TINA doctrine is evidence of the power of ideas. If arrangements are believed to be unviable, they will not get a political hearing and not be tried.

The political economic system is placed within those two ovals. It consists of the political system, the economic box, and the set of economic outcomes generated by the economy. The two outer rings constitute the context within which the system is set. The factors represented by those rings influence the behaviors of both economic and political actors, as symbolized by the inward arrows.

The political economic system constitutes a loop whereby the political system impacts the design of the box, which impacts economic outcomes that then feed back to impact political outcomes. Palley (2007; 2013, chs 1 and 12; 2021a) shows how financialization has been driven by financial interests pushing policies that changed the structure of the economy, thereby changing economic outcomes which in turn feed back to impact political power. The looping process is also analysed by Palley (2017/2018) in the context of the problem of lock-in, which is discussed in Section 7.4 below. Political developments can lock-in changes in the economy and vice versa. Acemoglu (2010) argues policy reforms in developing economies cause economic changes that may cause further (perhaps offsetting) policy changes. In a closer vein, Acemoglu and Robinson (2013) illustrate how policy reforms recommended by economists have economic impacts that feed back to affect political equilibrium in the political sector.

Political science has traditionally focused on the interaction between electoral politics and macroeconomic performance (see Hibbs 1987). The electorate rewards or punishes politicians for economic outcomes, which leads politicians to devise economic strategies that please voters in a way that creates a winning coalition. Now, there is growing awareness of the importance of politics for VoCs analysis (see Hall and Thelen 2009; Thelen 2012; Hall 2020). The box makes clear the reason for that. It substantially defines the VoC, which is significantly a political creation. Applying traditional political science logic, politicians in democratic polities will have an incentive to adjust the box in ways that foster a winning coalition of voters. Conventional coalition interest group politics and the determinants thereof should therefore be an important consideration in explaining the box and its evolution.

There are three critical features to Figure 10. First, the endowment (economic, social, and political) influences the structure of the economy. It does so by influencing the understandings and behaviors of political system actors, thereby directly impacting the design of the box. The endowment also impacts behaviors of economic agents which determine economic outcomes, thereby influencing the political system and indirectly influencing the design of the box. The influence of history and societal values is a recurrent theme in the VoCs literature. The model in Figure 10 explains that influence, which is represented by the arrows of influence from the endowment into the political economic system. Shonfield (1965) emphasized the importance of France's statist tradition and administrative capacity in explaining France's superior use of the interventionist tool set compared to the UK. That tradition and capacity have roots in France's history of absolute monarchy. Hall and Soskice (2001) emphasize the historical path of economic development in explaining the practices of CMEs. Differences in history, political tradition, and beliefs are also relevant to explaining why neo-corporatist wage-setting arrangements prevail in some countries and not in others.

Second, the looping process in Figure 10 directs attention to power, both economic and political. The political system substantially designs the economy, while the economy influences outcomes in the political system. That renders politics and economics inseparable, and power is the essential bond between the two. Political power determines political outcomes, which shape the box and economic outcomes, thereby influencing the distribution of economic power. The latter then influences political power and political outcomes. That looping process is central to the findings of Bartels (2008) and Gilens (2012) regarding the connection between economic inequality and political inequality.

Third, the system is highly dynamic. Internal developments and external shocks to both the economy and the political system can cause changes in the design of the box via the above mechanism. Capitalism is a live system which is constantly being adjusted and recalibrated in response to changing circumstances. That raises questions of how to assess and categorize such changes, which is discussed in Section 7.3 below.

7.2 Political systems as a characteristic of VoCs?

Figure 10 shows the political system having a significant impact on the economy via influence on the design of the box. That raises the question of whether there is a systematic relationship between the character of the political system and VoCs, and whether the political system constitutes a marker of capitalism? That argument is made by Milanovic (2019), who distinguishes between 'liberal democratic capitalism' and 'state capitalism' in his thesis of 'capitalism alone' (that is, capitalism as the globally hegemonic economic form).

Milanovic's focus is geopolitical competition and whether the developing world will follow the US model or the Chinese model. He argues the latter has the current advantage of fast growth, but it faces future economic challenges from the deleterious effects of corruption. Siegle et al. (2004) make a different argument, which is that liberal democracy avoids policy-induced economic black holes. Democracy is a mechanism for correcting policy mistakes. Authoritarian polities lack that course-correction mechanism. Consequently, they tend to get locked into failing policies.

A binary political framing is very parsimonious. Instead, capitalism might be quarterized politically into liberal democratic capitalism (for example, the UK, Canada, Australia), neo-corporatist democratic capitalism (for example, Western Europe), plutocratic democratic capitalism (for example, the USA), and state capitalism (for example, China). That expanded framing introduces additional political markers.

China's state capitalist political system has a large state-owned industrial sector – what used to be called 'nationalized industries.' It is also characterized by a greater degree of planning, reflected in extensive public infrastructure investment. France, with its statist political pedigree, has a history of emphasizing economic planning and it also supports national industrial champions. Germany and Northern European countries (neo-corporatist democratic capitalism) are more supportive of worker council representation within firms and sector wage bargaining. Lastly, the US (plutocratic democratic capitalism) has embraced 'hardcore' Neoliberalism, whereas the other Anglo-Saxon economies (liberal democratic capitalism) have embraced 'softcore' Neoliberalism.

Anglo-Saxon countries have a history of constitutional monarchy, a common law legal tradition, and democracy is organized on a parliamentary first-past-the-post principle. Western Europe has a history of absolutist monarchy, a Roman law legal tradition, and democracy is organized on proportional representation. Since all have roughly the same level of economic development, that suggests those political and legal differences may contribute to explaining differences in varietals of capitalism.

There is logic to that as the political system fundamentally impacts the economy via the design of the box. Employment relations are a form of political problem, and it makes sense that countries would seek to solve them in a similar way to how they solve other political problems. The implication is the political system may be another meaningful marker for both varieties and varietals of capitalism.[37]

7.3   Theorizing change within and of VoCs

The discussion of Figure 10 emphasized how capitalism is a dynamic changing system. That begs a theory of change, the first step of which is to identify what constitutes change. That question relates to the distinction between varieties and varietals. There is a need to distinguish between (i) changes of variety, (ii) changes of varietal, and (iii) changes within a varietal. Note, that framing introduces a distinction between 'of' and 'within.'

Regarding changes within a varietal, governments respond to the ordinary course of events and make policy changes. For instance, the monetary policy authority may decide to change its inflation target or interest-rate-setting policy guideline. Governments also turn over through the normal political process, which may deliver policy change that affects the box. For instance, a new government may raise the minimum wage, which impacts the 'labor market and employment relations' side of the box. Such policy recalibrations constitute changes within a varietal and are commonplace. For a democracy, they can be explained by the conventional political science of electoral politics and interest group competition.

A more difficult task is to define changes of varietals of capitalism. That begins with acceptance of the proposed 'variety vs varietal' distinction. A change of varietal corresponds to substantive change of the box, yet still leaves the overall character unchanged. As for the politics of varietal change, they too fall within the confines of conventional political science coalition interest group analysis. The impulse for change is the forces that make for changing power of interest groups and changing interest group demands, which then change political outcomes.[38]

Change of variety constitutes more fundamental change. Recalling Figure 4's stylized history of North Atlantic capitalism, variety change can be driven by technology, business practice, and politics. The shift to Victorian factory capitalism was driven by changed technology. Victorian globalized capitalism was driven by a combination of politics and technological advance. The shift to managerial mass market capitalism

---

37.   The political taxonomy begs the questions of whether it is sufficient to incorporate the political systems of East Asia and Latin America, and whether their political systems impact their capitalism?

38.   Drawing on current events, President Biden's economic program can be viewed as a change of varietal. His Build Back Better program proposes the introduction of universal pre-kindergarten education, an expanded permanent child tax credit, significant climate-change-related investment, marginal changes to low-cost housing provision, and marginal changes to Medicare that expanded coverage and lowered costs. Additionally, the Biden administration supports a significant increase in the minimum wage and passage of The Protecting the Right to Organize Act. The US would remain characterized by Neoliberal capitalism. However, the program would deliver a 'softer' version, constituting a change of varietal. The Biden administration's difficulty getting its agenda passed reflects its insufficient coalition strength, and it is also hobbled by the US political system which permits gerrymandering of Congressional districts and gives excessive Senate representation to conservative rural states.

was driven by changed business practice, while the shifts to both social democratic Keynesian capitalism and Neoliberal capitalism were politically driven.[39]

Events and ideas matter for politically driven change of variety. Dislocating events were critical for both the shift to social democratic Keynesian capitalism and the shift to Neoliberalism. The Great Depression was critical for the former, while the stagflation of the 1970s was critical for the latter. Changed ideas are also critical. The Keynesian revolution in macroeconomics was critical for the shift to social democratic Keynesian capitalism, while the shift to Neoliberalism was assisted by the rise of the Chicago School of economics. Both dislocating events and changed ideas foster the political demand for and supply of change.[40]

7.4   Policy space and policy lock-in

Varieties and varietals of capitalism reflect politically shaped societal choices. That makes the choice set a key issue, which connects to the issue of policy space. That issue has been raised in connection with Neoliberal globalization, which is argued to reduce and twist policy space (Palley 2021c). It does so by rendering unfeasible policies which were previously feasible. That can be either by changing the cost–benefit profile of policies, or via international agreements that explicitly make certain policies illegal (for example, tariffs and subsidies).

Rodrik (1997; 2011) notes how globalization creates economic winners and losers, while making it more difficult to implement policies that compensate and protect losers. In effect, it raises the costs and lowers the benefits of policy interventions that compensate. Chang (2002) characterizes international trade agreements of the past 40 years as 'kicking away the ladder' by making illegal previously effective development policies. Those examples illustrate the policy space issue and connect with the discussion in Section 3.8 regarding the designed character of the center–periphery relationship.

Another mechanism whereby globalization has shrunk policy space is via intellectual monopoly, which connects with the earlier discussion of the Washington Consensus. Part of globalization has been intellectual globalization whereby technocrats from around the world are trained at elite institutions such as Harvard University's Kennedy School. They then take that training back to their countries where they shape policy according to what they have been taught. The International Monetary Fund, the World Bank, and other multilateral institutions are also part of this mechanism, providing conduits for global implementation and enforcement of dominant ideas.[41]

39.   It could be argued that the Neoliberal era has witnessed a change of variety through Neoliberal globalization. The first 20 years corresponded to national Neoliberal capitalism. Since the mid 1990s, there has been a shift to global Neoliberal capitalism driven by the founding of the World Trade Organization, the North American Free Trade Agreement, and the full admission of China into the global trading system.
40.   In both instances, there were also other supportive political developments. In the 1930s and 1940s it was the political competition and threat provided by communism and the Soviet Union. In the 1970s it was the social backlash spurred by the civil rights movement, the peace movement against the Vietnam War, and the anti-establishment counterculture movement.
41.   That mechanism is exemplified by Chile's infamous 'Chicago boys' episode in the 1980s, when former students of Milton Friedman implemented a Neoliberal economic program for the Pinochet dictatorship along lines suggested by the Chicago School of Economics.

As regards VoCs analysis, shrinking policy space has two important implications. First, reduced policy space will tend to reduce heterogeneity of capitalism. A smaller choice set means less variation of choice outcomes. That is very relevant for the evolution of varietals of capitalism and would predict economies display increasing similarity under Neoliberal capitalism. Second, reduced policy space cuts off paths of development. Consequently, emerging market economies may get trapped and rendered unable to close the gap with developed economies. In terms of core–periphery theory, shrinking policy space cements the existing structure.

The issue of policy space connects with the issue of policy lock-in and lock-out (Palley 2017/2018). The logic of policy lock-in is that policies may be very hard to reverse, and even if they are reversed, the economy may not revert to its initial condition. Consequently, policy decisions regarding design of the box may near-irrevocably change the economy's structure, changing both the economy's performance and future policy possibilities.

Policy lock-in is illustrated by the euro and trade agreements which have created new institutional arrangements and business patterns that are very costly to reverse. Those costs lock-in the new arrangements. In the US, globalization has resulted in evisceration of manufacturing labor unions. Those unions were formed in a different political era and reversing globalization policy would not bring them back in full. Even standard macroeconomic policy may have hysteretic effects by causing changed economic outcomes that impact the distribution of wealth and income, thereby causing changes in political power that may lock-in the changed policy.

Lock-in is also important for understanding financialization (Palley 2021a, pp. 487–489), as it has increased stock market participation and home ownership, which has changed people's economic interests and political economic identification. Additionally, lock-in helps explain the political economics of the welfare state (Palley 2020, pp. 603–605), as the creation of benefits and entitlements creates new political constituencies that make repeal of such changes difficult.

As regards VoCs analysis, lock-in helps explain the durability and persistence of both varieties and varietals of capitalism, which can endure even if performance is poor. Lock-in also explains why cross-country differences may persist, as lock-in keeps countries different once they have gone down different paths. Lastly, and counter-intuitively, lock-in also explains homogeneity because diversity may be hard to recover once lost. In effect, lock-in can be a form of quasi-extinction mechanism. Thus, if shrinking policy space reduces 'softer' varietals of Neoliberal capitalism, lock-in makes it hard to recover those varietals.

8   CONCLUSION: TAKING STOCK

The VoCs approach to capitalism has the potential to transform economics. It implicitly emphasizes the plasticity of economies, whereby their character and outcomes are significantly a matter of choice. The paper augmented VoCs theory to include a distinction between varieties and varietals of capitalism. Drawing on biology, varieties correspond to species, and varietals correspond to sub-species. Varieties are rarer, whereas varietals are plentiful. Ironically, varietals may be far more important, as economies are characterized by a given variety at each moment in time, and change of varietal is easier and more common.

The paper proposed an analytical framework that unifies VoCs theory. It adds a mesoeconomics that links macroeconomics and microeconomics. Mesoeconomics concerns institutions, behavioral norms, rules and regulations, and policies that characterize the economy and influence its performance. The mesoeconomic structure was described using the metaphor of a box, the six sides of which correspond to the major dimensions of capitalist economies, with globalization being a special side. The box metaphor illustrates how economic arrangements can favor capital or labor.

The design of the box is the product of societal and political choices, which places politics and power at the center of VoCs analysis. Policy space and policy lock-in are important concerns as they impact the choice set. Since the box is a product of sociopolitical choice, country capitalisms are marked by their political and legal traditions.

The fact that economies inevitably involve choice means there is an inescapable implicit normative question regarding what type of capitalism society will have? Mrs Thatcher's TINA argues for Neoliberal capitalism and uses the rhetorical trick that it is the only viable form. Mainstream economics has helped promote that view. VoCs analysis potentially frees economics from the TINA straitjacket. In doing so, it creates a research agenda that is a blend of positive and normative economics. The positive agenda is to understand the workings of alternative varieties and varietals of capitalism. The normative agenda is to help guide society in its deliberations regarding different varieties and varietals. My personal take on that agenda is what I term 'economics for democratic and open societies.' At a time when democracy is threatened by a rising tide of political intolerance and proto-fascism, it is vital we understand what economic arrangements are needed to support democracy and open society.

REFERENCES

Acemoglu, D. (2010), 'Theory, general equilibrium, and political economy in development,' *Journal of Economic Perspectives*, 24(3), 17–32.

Acemoglu, D. and J.A. Robinson (2013), 'Economics versus politics: pitfalls of policy advice,' *Journal of Economic Perspectives*, 27(2), 173–192.

Aglietta, M. (1979), *A Theory of Capitalist Regulation*, London: NLB.

Akkermans, D., C. Castaldi, and B. Los (2009), 'Do "liberal market economies" really innovate more radically than "coordinated market economies"? Hall and Soskice reconsidered,' *Research Policy*, 38(1), 181–191.

Amin, S. (1976), *Unequal Development*, Brighton, UK: Harvester Press.

Amsden, A.H. (1989), *Asia's Next Giant: South Korea and Late Industrialization*, New York: Oxford University Press.

Arrow, K.J. and G. Debreu (1954), 'Existence of an equilibrium for a competitive economy,' *Econometrica*, 22(3), 265–290.

Azariadis, C. (1975), 'Implicit contracts and underemployment equilibria,' *Journal of Political Economy*, 83(6), 1183–1202.

Baccaro, L. and C. Howell (2017), *Trajectories of Neoliberal Transformation: European Industrial Relations Since 1970*, Cambridge, UK: Cambridge University Press.

Baccaro, L. and J. Pontusson (2016), 'Rethinking comparative political economy: the growth model perspective,' *Politics & Society*, 44(2), 175–207.

Baily, M.N. (1974), 'Wages and employment under uncertain demand,' *Review of Economic Studies*, 41(1), 37–50.

Barro, R.J. (1974), 'Are government bonds net wealth?,' *Journal of Political Economy*, 82(6), 1095–1117.

Bartels, L.M. (2008), *Unequal Democracy: The Political Economy of the New Gilded Age*, New York and Princeton, NJ: Russell Sage Foundation and Princeton University Press.

Berger, S. (1982), *Organizing Interests in Western Europe*, New York: Cambridge University Press.

Bhaduri, A. and S.A. Marglin (1990), 'Unemployment and the real wage: the economic basis for contesting political ideologies,' *Cambridge Journal of Economics*, 14(4), 375–393.

Blyth, M. (2014), *Austerity: The History of a Dangerous Idea*, Oxford: Oxford University Press.

Blyth, M. and M. Matthijs (2017), 'Black swans, lame ducks, and the mystery of IPE's missing macroeconomy,' *Review of International Political Economy*, 24(2), 203–231.

Bowles, S. and R. Boyer (1989), 'Labor discipline and aggregate demand,' *American Economic Review*, 78(2), 395–400.

Bowles, S. and H. Gintis (1990), 'Contested exchange: new microfoundations for the political economy of capitalism,' *Politics & Society*, 18(2), 165–222.

Boyer, R. (1990), *The Regulation School: A Critical Introduction*, C. Charney (trans.), New York: Columbia University Press.

Braudel, F. (1979 [1992]), *Civilization and Capitalism, 15th–18th Century: Vol III, The Perspective of the World*, Berkeley, CA: University of California Press.

Calmfors, L. and J. Drifill (1988), 'Bargaining structure, corporatism and macroeconomic performance,' *Economic Policy*, 3(6), 13–61.

Carvalho, L. and A. Rezai (2016), 'Personal income inequality and aggregate demand,' *Cambridge Journal of Economics*, 40(2), 491–505.

Chandler, A.D., Jr (1977), *The Visible Hand: The Managerial Revolution in American Business*, Cambridge, MA: Belknap Press of Harvard University Press.

Chang, H.J. (2002), *Kicking Away the Ladder: Development Strategy in Historical Perspective*, London: Anthem Press.

Coase, R.H. (1937), 'The nature of the firm,' *Economica*, 4(16), 386–405.

Dullien, S. (2009), 'The New Consensus from a traditional Keynesian and Post-Keynesian perspective: a worthwhile foundation for research or just a waste of time?,' Working Paper 12/2009, IMK Macroeconomic Policy Institutte, Dusseldorf, Germany.

Dutt, A.K. (1984), 'Stagnation, income distribution, and monopoly power,' *Cambridge Journal of Economics*, 8(1), 25–40.

Eisner, M.A. (2011), *The American Political Economy: Institutional Evolution of Market and State*, New York: Routledge.

Epstein, G. (1992), 'A political economy model of comparative central banking,' *Review of Radical Political Economics*, 24(1), 1–30.

Esping-Andersen, G. (1990), *The Three Worlds of Welfare Capitalism*, Princeton, NJ: Princeton University Press.

Fischer, A.M. (2010), 'Is China turning Latin? China's balancing act between power and dependence in the lead up to the global crisis,' *Journal of International Development*, 22(6), 739–757.

Fischer, A.M. (2015), 'The end of peripheries? On the enduring relevance of structuralism for understanding contemporary global development,' *Development and Change*, 46(4), 700–732.

Frank, A.G. (1966), 'The development of underdevelopment,' *Monthly Review*, 18(4), 17–31.

Furtado, C.M. (1963), *The Economic Growth of Brazil: A Survey from Colonial to Modern Times*, Los Angeles: University of California Press.

Galbraith, J.K. (2008), *The Predator State: How Conservatives Abandoned the Free Market and Why Liberals Should Too*, New York: Free Press.

Garfinkel, I. and T. Smeeding (2015), 'Welfare state myths and measurement,' *Capitalism and Society*, 10(1), Article 1.

Gerschenkron, A. (1952 [1962]), 'Economic backwardness in historical perspective,' in A. Gerschenkron, *Economic Backwardness in Historical Perspective: A Book of Essays*, Cambridge, MA: The Belknap Press of Harvard University, pp. 5–30.

Gilens, M. (2012), *Affluence and Influence: Economic Inequality and Political Power in America*, Princeton, NJ: Princeton University Press.

Gordon, D.M., R.C. Edwards, and M. Reich (1982), *Segmented Work, Divided Workers: The Historical Transformation of Labor in the United States*, New York: Cambridge University Press.

Hall, P.A. (2020), 'The electoral politics of growth regimes,' *Perspectives on Politics*, 18(1), 185–199.

Hall, P.A. and D. Soskice (2001), 'An introduction to varieties of capitalism,' in P.A. Hall and D. Soskice (eds), *Varieties of Capitalism: The Institutional Foundations of Comparative Advantage*, Oxford: Oxford University Press, pp. 1–70.

Hall, P.A. and K. Thelen (2009), 'Institutional change in varieties of capitalism,' *Socio-Economic Review*, 7(1), 7–34.

Hassel, A., B. Palier, and S. Avlijaš (2020), 'The pursuit of growth regimes, growth strategies, and welfare reform in advanced capitalist countries,' *Stato e Meracto*, Fasciolo, 1 April.

Hein, E. (2015), 'Finance-dominated capitalism and the re-distribution of income: a Kaleckian perspective,' *Cambridge Journal of Economics*, 39(3), 907–934.

Hein, E. and J. Martschin (2021), 'Demand and growth regimes in finance-dominated capitalism and the role of the macroeconomic policy regime: a post-Keynesian comparative study on France, Germany, Italy and Spain before and after the Great Financial Crisis and the Great Recession,' *Review of Evolutionary Political Economy*, 2(3), 493–527.

Hein, E., W. Paternesi-Meloni, and P. Tridico (2021), 'Welfare models and demand-led growth regimes before and after the financial and economic crisis,' *Review of International Political Economy*, 28(5), 1196–1223.

Hein, E. and T. van Treeck (2010), 'Financialization in post-Keynesian models of distribution and growth: a systematic review,' in M. Setterfield (ed.), *Handbook of Alternative Theories of Economic Growth*, Cheltenham, UK and Northampton, MA: Edward Elgar Publishing, pp. 277–292.

Hibbs, D.A., Jr (1987), *The American Political Economy: Macroeconomics and Electoral Politics*, Cambridge, MA: Harvard University Press.

Hope, D. and D. Soskice (2016), 'Growth models, varieties of capitalism and macroeconomics,' *Politics & Society*, 44(2), 209–226.

King, L.P. (2007), 'Central European capitalism in comparative perspective,' in B. Hancké, M. Rhodes, and M. Thatcher (eds), *Varieties of Capitalism: Conflict, Contradictions, and Complementarities in the European Economy*, Oxford: Oxford University Press, pp. 307–327.

Kohler, K., A. Guschanski, and E. Stockhammer (2019), 'The impact of financialization on the wage share: a theoretical clarification and empirical test,' *Cambridge Journal of Economics*, 43(4), 937–974.

Lazonick, W. and M. O'Sullivan (2000), 'Maximizing shareholder value: a new ideology for corporate governance,' *Economy and Society*, 29(1), 13–35.

Marglin, S.A. (1974), 'What do bosses do? The origins and functions of hierarchy in capitalist production, Part I,' *Review of Radical Political Economics*, 6(2), 60–112.

McDonough, T., M. Reich, and D.M. Kotz (2010), 'Introduction: Social Structure of Accumulation theory for the 21st century,' in T. McDonough, M. Reich, and D.M. Kotz (eds), *Contemporary Capitalism and its Crises: Social Structure of Accumulation Theory for the 21st Century*, Cambridge, UK: Cambridge University Press, pp. 1–19.

Milanovic, B. (2019), *Capitalism Alone: The Future of the System that Rules the World*, Cambridge, MA: The Belknap Press of Harvard University Press.

Mirowski, P. (1988), *More Heat Than Light: Economics as Social Physics, Physics as Nature's Economics*, New York: Cambridge University Pres.

Molina, O. and M. Rhodes (2007), 'The political economy of adjustment in mixed market economies; a study of Spain and Italy,' in B. Hancké, M. Rhodes, and M. Thatcher (eds), *Varieties of Capitalism: Conflict, Contradictions, and Complementarities in the European Economy*, Oxford: Oxford University Press, pp. 223–252.

Noble, D.F. (1977), *America by Design: Science, Technology and the Rise of Corporate Capitalism*, New York: Knopf.

Palley, T.I. (1998a), 'Macroeconomics with conflict and income distribution,' *Review of Political Economy*, 10(3), 329–342.

Palley, T.I. (1998b), *Plenty of Nothing: The Downsizing of the American Dream and the Case for Structural Keynesianism*, Princeton, NJ: Princeton University Press.

Palley, T.I. (1998c), 'Restoring prosperity: why the U.S. model is not the right answer for the U.S. or Europe,' *Journal of Post Keynesian Economics*, 20(3), 337–354.

Palley, T.I. (2007), 'Financialization: what it is and why it matters,' Levy Economics Institute of Bard College Working Paper No 525, Bard College, NY. (Published in E. Hein, T. Niechoj,

P. Spahn, and A. Truger (eds) (2008), *Finance-Led Capitalism? Macroeconomic Effects of Changes in the Financial Sector*, Marburg: Metropolis-Verlag, pp. 29–60.)

Palley, T.I. (2011), 'America's flawed paradigm: macroeconomic causes of the financial crisis and Great Recession,' *Empirica*, 38(1), 3–17.

Palley, T.I. (2012), *From Financial Crisis to Stagnation: The Destruction of Shared Prosperity and the Role of Economics*, Cambridge, UK: Cambridge University Press.

Palley, T.I. (2013), *Financialization: The Macroeconomics of Finance Capital Domination*, New York: Macmillan/Palgrave.

Palley, T.I. (2017), 'Wage- vs. profit-led growth: the role of the distribution of wages in determining regime character,' *Cambridge Journal of Economics*, 41(1), 49–61.

Palley, T.I. (2017/2018), 'A theory of economic policy lock-in and lock-out via hysteresis: rethinking economists' approach to economic policy,' *Economics: The Open-Access, Open-Assessment E-Journal*, 11(July), 1–18.

Palley, T.I. (2018), 'Three globalizations, not two: rethinking the history and economics of trade and globalization,' *European Journal of Economics and Economic Policies*, 15(2), 174–192.

Palley, T.I. (2020), 'Re-theorizing the welfare state and the political economy of Neoliberalism's campaign against it,' *Journal of Economic Issues*, LIV(3), 588–612.

Palley, T.I. (2021a), 'Financialization revisited: the economics and political economy of the vampire squid economy,' *Review of Keynesian Economics*, 9(4), 461–492.

Palley, T.I. (2021b), 'Introduction: Neoliberalism as a variety of capitalism,' in T.I. Palley, *Neoliberalism and the Road to Inequality and Stagnation: A Chronicle Foretold*, Cheltenham, UK and Northampton, MA: Edward Elgar Publishing, pp. 1–8.

Palley, T.I. (2021c), 'National policy space: reframing the political economy of globalization and its implications for national sovereignty and democracy,' *Brazilian Journal of Political Economy*, 41(3), 447–465.

Pérez Caldentey, E. and M. Vernengo (2016), 'Raúl Prebisch and economic dynamics: economic growth and center–periphery interaction,' *CEPAL Review*, 118, 9–24.

Pistor, K. (2019), *The Code of Capital: How Law Creates Wealth and Inequality*, Princeton, NJ: Princeton University Press.

Podkamminer, L. (2021), 'Dynamic stochastic general equilibrium: macroeconomics at a dead end,' *Bank y Kredit*, 52(2), 97–122.

Prebisch, R. (1950), *The Economic Development of Latin America and its Principal Problem*, Santiago: UNECLA.

Rodrik, D. (1997), *Has Globalization Gone Too Far?*, Washington, DC: Peterson Institute for International Economics.

Rodrik, D. (2011), *The Globalization Paradox: Democracy and the Future of the World Economy*, New York: W.W. Norton.

Rowthorn, R. (1981), 'Demand, real wages and economic growth,' Thames Papers in Political Economy, Autumn, No TP/PPE/81/3.

Schasching, J. (1998), 'Catholic social teaching and labor,' *The Future of Labor and Labor in the Future: Pontificiae Academiae Scientiarum Socialium Acta*, 2, 53–80.

Schmitter, P. (1974), 'Still the century of corporatism,' *Review of Politics*, 36(1), 85–131.

Schumpeter, J.A. (1942), *Capitalism, Socialism and Democracy*, New York: Harper & Brothers.

Shonfield, A. (1965), *Modern Capitalism: The Changing Balance of Public and Private Power*, Oxford: Oxford University Press.

Siegle, J.T., M.M. Weinstein, and M.H. Halperin (2004), 'Why democracies excel,' *Foreign Affairs*, 83(5), 57–71.

Singer, H. (1950), 'The distribution of gains between investing and borrowing countries,' *American Economic Review (Papers and Proceedings)*, 40(2), 473–485.

Smith, A. (1776 [2004]), *The Wealth of Nations*, New York: Barnes and Noble.

Solow, R.S. (1985), 'Economic history and economics,' *American Economic Review*, 75(2), 328–331.

Stockhammer, E. (2004), 'Financialization and the slowdown of accumulation,' *Cambridge Journal of Economics*, 28(5), 719–741.

Stockhammer, E. (2021), 'Post-Keynesian macroeconomic foundations for comparative political economy,' *Politics & Society*, advance access, 15 April, available at: https://journals.sagepub.com/doi/full/10.1177/00323292211006562.

Stockhammer, E. and Ö. Onaran (2013), 'Wage-led growth: theory, evidence, policy,' *Review of Keynesian Economics*, 1(1), 61–78.

Stolper, W.F. and P. Samuelson (1941), 'Protection and real wages,' *Review of Economic Studies*, 9(1), 58–73.

Storm, S. (2021), 'Cordon of conformity: why DSGE models are *not* the future of macro-economics,' *International Journal of Political Economy*, 50(2), 77–98.

Tabb, W.K. (2010), 'Financialization in the contemporary social structure of accumulation,' in T. McDonough, M. Reich, and D.M. Kotz (eds), *Contemporary Capitalism and its Crises: Social Structure of Accumulation Theory for the 21st Century*, Cambridge, UK: Cambridge University Press, pp. 145–167.

Thelen, K. (2012), 'Varieties of capitalism: trajectories of liberalization and the new politics of solidarity,' *Annual Review of Political Science*, 15(1), 137–159.

Wade, R. (1990), *Governing the Market: Economic Theory and the Role of Government in East Asian Industrialization*, Princeton, NJ: Princeton University Press.

Wallerstein, I. (1974), *The Modern World – System I: Capitalist Agriculture and the Origins of the European World – Economy in the Sixteenth Century*, Berkeley, CA: University of California Press.

Williamson, J. (1990), *Latin American Adjustment: How Much has Happened?*, Washington, DC: Institute for International Economics.

Williamson, O.J. (1975), *Markets and Hierarchies: Analysis and Antitrust Implications*, New York: Free Press.

Williamson, O.J. (1985), *The Economic Institutions of Capitalism*, New York: Free Press.

Review of Keynesian Economics, Vol. 10 No. 2, Summer 2022, pp. 39–55

In search of varieties of capitalism: hardy perennial or troublesome weed?

Mark Blyth*
Watson Institute for International and Public Affairs, Brown University, Providence, RI, USA

Herman Mark Schwartz**
Politics Department, University of Virginia, Charlottesville, VA, USA

Are varieties of capitalism real things in the world, or analytic artifacts that scholars project into the world? The first part of this essay considers the utility of sorting different capitalist economies into different types. We build upon Hay (2020) to argue that some varietals are both more real and more useful than others. Specifically, we argue that recent work on growth models (Baccaro and Pontusson 2016) marks a progressive extension of the Comparative Political Economy research program on advanced capitalist states. But from an International Political Economy perspective, this research program can only reach its potential by clearly determining whether the causal origins of variety lie in either unit or system-level characteristics. We argue for incorporating a more system-led explanation of variety that focuses upon fallacies of composition, power asymmetries, and credit cycles. To show this, we walk through four different arguments about system–unit relations – the 'four Galtons' – and add in Minsky's argument about financial crisis cycles.

Keywords: *varieties of capitalism, growth models, system–unit relations*

JEL codes: *F02, F6, G01, P1, P51*

1 INTRODUCTION

The discipline of political science tends to push political economists who end up working there (rather than in economics or sociology) into one of two sub-field identities early in their careers: 'comparative politics' or 'international relations.' Choosing comparative politics incentivizes them to engage with a sub-field called 'Comparative Political Economy' (CPE), where one of the largest research programs over the past 40 years involves sorting capitalist states into different functional types or varieties. By contrast, choosing 'International Relations' (IR) initially groups them with colleagues who tend to see states as behaviorally similar and differentiated only by the 'distribution of capabilities' in the system (Waltz 1979). This reductionism incentivizes them to join a sub-field called 'International Political Economy' (IPE), where varieties also exist (core vs periphery, revisionist vs status quo, for example) but are of an altogether different kind from CPE's varieties.

Where CPE's varieties are largely complementary and arise from functional specialization, IPE's varieties arise from differences in relative power manifested through

* Email: Mark_Blyth@brown.edu.
** Email: schwartz@virginia.edu.

Journal compilation © 2022 Edward Elgar Publishing Ltd
The Lypiatts, 15 Lansdown Road, Cheltenham, Glos GL50 2JA, UK
and The William Pratt House, 9 Dewey Court, Northampton MA 01060-3815, USA

hierarchy in the global system. Consequently, these two approaches tend to produce quite different answers about why, for example, German capitalism differs from American capitalism (see, for example, Katzenstein 2005 versus Hall and Soskice 2001). This article tries to strengthen how we think about variety, to be clearer about what is at stake when we posit varieties or types, and thus to partially remedy or reduce this analytic tension between CPE and IPE.

Sections 2 and 3 of this essay consider whether sorting different capitalist economies into different types is useful. We concur with Hay (2020) that while one can undoubtedly scatter-plot or cluster capitalist economies using numerous vectors (the degree of economic efficiency versus the degree of inequality, for example, in Hopkin and Blyth 2011), we should be wary about declaring clusters as distinct 'varieties' or types. 'Varieties' implies similarity in genetic origins and internal functional feedback loops that sustain differences. The search for varieties encourages us to impute rather than directly observe those equilibrium mechanisms. But as convergent evolution – for example, 'carcinization'[1] – demonstrates, superficial morphological similarities can arise from diverse genetic origins and be maintained through external selective pressure rather than internal feedback.[2]

Sections 4 and 5 of this essay build on this discussion to examine how CPE cultivates varieties. We contrast the canonical Varieties of Capitalism (VoC) approach (Hall and Soskice 2001) with the more recent 'Growth Models' (GM) research program (Baccaro et al. 2022). We argue that while the GM approach better avoids misidentification of types and mechanisms, it does not go far enough in integrating insights from IPE.

Sections 6 through 12 of the essay discuss those insights in the form of five conditions that shape how we should think about variety. Drawing on Schwartz and Blyth (2022), we use four 'Galtons' and a 'Minsky' to elaborate how to think about variety.

The Galtons specify four different ways to think about the nature of interaction effects among national capitalisms, and thus where to locate the causal origins of variety in specific cases as well as in general. As we shall demonstrate, most views of variety in CPE, and even more so in economics, tend to ignore what we will call the third and fourth type of Galtonian interdependency. They similarly downplay Minskyan dynamics around the interpenetration of local and global credit cycles, and how that differentially shapes national capitalisms over time. We conclude by suggesting where these insights can be best integrated into existing models of variety without succumbing to the temptation to see real, useful, and hardy perennial types where there are in fact only deductively derived, chimerical types that, weed-like, choke the garden of CPE.

2   TYPES, CLUSTERS, AND VARIETIES

Hay (2020) profoundly challenges the notion that different national capitalisms constitute necessarily distinct and stable varieties. He argues that a pre-commitment to the idea that varieties exist, and thus should be discerned, confuses ideal and real types. This leads analysts to deductively impute a common but potentially chimerical set of causally important institutions to any cluster of countries with some discernable shared

---

1.   Carcinization is the tendency of non-crab-like crustacea to evolve into crab-like forms through convergent evolution.
2.   That said, we by no means want to argue that reifications like 'globalization' or 'neoliberalism' ineluctably lead to morphological convergence in capitalist economies.

statistical characteristics. A brief precis of Hay's critique helps us more accurately frame what we should be looking for when we posit varieties of national capitalisms.

Hay elaborates three analytic constructs for recognizing variety: Max Weber's two 'ideal' types and one 'real' type. Hay notes that Weberian ideal types can be agential (micro) or structural (macro). 'Homo economicus' exemplifies the micro or agential type of analytic abstraction. Chicago School economists aside, no one thinks that such people exist, but the theoretical construct provides a benchmark against which real behavior can be compared. The 'market economy' exemplifies the pure macro type, where 'the analyst seeks to capture … through abstraction certain features of the whole to which attention is being drawn in a pure … way' (Hay 2020, p. 306). Finally, Hay draws attention to 'real types.' These are arrived at inductively, 'from the patterned dispersion … of actually existing cases … [and are] … invariably … a statistical archetype' (ibid., p. 306).

Hay argues that conceptual slippage across these analytics arises precisely when we start looking for varieties. Starting with homo economicus can get you to an idealized market economy and vice versa. You can imagine such an agent, and then deduce what type of world they must live in. But doing so does not mean that in building the former construct you can logically infer the existence of any 'real type' that corresponds to the latter. If an ideal type is 'at best, a stylized extrapolation from processes … present in real cases,' one cannot backwardly induce that real cases are only 'real' – and therefore worthy of investigation – if they correspond to these extrapolations (ibid., p. 308). If we do so, we run into trouble insofar as, to paraphrase Bellow's Ravelstein, 'a thing is not a thing until it corresponds to the ideal type.'

3   CPE AND VARIETY

Hay's critique of 'variety hunting' offers an interesting vantage on how CPE views variety and why it has difficulty incorporating the type of scale and system effects IPE scholars tend to frontload in their work. For example, much of the early CPE literature sought to delineate national models of capitalism based on the different roles played by government, business, and organized labor in different economies (Schwartz and Trangøy 2019). Shonfield (1965), for example, developed the idea that the structure of interest groups and institutionalized relations among unions, employers, and the state differed across capitalist economies in ways that mattered for macroeconomic growth outcomes. The subsequent literature shared a broad consensus on a threefold typology of liberal, statist, and corporatist advanced capitalist political economies (Hall 1986; Katzenstein 1985; Zysman 1983).

These typological exercises reached their most advanced form in Hall and Soskice's canonical *Varieties of Capitalism* (2001), which integrated prior insights into a single analytical model. While implicitly founded on Weberian agential ideal types – firms, not states, are the unit of analysis – it produced two structural ideal types: liberal market economies (LMEs) and coordinated market economies (CMEs). To produce those types, Hall and Soskice contend that firms confront five key coordination problems: eliciting cooperation from employees while securing wage restraint, securing a supply of workers with the relevant skills, financing investment, managing relations with owners, and, finally, managing relations with sub-contractors and competitors. Firms' divergent solutions to these coordination problems generate their two ideal types of capitalism.

LMEs solve these problems through markets. CMEs solve them through institutionalized strategic coordination among labor and product market partners. These institutional arrangements become self-reinforcing equilibria. If some firms generate solutions that constitute a Pareto improvement over the initial position of all agents, all agents will eventually adopt those solutions. Iteration produces self-reinforcing institutional complementarities through increasing returns and lock-in through feedback. In short, decisions taken by firms in, for example, an LME, *precisely because it is an LME*, reinforce the selection of specific LME strategies over time, resulting in distinct and diverging institutional clusters of LMEs versus CMEs locked into path-dependent trajectories (Pierson 2000) that emerge endogenously from local conditions.

Hall and Soskice (2001) therefore did not simply describe particular varieties, as previous CPE scholars had done, but also sought to explain how these clusters emerge and reproduce themselves through self-selection. The concepts of 'institutional complementarities,' whereby homeostatic feedback mechanisms tightly bind institutions and their outputs in equilibrium, and 'comparative institutional advantage,' whereby such institutional clusters allow variation across the two main possible types of CME and LME, drove their explanatory framework. Consequently, institutional solutions to key coordination problems explained discrete institutional outcomes, such as firms' innovation strategies, or the choice of social and public policies favored in a particular state.

VoC's two 'varieties' of capitalism thus also diverge in terms of the economic activities that generate growth. The LME institutional framework favors the expansion of low-wage services and high-tech sectors engaged in radical product innovation; the CME institutional framework favors incremental process-focused innovation in manufacturing. Perhaps most importantly, VoC strongly implies that increased international competition leads to a crystallization of LME–CME differences, as firms double down on economic activities and production profiles that mesh with existing institutions. VoC thus implies that governments should promote growth by engaging in reforms that render their institutional frameworks more coherent, thereby enhancing existing institutional complementarities.[3] Growing grapes that don't fit the *terroir* will lead to mediocre wines.

4   BEYOND VoC: GROWTH MODELS (GMs) AND VARIETY

The emerging literature on GMs (Baccaro and Pontusson 2016) precisely targets VoC's reliance on a supply-side/neoclassical understanding of the overall macroeconomy, its assumption of equilibrium outcomes, and its conclusion that comparative institutional advantage is the source of national competitiveness. The GM literature instead uses Post-Keynesian economics to generate varieties of national growth models that are demand-driven and in dis-equilibrium. The GM literature begins with the breakdown of the wage-led Fordist political economies of the 1970s and 1980s (Bhaduri and Marglin 1990) – effectively the same territory as the neo-corporatist literature mentioned above – but draws rather different inferences from these cases.

As a declining wage share of GDP led to lower growth and greater inequality across the OECD, the collapse of demand-driven growth caused Shonfield's relatively homogenous wage-led Fordist economies to mutate into a 'variety' of different national growth models by the 1990s. Those vary from debt-financed consumption-led Britain

---

3.   Soskice (1999) supports this general line of argument by suggesting that multinational corporations engage in 'institutional arbitrage,' locating different activities in countries with different institutional configurations.

                                   Journal compilation © 2022 Edward Elgar Publishing Ltd

and America, FDI-led Hungary and Ireland, export-led Germany and Eastern Europe, the occasionally 'balanced' Sweden, and on to cases with no discernable coherent growth model such as Italy or Greece (Baccaro et al. 2022).

The GM approach eschews the idea that complementary institutions in equilibrium drive divergence between VoC's two varieties. The GM approach instead identifies Hay-sian (2020) *real types* by asking what sectors of a given economy generate value added, and what coalitions support the interests of these sectors in public policy and politics. Thus Baccaro and Hadziabdic (2022) decompose national accounting GDP data to identify the demand drivers in an economy and its dominant growth coalition. Here an understanding of the different types of GM emerge inductively rather than deductively, as in VoC.

This move partially enables the GM approach to avoid methodological nationalism in its conception of variety. For example, it can identify regional-level GMs, such as China's twin GMs (FDI and state-led investment) (Tan and Conran 2022) and it can identify the huge reliance on externally generated demand for commodities for most of Latin America (Sierra 2022). Nonetheless, Hay's critique about 'variety hunting' pertains as much to the GM approach as to VoC, albeit in a different way. Where VoC conflates agential and structural ideal types, the GM approach is vulnerable to the claim that the morphological similarities of its various real types emerge from an overly strong bias towards unit-level causal factors. It is precisely here that IPE scholarship can potentially supply a cure for the issue of why and how varieties emerge.

5   WHAT'S AT STAKE IN DIFFERENT FORMS OF 'VARIETY HUNTING'?

The VoC approach implicitly assumes that distinct varieties are there waiting to be found. Yet what it finds are not 'real types' discovered via statistical analysis. Rather, what VoC posits and discovers is a micro ideal type in the form of firms whose decisions scale up without any fallacy of composition to form a distinct capitalist variety, and a macro 'ideal type' in the form of a set of institutional complementarities that determine the persistence and growth of that variety.

Hay's critique supplies a covering analysis for the many empirical studies showing that many, if not most, actual capitalist economies fit neither VoC ideal type (see, for example, Campbell and Pedersen 2007). First, as Hay notes, fitting things into ideal types risks confusing the real and the ideal. Second, the focus on firms obscures the role of other actors (the state, the electoral system, the financial system, etc.) that might equally well explain the real types of national models and growth trajectories.

GM theory attempts to solve this problem by ignoring it and/or bypassing it. Rather than producing ideal types, the framework generates its *real types* through GDP decomposition and comparative historical analysis. These data then score country Y or Z by how much it resembles the real type of GM X (say, export-led growth). While GM analysts try to find broad categories of growth drivers and then group states with reference to those drivers, there is no *a priori* attempt to find ideal forms of varieties that may not exist. Here, things can be things without fitting into types, and types do not necessarily generate things.

The move to GM analysis from VoC therefore constitutes a progressive extension of CPE's comparative capitalism research program, but with one crucial limit. States are neither hermetically sealed units with discrete national economies, nor are they similarly endowed actors who interact on a neutral playing field. The GM approach is more attuned to questions of power than the VoC approach, but still has trouble dealing with scale effects, hierarchy and power, and how the drivers of demand shift over time. For example, whatever drives changes in gross value added in the Latvian economy is probably not relevant for changes in US gross value added, but the reverse is probably not true. To incorporate those factors, we turn from a CPE to an IPE perspective.

6   GOING GALTON: THINKING ABOUT SYSTEMS AND UNITS

The IPE approach primarily differs from CPE, and especially VoC, by asking about the sources of demand rather than of supply, asking about sources of growth exogenous to countries (units), and, in some cases, by examining system-level constitutive effects. These are all questions about how to weight and prioritize unit-level versus system-level factors in a GM framework. We provide five possible pathways – 'four Galtons and a Minsky' – for doing so.

The four Galtons we set out here recast sources of growth and the causes of unit-level variation with increasingly strong system-level effects, so as to avoid fallacies of composition.[4] Our 'Minsky' provides a similar but finance-oriented system-level approach because the credit cycles integral to both expansion and recession are no longer purely or mostly unit-level phenomena, and arguably were not unit-level phenomena in the nineteenth century (Jordà et al. 2019). Rather, system-level credit cycles deeply affect which and why different growth models experience growth at different historical moments. The strongest version of 'Galton' – a Galton 4 – reverses the relationship between system and unit level found in VoC: varieties are simply expressions of a global division of labor that defines the available set of production niches, and plausibly dictates much of how production occurs in those niches. In the conclusion, we suggest which Galtons are most directly applicable to any study of real varieties.

7   GEOGRAPHY LESSONS FOR VARIETY CULTIVATORS

The methodological issue at the heart of our discussion parallels Francis Galton's critique of Edward Burnett Tylor's explanation for the presence of similar sets of cultural practices in Pacific Island societies (Hammel 1980). Like VoC, Tylor argued that similar practices represented functional, complementary responses ('adhesions') to similar problems in all these societies, and so for statistical purposes they could be considered independent events. Galton, in contrast, argued that rather than springing up independently, these sets of practices had originated in a single spot and then diffused mimetically or by imposition. Galton argued that Occam's razor favored external causality, as the odds of independent similar emergence were low. Units were not independent.

Galton's critique can be extended to understand GM's units and growth in today's increasingly complex global division of labor. For example, in the Baccaro and Pontusson (2016) version of GMs, most countries initially exhibited wage-led growth but diverged after the 1970s. But did unit-level or system-level factors drive similarity before 1970–1980 and then diversity afterward? This debate has any number of classic formulations, but a key touch point is the debate between Robert Brenner (1977) and

---

4.   Specifically, that what is true at the unit level will be aggregately true at the system level as well.

Immanuel Wallerstein (1974) over the causes for the rise of a world economy differentiated into distinct production zones.

Brenner, like VoC, generated a unit-level account where local class struggles produced specific production and class configurations that then aggregated to produce a world economy characterized by trade. Wallerstein, by contrast, generated a system level account in which an expanding global division of labor automatically called into existence the appropriate – and different – forms of production and state structure needed in any given locale. Wallerstein never really specified the mechanism by which the system generated units, but his analysis drew heavily on the French *Annales* school's studies of European agricultural zones, which, in turn, rested on Thünen's *Der isolierte Staat* (1826 [1966]), the *ur*-text of economic geography.

Thünen's abstract model posited a market-based economy in which farmers located on a plain with uniform fertility and monotonically increasing transportation costs that responded to the food demands of a central town. He showed that market forces would produce zones differentiated not only by their products, but also – *and here is the really important part* – by their production methods, including the degree of capital and labor intensity (Schwartz 2007). In Thünen's model (see also Krugman and Venables 1995), the market eliminates actors who choose the wrong product or production technique. This generates production profile homogeneity – what we might call unit-level growth models – but system-level diversity. Given demand on scale A, the market will create niches for products X, Y, and Z, and someone/someplace will emerge to serve that demand. Idiosyncratic local factors might determine which of several potential producers became a dominant producer, but it was the fact that the system generated the niche for that producer that is analytically key.

This is not to say that unit-level variables lack any causal significance, but rather that unit-level variables are brought into play and activated by system-level mechanisms. As such, they should not be understood in isolation from systemic mechanisms. To take two obvious examples, export specialization requires a division of labor large enough to sustain that specialization. Export-led economies can only be export-led to a significant degree if there are import-surplus economies out there, which immediately implicates a global financial system, and perhaps a dominant currency. The next section casts the specific arguments in CPE GMs as the more minimalist Galton 1 and 2 arguments before turning to the more system-oriented, maximalist Galtons 3 and 4.

8   GALTONS 1 AND 2: FROM UNIT CAUSES TO SYSTEM CAUSES

Galtons 1 and 2 are essentially Tylor's and Galton's positions respectively, with VoC closer to Galton 1 and GM closer to Galton 2. This can be seen in the differing ways that VoC and GM deal with the origins of the plausibly uniform post-war Fordist growth models theorized by Boyer and Saillard (2005; Bhaduri and Marglin 1990) and the transition to today's more variegated models.

CPE's GM theory brings three useful insights that are ultimately compatible with existing work in IPE. First, per Keynes, Kaldor, and Post-Keynesian models, Say's law is backwards. Rather than supply creating its own demand, demand induces the expansion of supply as firms opt to invest when excess capacity is absorbed (Baccaro and Pontusson 2016). Second, per Keynes, the income distribution matters since the marginal propensity to consume declines with rising income. Third, per both Hayek and the Post-Keynesians, apparent institutional stability conceals the likelihood that economies can be in permanent disequilibrium because growth changes the availability of the different material and social resources powering those economies, and because capitalism is inherently conflictual (Schwartz and Tr3nøy 2019). In sum, demand drives supply due to differences in the ability and propensity to consume, and the more skewed the income distribution, particularly in moments of heightened investment uncertainty or class conflict, the weaker the domestic growth impulse (Lavoie and Stockhammer 2013). All of these plausibly operate at either a global or a unit level.

But both the VoC and, to a lesser extent, the GM approaches retain a strong unit-level starting point. Consider their explanations for the transition from what they see as relatively homogenous Fordist political economies to the current variegated Post-Fordist political economies. The GM literature, drawing on Blyth and Matthijs (2017), argues that this transition emerged from a Kaleckian stand-off between investors and workers over the effects of inflation on profits and on future investment at the level of the system as a whole. Those Kaleckian stand-offs in the 1960s and 1970s exacerbated the pre-existing but mild global inflationary pressures that eventually motivated oil exporters to raise prices and thus trigger what looked like uncontrollable inflation. This shifted what CPE theorists would see as relatively homogenous, Fordist wage-led regimes – where the policy target was full employment – to a set of more heterogeneous and specialized profit-led regimes – where price stability became the key policy target, and the restoration of profits became the key concern of elites.

Similar Kaleckian causal mechanisms drive the GM (Baccaro and Pontusson 2016) and IPE (Blyth and Matthijs 2017) versions of the shift away respectively from a wage-led to a profit-led regime and from the post-war full-employment regime to a neoliberal regime. The CPE version rests upon the insights of Post-Keynesian/Neo-Kaleckian macroeconomics regarding variation in wage shares and thus demand in unit-level economies. The IPE version rests upon a breakdown in the capital–labor productivity bargain underlying the regime at the level of critical components at the global level (but not the system as such). Both versions thus present a 'Galton 1' scenario of independent, local responses to the functional problems of managing mass production, which in turn produced the inflation 'bug' that crashed discrete national systems.

But a plausible 'Galton 2' understanding would focus instead on a global-level fallacy of composition that these homogenous unit-level national growth models generated endogenously (Schwartz and Tranøy 2019). Fordist domestic growth in most OECD economies rested on tightly coupled material production systems (Piore and Sabel 1984). Tight coupling could only work in the presence of stable prices, stable access to labor power, stable consumption, and stable inputs. Fordist *domestic* stability therefore relied on a stable class compromise or incomes policy in which wages grew with productivity (and sometimes inflation), as Galton 1 stresses. But Fordist growth relied on equivalent *global* compromises securing a stable and predictable supply of raw materials, particularly oil. Here the fallacy of composition emerges.

The dual political compromises around materials supply involved the US and ex-imperial European states supporting governments in recently decolonized polities in exchange for a ceiling on prices on the one hand, and major resource firms restraining output to set a floor on the other hand (Parra 2004, p. 39). At the beginning of the 1960s the problem was largely one of preventing price declines. But as Fordist production practices and consumption norms spread to Europe and Japan, the demand for oil for transport and plastics began to exceed supply, shifting the problem to one of preventing price increases that might trigger global inflation.

Put differently, institutional mimesis around the Fordist growth model could occur at a national level from the 1950s to 1970 because economies were relatively closed for historical reasons, and because economies of scale in critical industries like transportation equipment were low enough to be satisfied in a national (or near-national – consider Scandinavia) market. Any one economy could plausibly have succeeded at Fordist production of transport equipment without stressing oil supplies. But if all rich countries adopted a Fordist model, then oil at cheap predictable prices would disappear, shocking tightly coupled production systems. Thus in Galton 2 a crisis emerges endogenously from simple aggregation, but the causal driver is no longer purely local. In Galton 2 (as in Galton 1) no central power directs the adoption of Fordism, yet local growth models cannot operate disconnected from global outcomes. Nonetheless, in Galton 2 the system is still largely the tail on the causal dog.

9   GALTON 3: ASYMMETRIC POWER AND HIERARCHY

In Galton 2, the fallacy of composition generates an unexpected or unintended outcome from individually rational and independent unit-level choices about GMs. But as International Relations (IR) scholars will tell you, the world is not composed of units of equal size, power, and resources. Thus 'Galton 3' shifts the source of diversity or homogeneity from mimesis to imposition. In Galton 3 a dominant actor(s) attempts to impose its preferred growth model on other units, or to control and (re)shape the market signals driving actors' behavior in their local economy. Galton 3 comes in instrumental and structural versions. Both imply that complementary local institutions in some equilibria matter less than system-level forces in shaping production profiles.

Farrell and Newman's (2016; 2018) New Interdependence Approach and particularly its related argument about 'weaponized interdependence' exemplify the instrumental version of Galton 3. Farrell and Newman argue that globalization created a world of overlapping rules and novel jurisdictions where policy in areas as diverse as financial affairs, digital privacy, and environmental regulation is no longer bound by the nation state. In these contested areas, 'rule overlap' empowers agents beyond the state as diverse as financial regulators, veterinarian scientists, and electric-plug standard-setters to engage in bargaining, which leads to new political and distributional cleavages at a system level. Given this, Farrell and Newman (2016; 2018) suggest that control of key institutions at the system level is a key source of asymmetric power among states that is not reducible to the unit level. Powerful states can use this power instrumentally if they can control critical nodes in the various networks linking otherwise discrete flows of finance, trade, and information.

These critical nodes function as what Farrell and Newman call 'chokepoints' or 'panopticons.' This privileges the United States, which controls many critical nodes, albeit not without some contestation. For example, the ability to monitor almost all internet traffic due to so much of it being routed through northern Virginia (conveniently close to US intelligence agencies), or the ability to exclude third parties from the SWIFT payment settlement system (despite it being based in Brussels), strongly suggests power lies at the system level in networks made possible by globalization. More subtly, the fact that about two-thirds of total global trade lately involves goods that cross national borders at least twice before reaching end users subjects all growth models to this kind of interdependence (Constantinescu et al. 2018), while privileging the handful of countries that headquarter the transnational firms dominating that trade. Here system-level control shapes unit-level behaviors.

Similarly, Lloyd Gruber's (2000) analysis of trade negotiations sits intermediately between an instrumental and a structural version of Galton 3. Gruber shows that the

                                   Journal compilation © 2022 Edward Elgar Publishing Ltd

United States and the European Union constructed institutions regulating global trade and then offered everyone else 'take it or leave it' access to those institutions. Participation in those institutions exposed third parties to market forces that reshaped their domestic production profiles. Here the system reshapes VoC's domestic institutions.

Consider Eastern Europe in relation to Germany. The Eastern European foreign-direct-investment-led (FDI) and (largely) export-dependent growth model is only possible because of its embeddedness in the wider EU-level macroeconomic regime (*pace* Blyth and Matthijs 2017). German firms deliberately constructed the Eastern European GMs, linking them to the Greater European Export Complex (Blyth 2016; see also Hirschman 1945). These commodity chains disproportionately return value to Germany rather than Eastern Europe.

The strongest structural version of Galton 3 implies that one powerful actor actually constructs the institutional equilibria in other societies, rather than those equilibria emerging endogenously, as VoC would have it. The United States, for example, has been consciously trying to reshape other countries' domestic political economies since the 1920s (Costigliola 1984; Maier 2015; Sørensen 2001; Wade 2003). Those efforts involved enforcing class compromise on societies then known for highly conflictual labor relations rather than VoC's cooperation. The United States also tried to reshape European and Japanese production along Fordist lines (Zeitlin and Herrigel 2000).

This version of Galton 3 would suggest that the world economy constitutes a single field of power shaped by a hegemonic actor. Both firms and states operate in this field of power, and the firms and associations of firms that provide both VoC's and GM's local social blocs are inseparable from an overarching global social bloc. On this view, the complementarity between GM's consumption/debt-led and export-led economies, or VoC's CMEs and LMEs, arises not from simple aggregation of units whose shape was determined by local forces alone. Rather, the strongest version of Galton 3 would argue that a single powerful actor shaped unit-level growth dynamics using control over the global trade and financial system. Complementarity is constructed, not emergent. CPE brackets this asymmetric power among states.

10   GALTON 4: A GLOBAL DIVISION OF LABOR CREATES PRODUCTION NICHES

Galton 4 presents an even stronger version of a system-level argument, abandoning the residual methodological nationalism in Galton 3 and perforce VoC's Galton 1 understanding of states, and to a lesser degree national economies, as discrete units. Here the Weberian macrostructural ideal type is close to that posed by Thünen and other economic geographers. Galton 4 posits an overarching global economy with a complex division of labor. The increasing depth of that division of labor generates ever more distinct potential economic niches. But the timing and nature of a given region's incorporation into that division of labor creates relatively durable social groups, dominant social blocs, and thus institutional complexes that shape its long-run production profile. Here the system constitutes units, and complementarity among units reflects system-level political and market pressures and system-level solutions to the problems of adequate aggregate demand.

Where VoC sees history as an iterated game causing convergence towards complementary institutions, Galton 4 sees history as an evolutionary process in which fitness at any given time implies neither efficiency nor equilibrium. Where VoC sees excess

LME consumption as a consequence of local institutions, Galton 4 sees a global hierarchy of currencies that allows a key country to exogenously generate extra global demand.[5] Examining the relationship between VoC's CMEs and its LMEs, and the nearly similar GM export-led and consumption/debt-led economies, shows this clearly.[6]

By definition, export-led economies must generate substantial net exports, while consumption/debt-led economies must generate – and pay for – substantial net imports corresponding to those exports. But this is not just by definition. From 1992 to 2017, the United States accounted for 50.6 percent of global current-account deficits, while Germany, Japan, and China accounted for 43.3 percent of global surpluses, roughly equal to the US deficit (Schwartz 2019, p. 495). Normally, large export surpluses would produce a substantial growth impulse. But, putting China aside (as VoC does with all developing economies), export-led economies generally exhibit lower rates of growth than consumption-led GMs. CPE's GM approaches try to accommodate this by asserting that consumption-led economies have excessive, debt-financed growth, implying that the normal state of affairs is low rates of growth, perhaps exacerbated by debt overhangs, and counter-factually, lower levels of consumption absent such financialization. This is perfectly plausible given that continual productivity growth means that deflation is the natural state in capitalism.

But this escape hatch leads VoC and GM into a different peril. Any GM with significant net exports necessarily accrues external assets. If they sell payments made in importers' currency to buy assets denominated in their own currency, they most likely drive up the exchange rate for their currency, thus pricing themselves out of the market while also transforming themselves into a financialized, consumption-led economy. Conveniently, developed country importers offer assets in their currency (as the numbers above show). But why would export-led polities continue to accept this debt, knowing that consumption-led economies do not generate enough tradeables to make good on those debts?

Indeed, this pain is real, not potential. As Hünnekes et al. (2019) show, foreign investment by Germany and other export-led economies in their 13-country data set not only underperforms that by consumption-led economies, particularly the United States, but often even underperforms local assets. Beck (2021) similarly shows that European banks must create balance sheets with considerable US dollar assets and liabilities in order to be globally competitive. Non-US banks' US-dollar-denominated liabilities – that is, deposits – accounted for more than 49 percent of all cross-border liabilities on average, between 1992 and 2017 (Schwartz 2019, p. 500).

In short, export-led economies can only exist in a world characterized not only by some globally acceptable currency, but one which is issued by a hegemonic polity with a credible claim to back that currency with future production and present power. The US majority share of cumulative current-account deficits demonstrates this. If this were not the case, chronic US current-account deficits would call into question both the viability of their associated global liabilities and the US dollar. The financialization of the US economy is thus not simply a mechanical counterpart to export-led growth elsewhere. Rather, it reflects a global political and monetary hierarchy in which US administrations and firms have consciously shaped a specific kind of integrated global

---

5. Here the core GM theorists (Baccaro et al. 2022) partly recognize how reserve currencies matter for global aggregate demand.
6. Conveniently, but not coincidentally, this directly connects to the subsequent section on Minsky.

 Journal compilation © 2022 Edward Elgar Publishing Ltd

economy – at a minimum, a Galton 3 story – where hierarchy and power matters. Similarly, without dollar credibility and the non-trivial 0.8 percent of global GDP (about $380 billion) *annual* stimulus to the global economy between 1992 and 2017 that the US current-account deficit provided, export-led growth would be difficult if not impossible – a Galton 4 story. This extra demand matters, because the constant productivity growth characteristic of capitalism expands supply faster than demand (Erten and Ocampo 2013; Grilli and Yang 1988), and as Keynes argued, Say's law does not operate: supply will not create its own demand.

11   GALTONS 3 AND 4: BRINGING HISTORY (AND COLONIALISM) BACK IN

The origins of VoC's LMEs and CMEs also show system-level constitutive effects of both the Galton 3 and 4 type. The LMEs are all products of Britain's colonization of and near genocide in thinly settled temperate-zone areas. In the nineteenth century, the 'mortgage revolution' that accompanied British expansion created billions of pounds worth of new aggregate demand on the basis of endogenous lending against the collateral of newly settled and productive agricultural land (Schwartz 2020). LMEs were born 'financialized,' and these new debts financed British industrial exports. This pattern has continued into the present. The US housing finance system was a critical source of global demand in the 2000s (Schwartz 2009).

Conversely, the export-led economies are all successful late developers who occupied niches that emerged as first Britain and then the United States pumped new demand into the global economy. As Gerschenkron (1962), Streeck and Yamamura (2001), and the subsequent developmental state literature argued, successful late developers generally mobilize capital for development by suppressing domestic demand. That capital is channeled into successively 'heavier' industries, which tends to starve agriculture, light industry, small and medium-sized enterprises, and the service sector of investment capital. While policy-driven mobilization of domestic resources can create viable, globally competitive firms at the technological frontier, it also leaves behind the scar of permanently deficient domestic demand (Höpner 2018). Relatively low household consumption in the late developers therefore forces firms to look outward for markets, which they find in the Anglo-LME economies, and in high-growth developing economies. As an outcome of late development, this is a structural and systemic factor more so than an expression of independent local choices. Germany can choose today to 'do more exports' in response to a financial shock, but that is possible precisely because the political and economic institutions that generated successful late development have never supported 'more consumption.' Thus, from a Galton 4 perspective, the relationship between export-led and consumption-led economies is more than a simple mechanical one emerging from local choices independent of the system *à la* Brenner (1977).

Rather, export-led GMs have their origins in a Stinchcombe-ian *historical cause*,[7] namely late development efforts triggered by the power imbalance first between Britain and the world, and, subsequently, the United States and the world. They have a Stinchcombe-ian *continuing cause* in the local structure of power, namely (excess) production and (suppressed) consumption built into firms and a local institutional environment shaped by late development and reinforced by the outcomes of two world wars. These export-led GMs make sense – that is, they can survive and prosper

---

7.   See Stinchcombe (1968).

– economically only because a global hegemon generates new demand (via new, globally acceptable debt) that validates the excess investment in export-led economies. In sum, from a Galton 4 point of view, GMs are not simply deeply interdependent, but rather are constituted by a global division of labor managed by a hegemonic power whose assets provide the additional aggregate demand needed to offset the chronic deflation characterizing capitalist economies.

Turning to the next section, the salience of financialization in generating extra aggregate demand points us towards Minsky's (1986) analysis of the dynamic nature of finance. CPE certainly does not ignore finance and debt, a crucial growth driver of the GM 'consumption/debt-led' type. But CPE accounts tend to view finance as a 'fix' that ameliorates insufficient aggregate demand in national economies that have shifted from wage-led to profit-led regimes of growth (Baccaro and Pontusson 2016; Streeck 2014), or, in VoC, as simply a corporate governance problem around how firms find capital (Hall and Soskice 2001). By contrast, Minsky allows us to understand the fallacy of composition around credit creation, why credit creation is a system-level phenomenon, and why credit creation tends towards endogenous crisis rather than towards VoC's institutional equilibria.

12   MINSKY AND THE GLOBAL DYNAMICS OF GROWTH

Minsky (1986) argued that endogenous credit cycles were both integral to and disruptive of growth, noting that 'stability breeds instability' over the long run. Financial crises typically caused regulators to drastically restrain permissible financial instruments and actions, producing extended periods of financial stability. Subsequently, actors mistake the lack of volatility as evidence of their own ability to successfully manage risk, and lobby to remove constraints. At the same time, stability encourages further expansion of the credit that Minsky terms hedge finance. In hedge finance, actors borrow in the expectation that cash flow will cover both interest and principal repayment.

A more liberal regulatory regime and credit expansion create a temporarily stable economy, with higher profits for finance and rising asset prices. New credit is a form of public good. It increases returns to existing investment, thus boosting its collateral value, and thus encourages and enables further credit emission. In turn, this encourages financial actors to begin speculative finance, where cash flow covers interest but not principal repayment. This second wave of credit expansion is, however, inherently unstable. It is itself predicated on realizing capital gains from rising asset prices that are financed out of new credit expansion so that principal repayment can occur.

In the last phase of the Minsky cycle – Ponzi finance – less sophisticated investors ('greater fools') and highly risk-accepting investors begin borrowing in the hope that capital gains will cover both principal repayment and accrued interest. In the Ponzi stage, the cycle becomes endogenously unstable. Returns on these hyper-inflated assets can no longer support their valuation, producing 'revulsion' – a crisis – as market actors all try to sell off assets at the top of the market. Minsky thus combines the fallacy of composition and endogenous decay.

Minsky analysed the US market, but, as many IPE scholars have noted, the same process characterizes various global crises as far back as the 1830s, and more obviously the 1982 Latin American debt crisis, the 1997 East Asian financial crisis, and the 2008–2010 global financial crisis. This is not a new insight. Schumpeter (1934, pp. 86–89, 134–137, 152–153, and 208) argued that new growth waves rely on exogenous credit creation. Minimally, then, Galton-3-type system-level credit dynamics cannot be ignored, because only a hegemonic actor can act as a global lender of last resort and bail out other actors with foreign-currency liabilities as the US Federal Reserve's $5 trillion in loans and guarantees to non-US banks showed clearly in 2008–2010 (Tooze 2018). Maximally, Galton 4 suggests that system-level credit creation (by a debt-led hegemonic actor and through endogenous credit creation in the hegemon's currency by other country financial actors) initiates and reinforces an export-led orientation in CMEs and/or export-led economies, rather than purely internal dynamics as VoC would have it.

13   CONCLUSION

Hay (2020) criticized VoC for deductively creating two ideal types of unit-level capitalist economies and then forcing real types into its ideal types. The GM approach partially remedied that, with an inductive assessment of the sources of growth, albeit still at the unit level. We built on Hay's critique, and GM's modification of VoC, by introducing system-level causes for the unit-level growth orientations and unit-level institutions observed in real types. Galton 1 and 2 understandings of the world each accommodate the unit-level causal focus in VoC and GMs. Specifically, VoC exemplifies a Galton 1 approach while the GM school incorporates both Galton 1 and Galton 2 processes and effects. Unit-level institutional configurations could result from internal processes involving either functional or mimetic responses to the emergence of new technological opportunities or social challenges. These plausibly aggregate into the pattern of current-account and growth outcomes we can observe. We then introduced Galtons 3 and 4, as well as Minsky, to provide system-level IPE-based accounts that supplement (or supplant) the unit-level causal stories central to the VoC and GM approaches.

Galtons 3 and 4 locate the origins of VoC's LME and CME types, and of GM's various types, in an expanding global division of labor fueled by system-level credit, usually created by a hegemonic polity that also might be actively selecting who benefits from that division of labor. That global division of labor creates various productive niches for different kinds of goods, but, consistent with Thünen and other economic geographers, rewards (punishes) firm-level actors who respectively adopt the appropriate (inappropriate) good and production process when they fill that niche.[8]

While these market pressures do not dictate a specific production profile on a one-for-one basis, they do limit the number of potential producers, and the range of potential production formats. Because the global division of labor expands secularly (so far), the origins of local economic institutions are therefore a function of incorporation into that global division of labor as much as, if not more than, they are due to endogenously determined growth drivers. The fact that Latin America as a whole has had a commodity-driven GM despite multiple national variations and 250 years of evolution and revolution speaks exactly to this point (Sierra 2022). Furthermore, the persistence of any given production complex and process cannot be taken for granted as new niches emerge and old niches become increasingly specialized. The institutional complexes in VoC and the growth drivers in GM are necessarily linked to events at the system level.

---

8.   That said, a focus on the global division of labor (or Marxist uneven and combined development arguments) immediately suggests that 'globalization = convergence' arguments are almost certainly incorrect except when cast as institutional mimesis arguments.

                    Journal compilation © 2022 Edward Elgar Publishing Ltd

Minsky likewise shows that the unit-level institutional equilibria central to both approaches are vulnerable to financial cycles generated at the system level. These financial cycles do not settle into any equilibrium that might leave institutional complexes reliant on credit unscathed – and almost all capitalist processes require credit. The hegemonic powers generating new credit impulses are the functional link between Galtons 3 or 4 and Minsky. Export-led economies in the aggregate necessarily accumulate foreign-currency assets. Because those in turn will largely come from the hegemonic power, there is nothing inevitable or permanent about export-led growth. All that said, we cannot hope to resolve the long-standing debate about the relationship between actors and structure (units and system). Rather, we hope we have shown why both VoC and GM as approaches need to take system-level causal factors and dynamic processes much more seriously, even if this means abandoning some of their core assumptions. As for the wider project of varieties and variety hunting? Let's just say that some weeds are hardier than others.

REFERENCES

Baccaro, L. and S. Hadziabdic (2022), 'Operationalizing growth models,' Max Planck Social Research Institute, Working Paper.

Baccaro, L. and J. Pontusson (2016), 'Rethinking comparative political economy: the growth model perspective,' *Politics and Society*, 44(2), 175–207.

Baccaro, L., M. Blyth, and J. Pontusson (eds) (2022), *Diminishing Returns: The New Politics of Growth and Stagnation*, New York: Oxford University Press, forthcoming.

Beck, M. (2021), 'Extroverted financialization: how US finance shapes European banking,' *Review of International Political Economy*, doi: 10.1080/09692290.2021.1949375.

Bhaduri, A. and S. Marglin (1990), 'Unemployment and the real wage: the economic basis for contesting political ideologies,' *Cambridge Journal of Economics*, 14, 375–393.

Blyth, M. (2016), 'Policies to overcome stagnation: the crisis, and the possible futures, of all things euro,' *European Journal of Economics and Economic Policies*, 13(2), 215–228.

Blyth, M. and M. Matthijs (2017), 'Black swans, lame ducks, and the mystery of IPE's missing macro-economy,' *Review of International Political Economy*, 24(2), 203–231.

Boyer, R. and Y. Saillard (eds) (2005), *Regulation Theory: The State of the Art*, London: Routledge.

Brenner, R. (1977), 'The origins of capitalist development: a critique of neo-Smithian Marxism,' *New Left Review*, 104, 25–92.

Campbell, J. and O. Pedersen (2007), 'The varieties of capitalism and hybrid success: Denmark in the global economy,' *Comparative Political Studies*, 40(3), 307–332.

Constantinescu, C., A. Mattoo, A. Mulabdic, and M. Ruta (2018), *Global Trade Watch 2017*, Washington, DC: World Bank.

Costigliola, F. (1984), *Awkward Dominion: American Political, Economic, and Cultural Relations with Europe, 1919–1933*, Ithaca, NY: Cornell University Press.

Erten, B. and J. Ocampo (2013), 'Super cycles of commodity prices since the mid-nineteenth century,' *World Development*, 44, 14–30.

Farrell, H. and A. Newman (2016), 'The new interdependence approach: theoretical development and empirical demonstration,' *Review of International Political Economy*, 23(5), 713–736.

Farrell, H. and A. Newman (2018), 'Linkage politics and complex governance in Transatlantic surveillance,' *World Politics*, 70(4), 515–554.

Gerschenkron, A. (1962), *Economic Backwardness in Historical Perspective: A Book of Essays*, Cambridge, MA: Harvard University Press.

Grilli, E. and M. Yang (1988), 'Primary commodity prices, manufactured goods prices, and the terms of trade of developing countries: what the long run shows,' *The World Bank Economic Review*, 2(1), 1–47.

Gruber, L. (2000), *Ruling the World*, Princeton, NJ: Princeton University Press.

Hall, P. (1986), *Governing the Economy: The Politics of State Intervention in Britain and France*, Cambridge, UK: Cambridge University Press.

Hall, P. and D. Soskice (eds) (2001), *Varieties of Capitalism*, New York: Oxford University Press.

Hammel, E. (1980), 'The comparative method in anthropological perspective,' *Comparative Studies in Society and History*, 22(2), 145–155.

Hay, C. (2020), 'Does capitalism (still) come in varieties?,' *Review of International Political Economy*, 27(2), 302–319.

Hirschman, A. (1945), *National Power and the Structure of Foreign Trade*, Berkeley, CA: University of California Press.

Hopkin, J. and M. Blyth (2011), 'What can Okun teach Polanyi: efficiency, regulation and equality in the OECD,' *Review of International Political Economy*, 19(1), 1–33.

Höpner, M. (2018), 'The German undervaluation regime under Bretton Woods, 1950–1973: how Germany became the nightmare of the world economy,' MPIfG Discussion Paper 19/1, Cologne: Max Planck Institute.

Hünnekes, F., M. Schularick, and C. Trebesch (2019), 'Exportweltmeister: the low returns on Germany's capital exports,' CEPR Discussion Paper No DP13863, Brussels: Centre for Economic Policy Research.

Jordà, Ò., M. Schularick, A. Taylor, and F. Ward (2019), 'Global financial cycles and risk premiums,' *IMF Economic Review*, 67(1), 109–150.

Katzenstein, P. (1985), *Small States in World Markets*, Ithaca, NY: Cornell University Press.

Katzenstein, P. (2005), *A World of Regions: Asia and Europe in the American Imperium*, Ithaca, NY: Cornell University Press.

Krugman, P. and A. Venables (1995), 'Globalization and the inequality of nations,' *Quarterly Journal of Economics*, 110(4), 857–880.

Lavoie, M. and E. Stockhammer (2013), *Wage-Led Growth*, London: Palgrave Macmillan.

Maier, C. (2015), *Recasting Bourgeois Europe: Stabilization in France, Germany, and Italy in the Decade after World War I*, Princeton, NJ: Princeton University Press.

Minsky, H. (1986), *Stabilizing an Unstable Economy*, New Haven, CT: Yale University Press.

Parra, F. (2004), *Oil Politics: A Modern History of Petroleum*, New York: IB Tauris.

Pierson, P. (2000), 'Increasing returns, path dependence, and the study of politics,' *American Political Science Review*, 94(2), 251–267.

Piore, M. and C. Sabel (1984), *The Second Industrial Divide: Possibilities for Prosperity*, New York: Basic Books.

Schumpeter, J. (1934), *The Theory of Economic Development*, Cambridge, MA: Harvard University Press.

Schwartz, H. (2007), 'Dependency or institutions? Economic geography, causal mechanisms and logic in understanding development,' *Studies in Comparative International Development*, 42(1), 115–135.

Schwartz, H. (2009), *Subprime Nation: American Power, Global Capital, and the Housing Bubble*, Ithaca, NY: Cornell University Press.

Schwartz, H. (2019), 'American hegemony: intellectual property rights, money, and infrastructural power,' *Review of International Political Economy*, 26(3), 490–519.

Schwartz, H. (2020), 'Covering the private parts: the (re-) nationalisation of housing finance,' *West European Politics*, 43(2), 485–508.

Schwartz, H. and M. Blyth (2022), 'Four Galtons and a Minsky: Growth Models from an IPE perspective,' in L. Baccaro, M. Blyth, and J. Pontusson (eds), *The New Politics of Growth and Stagnation*, New York: Oxford University Press, forthcoming.

Schwartz, H. and B. Tranøy (2019), 'Thinking about thinking about comparative political economy: from macro to micro and back,' *Politics and Society*, 47(1), 23–54.

Shonfield, A. (1965), *Modern Capitalism: The Changing Balance of Public and Private Power*, New York: Oxford University Press.

Sierra, J. (2022), 'The politics of growth model switching: why Latin America tries, and fails, to abandon commodity-driven growth,' in L. Baccaro, M. Blyth, and J. Pontusson (eds), *The New Politics of Growth and Stagnation*, New York: Oxford University Press, forthcoming.

Sørensen, V. (2001), *Denmark's Social Democratic Government and the Marshall Plan, 1947–1950*, Aarhus, Denmark: Museum Tusculanum Press.

Soskice, D. (1999), 'Divergent production regimes: coordinated and uncoordinated market economies in the 1980s and 1990s,' in H. Kitschelt, P. Lange, G. Marks, and J.D. Stephens (eds), *Continuity and Change in Contemporary Capitalism*, Cambridge, UK: Cambridge University Press, pp. 101–134.

Stinchcombe, A. (1968), *Constructing Social Theories*, New York: Harcourt Brace.

Streeck, W. (2014), *Buying Time: The Delayed Crisis of Democratic Capitalism*, London: Verso Books.

Streeck, W. and K. Yamamura (eds) (2001), *The Origins of Nonliberal Capitalism: Germany and Japan in Comparison*, Ithaca, NY: Cornell University Press.

Tan, Y. and J. Conran (2022), 'China's growth models in comparative and international perspective,' in L. Baccaro, M. Blyth, and J. Pontusson (eds), *The New Politics of Growth and Stagnation*, New York: Oxford University Press, forthcoming.

Thünen, J.H. von (1826 [1966]), *The Isolated State [Der isolierte Staat]*, P. Hall (ed.) and C.M. Wartenberg (trans.), New York: Pergamon Press.

Tooze, A. (2018), *Crashed: How a Decade of Financial Crises Changed the World*, London: Penguin.

Wade, R. (2003), 'What strategies are viable for developing countries today? The World Trade Organization and the shrinking of "development space",' *Review of International Political Economy*, 10(4), 621–644.

Wallerstein, I. (1974), *The Modern World – System I: Capitalist Agriculture and the Origins of the European World-Economy in the Sixteenth Century*, Berkeley, CA: University of California Press.

Waltz, K. (1979), *Theory of International Politics*, Reading, MA: Addison-Wesley.

Zeitlin, J. and G. Herrigel (eds) (2000), *Americanization and its Limits: Reworking US Technology and Management in Post-War Europe and Japan*, New York: Oxford University Press.

Zysman, J. (1983), *Governments, Markets, and Growth: Financial Systems and the Politics of Industrial Change*, Ithaca, NY: Cornell University Press.

Review of Keynesian Economics, Vol. 10 No. 2, Summer 2022, pp. 56–75

Learning from distant cousins? Post-Keynesian Economics, Comparative Political Economy, and the Growth Models approach

Engelbert Stockhammer*
King's College London, UK

Karsten Kohler**
Leeds University Business School, University of Leeds, UK

Since the global financial crisis there has been growing interest in Post-Keynesian macroeconomic theory by political economists. In particular, the recent Growth Models approach in Comparative Political Economy (CPE) draws heavily on Kaleckian macroeconomics of demand regimes. This paper, firstly, traces the disintegration of nineteenth-century political economy and highlights that many streams within heterodox economics are a continuation of the political economy project, as are the sub-fields of CPE and International Political Economy in the social sciences. Secondly, the paper gives an over-view of the Growth Models approach and its relation to Post-Keynesian Economics (PKE). It clarifies different strategies of identifying growth models empirically, namely GDP growth decomposition versus analysing growth drivers, and it highlights changes in growth models since the global financial crisis. Finally, it identifies opportunities and challenges that emerge from a continued engagement of PKE with political economy and with CPE in particular.

Keywords: *Post-Keynesian Economics, Comparative Political Economy, Growth Models, Varieties of Capitalism*

JEL codes: *B2, B5, E12, O43, P51*

1 INTRODUCTION

Since the global financial crisis (GFC) there has been a growing interest in Post-Keynesian Economics (PKE) from the side of social scientists.[1] In the field of Comparative Political Economy (CPE), which had previously been dominated by the Varieties of Capitalism (VoC) approach, Baccaro and Pontusson (2016) have proposed the Growth Models approach that builds on Post-Keynesian (PK) macroeconomics.

---

*   Email: engelbert.stockhammer@kcl.ac.uk.
**   Email: k.kohler@leeds.ac.uk.
1.   While economics ought to be considered a social science, in this article we will use the term 'social sciences' to refer to political science, international relations and sociology, and will contrast these with economics (see Section 2).

Journal compilation © 2022 Edward Elgar Publishing Ltd
The Lypiatts, 15 Lansdown Road, Cheltenham, Glos GL50 2JA, UK
and The William Pratt House, 9 Dewey Court, Northampton MA 01060-3815, USA

It marries the analysis of demand regimes with the institutional focus of CPE and is part of a broader trend of engagement of political economy with heterodox economics and PKE in particular. In International Political Economy (IPE), Blyth and Matthijs (2017) have made a forceful statement that IPE needs to re-engage with critical Keynesian approaches. This raises interesting questions about the mutual relationship between PKE and CPE: what can CPE and PKE learn from each other? And, more generally, is PKE part of the political economy tradition and what is the significance of its engagement with current political economy approaches in the social sciences? The aim of this paper is to take stock of the recent engagement of CPE and PKE and to identify areas for further dialogue.

This paper makes three points. Firstly, we clarify the historical origins of PKE and CPE in the nineteenth-century political economy tradition and the subsequent split of political economy into distinct fields of economics and the social sciences. PKE and heterodox economics more generally are part of the political economy tradition, but have become narrower in the type of questions they investigate due to pressures of discipline. CPE forms a sub-field of political science and sociology and considers economic, institutional and political phenomena. It thus resurrects ambitions of the original political economy approach, but comes from the modern social sciences. In this sense, PKE and CPE are natural complements, in that both are situated in the political economy approach, but depart from different disciplinary backgrounds. We argue that they are best thought of as distant cousins, but that their different departure points also generate difficulties for communication.

Secondly, we highlight the contributions of PKE to CPE in general and the Growth Models approach specifically. We give an overview of the development of the Growth Models approach and how it builds on PK analysis of demand regimes. We clarify the key concepts of demand regimes, growth drivers and growth models theoretically, and then discuss different ways to empirically identify them. We argue that while the Growth Models approach got traction via the export-led/debt-led growth models distinction, this typology should not be confused with the Growth Models approach itself. Analyses of growth models need to be based on a comprehensive set of potential growth drivers and their dynamic properties. Specifically, we argue that finance-led growth comes with cycles and that there are forms of state-led growth.

Finally, we explore the potential benefits for PKE of engaging with CPE (or with political economy more generally). While PKE is part of the political economy tradition, it has become narrower over the past decades. While it frequently refers to power and institutions as explanatory factors, they are not subjects of analysis themselves. One area where this is particularly important is regarding state policies, which are often treated as exogenous in PKE. Thus engagement with CPE (or political economy more generally) allows PKE to build towards historically and institutionally specific analysis. We illustrate potential benefits using the Sraffian supermultiplier approach, Institutionalist PKs, and Minskyans as examples.

The paper is structured as follows. Section 2 traces the bifurcation of the political economy approach into separate fields of economics and social sciences, and situates PKE and CPE within these. Sections 3 and 4 give an overview of the debates within CPE and how the Kaleckian-inspired Growth Models approach emerged. Section 5 clarifies the notion of growth models and discusses their empirical identification. Section 6 analyses changing growth drivers since the GFC. Finally Section 7 concludes by highlighting challenges as well as opportunities of a continued conversation between PKE and political economy.

                    Journal compilation © 2022 Edward Elgar Publishing Ltd

2   FROM POLITICAL ECONOMY TO POST-KEYNESIAN ECONOMICS AND COMPARATIVE POLITICAL ECONOMY

Today, PKE and CPE seem like rather different fields. However, they share a common origin in nineteenth-century political economy and, we argue, they are best understood as distant cousins. The nineteenth century saw a broad field of political economy that analysed economic and political phenomena, typically with a strong awareness of the historical and institutional circumstances. For most proponents, the existence of classes and class conflict was a given. It encompassed a variety of different theoretical and political positions ranging from liberalism and the German Historical School to Karl Marx. Notably, that was before the formation of modern academic disciplines. This tradition of political economy came to an end with the rise of neoclassical economics and the separation of economics and social sciences. The use of the term 'pure economics' in the title of Leon Walras's most famous work is indicative here.[2] Figure 1 gives a graphical representation of the bifurcation of nineteenth-century political economy into different disciplines and sub-fields.

The separation of disciplines would have a profound impact on the type of questions economists ask and the framing they use in their analysis. Most specifically it justified excluding the analysis of power relations, and mainstream economics would only return much later to the analysis of institutions in the form of New Institutional Economics (Williamson 2000). The pathways to the dominance of modern (Neoclassically informed) mainstream economics varied by country, with dissenting views surviving in many cases for a long time. In the 1930s economics was shaken by the Keynesian revolution. Keynesianism allowed for non-rational behaviour and thus gave prominence to social conventions and institutions that would stabilise the formation of expectations. It also highlighted fallacies of composition that undermined the Neoclassical project of rational-actor microfoundations. Within the mainstream the

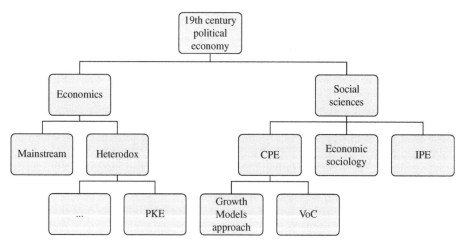

Figure 1   The bifurcation of political economy research

2.   Walras uses 'pure economics' in contrast to 'applied economics' and 'social economics', which were concerned with what is true, useful and just, respectively (Jaffe 1956). The second and third are much closer to political economy.

   Journal compilation © 2022 Edward Elgar Publishing Ltd

Keynesian challenge was resolved uneasily with the Neoclassical–Keynesian Synthesis, which used a long-run/short-run dichotomy to reconcile these strands. In the short run, prices would be rigid, which gave rise to Keynesian results. However, that did not solve the theoretical tensions. What would later become PKE rejected the Synthesis; the more radical wing of the mainstream (for example, Milton Friedman and Robert Lucas) attacked the Keynesian elements from the Neoclassical side.

The second big transformation of economics came in the 1970s with the Monetarist and New Classical counter-revolution. The Synthesis Keynesians were attacked by the Monetarists in economic policy and by the New Classicals theoretically. From then onwards we observe a substantial narrowing of what is considered an acceptable theoretical framework, in particular an insistence on Neoclassical 'microfoundations'. Neoclassical economics also branched out into other social sciences with the 'economic approach' applied to questions outside the field of economics (Becker 1957), sometimes referred to as economic imperialism.

The Monetarist counter-revolution marginalised those outside the mainstream, most acutely the Post-Keynesians.[3] Their school formation dates from this period of a growing sense of exclusion from the economics journals and grant agencies; and PKs started forming their own journals, conferences, etc. From this point, economics was characterised by a very strong (and repressive) mainstream and a multitude of small heterodox niches, which included Feminist Economics, (old) Institutionalism, Ecological Economics, Marxism, Evolutionary Economics, Agent-Based Modelling, etc., which negatively relate to the mainstream, but much less to each other (Dobusch and Kapeller 2012). Effectively these fragmented heterodox approaches continue the project of political economy; however, since the later 1990s the term 'heterodox economics' has often been used.[4]

While the narrowing of economics suited the mainstream, it created tensions within PKE. PKE is often based on a class analytic approach, which emphasises the importance of institutions and gives prominence to power relations (for example, in the determination of income distribution, but arguably also in finance). However, these power relations (and institutions) are usually taken as given and not subject to analysis. To some extent that is unavoidable: in a field where most published pieces face an 8000-word limit, a certain division of labour is necessary. However, it also reflects a narrow set of questions that PKE is asking, which typically focus on pure economic issues. To be clear, this 'narrowness' has also been a strength of PKE, which has arguably more theoretical coherence than other parts of heterodox economics; however this coherence is a weakness insofar as it limits the explanatory range of PKE. Where this sidelining of the political economy dimension is most obviously detrimental to PKE's own research agenda is in the treatment of the state. Overwhelmingly, state policies are taken as exogenous in PKE. Often that is for analytical clarity and to highlight that state policy has different options. However, it also means that there is very little analysis of actual policy regimes (as in, say, the New Keynesian discussions of monetary policy rules) and there is even less discussion of endogenous changes in policy regimes.

3.   PKs had a foothold in Cambridge, UK, and in the 1950s and 1960s had the status of dissident economists, that is, outside the mainstream, while the mainstream remained in communication (PKs were able to publish in leading journals), most famously in the Cambridge capital controversies.
4.   However, the largest European network of heterodox economics, the European Association of Evolutionary Political Economy, founded in the early 1980s, uses the term 'political economy'.

Interestingly, until around 1980, PKs often used the term 'political economy'. For example, one of the first book-length introductions to PKE was Kregel's *The Reconstruction of Political Economy* (1973). We are not aware of a study of where and when in the institutionalisation of PKE there was a clear shift to PKE rather than 'PKPE'. It might well have been the establishment of the *Journal of Post Keynesian Economics* that tilted the balance.[5]

The split of political economy also impacted the social sciences, which would form the disciplines of political science, international relations, and sociology. From the 1970s onward we see research areas form at the intersection of economics with various social sciences, that is, they occupy the space that the demise of political economy has vacated. These include IPE at the intersection of international relations and international economics; CPE which builds on industrial relations, welfare-state regimes and economics (Schwartz and Tranoy 2019); and economic sociology.[6] Among these, IPE is the most firmly established, but is usually located within international relations or political science departments. A number of universities offer degrees in IPE. By contrast, CPE is less institutionalised. While there is a clear stream of academic literature and some textbooks (Clift 2014), there are few corresponding degrees or academic units.[7]

Thus we find a situation where both in economics and in the social sciences there are descendants of political economy. However, there is a notable lack of, or at least an unevenness, of communication. Firstly, heterodox economics is a fragmented and marginalised field that has limited visibility to non-specialists. Furthermore, many of the heterodox economists (and indeed many of the PKs) are trained economists who, in line with the standards of the field, use advanced mathematical and statistical modelling, which constitutes a barrier for many political economists. Heterodox economists, despite a basic sympathy for the social sciences, often lack systematic knowledge in

---

5.   Within the PKs, the Cambridge and Sraffian wings, which also had links with the Marxist tradition, used the term political economy. The monetary PKs, who would become important after the demise of Cambridge as the PK centre, seemed to have been less inclined to use the term. It is less clear why the Kaleckians, who played an important role in the 1980s, did not use the term. Note that, of the other journals founded at a similar time as the *Journal of Post Keynesian Economics*, the *Review of Political Economy* has 'political economy' in the name; and the *Cambridge Journal of Economics* has 'economics' in the name, but it is owned by Cambridge Political Economy Society and explicitly encourages submissions from heterodox economics and the social sciences.

6.   There are other, often less institutionalised, fields of political economy research that transcend the economics/social-sciences divide. One of the most important ones is the debate on financialisation (no academic units yet), which draws heavily on heterodox economics as well as on insights from the social sciences. Other fields that could be listed include aspects of gender studies, development, and economic geography.

7.   As a simple measure of the relative size and frequency of use of the terms, we check the respective citations in the Google Scholar fields. That is based on the self-declaration of researchers, and thus to some extent measures the strength of identity of a field. As a measure, admittedly *ad hoc*, we take the citations of the tenth researcher ranked under each field. This measure is a mix of the willingness of researchers to list a certain field as their research area and the citations of the respective researcher. For CPE, that person has a citation count of 8391, for IPE 14412, and for economic sociology 29292. By comparison, for heterodox economics the value is 2926, and for PKE 576; 'New Keynesian economics' only has two researchers listed, which probably reflects that New Keynesians would identify their field as 'macroeconomics' rather than 'New Keynesian'. Thus a lower degree of institutionalisation does not necessarily represent a weakness (accessed 12 November 2021).

the canonical theories in the social sciences and are not familiar with their recent debates. Moreover, restrictive promotion criteria often discourage publishing outside economics journals.[8] Thus decades of disciplinary division have led to substantial communication barriers between heterodox economics and the social sciences.

3   COMPARATIVE POLITICAL ECONOMY AND VARIETIES OF CAPITALISM

Comparative Political Economy emerged as a field within the social sciences that compares economic performance, institutions, and political dynamics across countries, and analyses the interaction between institutions and economic growth. It thus needs a theory of growth (that is, economics) as well as a theory of institutions and politics. Schwartz and Tranoy (2019) give an overview of the development of CPE and highlight that in terms of the economic underpinning, there has been a steady shift from a focus on demand formation to a focus on supply-side institutions.

The narrowing of CPE's research agenda in favour of the supply side manifested itself with the Varieties of Capitalism approach that came to dominate CPE in the 2000s. The VoC approach emerged from debates in comparative industrial sociology and argued that globalisation does not necessarily give rise to one (liberal) model of capitalism, but that different versions are feasible. Theoretically it builds on Neo-Institutionalist theory (Hall and Soskice 2001) and analyses how different institutional configurations can provide a comparative advantage to firms. One of VoC's achievements is that it synthesises literatures on industrial-relations regimes, welfare-state regimes, and differences in financial systems and national innovation systems into a comparative country typology. At the core is the distinction between liberal market economies (LMEs) and coordinated market economies (CMEs): the USA and UK vs Germany and Japan. Later, mixed market economies (MMEs), mostly Southern European countries, have been added. Despite ongoing debates and questions on whether these typologies are still valid, it is fair to say that the country classification has been one of the most enduring impacts of VoC, while its theoretical analysis now features less prominently.

VoC has been criticised for being functionalist, firm-centred, and methodologically nationalist (see, for example, Bohle and Greskovits 2009). From a PKE perspective, the absence of a serious analysis of demand formation is notable. Essentially VoC offers a version of supply-side socioeconomics that identifies institutional sources of microeconomic efficiency. We also note an absence of issues of financial instability or of financial factors more generally. The analysis of the market-based, bank-based distinction refers to corporate finance (that is, the financing of investment, including R&D and skills upgrading); but there is no housing finance, no speculation, etc. Rather than a general analysis of demand formation, VoC is concerned with international competitiveness (almost as if foreign demand is the only one worth considering).

The supply-side and competitiveness focus of VoC becomes apparent in their contributions on the euro crisis (Hall 2014; Johnston et al. 2014). These essentially interpret the euro crisis as the outcome of cost divergences. CMEs have coordinated wage-bargaining systems, which leads to wage constraint (in line with export sectors),

---

8.   The main qualification to that is that, in the UK, business schools to some extent do encourage heterodox economists to consider non-economics journals as there are hardly any well-ranked heterodox economics journals.

                                              Journal compilation © 2022 Edward Elgar Publishing Ltd

whereas MMEs have less coordination among unions, hence non-tradable sectors push for higher wages, which results in a loss of competitiveness. At the core, the explanation is a trade-driven story (in line with the core theoretical framework). As a side-note, LME and MME also rely on credit to finance domestic demand, but financialisation or financial booms clearly take a subordinate role in the analysis. Restrictive fiscal policy is reported and considered unhelpful, but plays no independent role in the escalation of the euro crisis.

Stockhammer (2022) provides a general discussion of CPE from a PK perspective. He identifies financialisation, financial cycles, the understanding of Neoliberal growth models and the political economy of central banks as areas where PKE can provide specific insights for CPE. In the following, we will focus on the impact of PKE on the Growth Models approach in CPE.

4   POST-KEYNESIAN ECONOMICS AND THE TURN TO GROWTH MODELS IN COMPARATIVE POLITICAL ECONOMY

While CPE was preoccupied with classifying countries into LMEs and CMEs, PKs (and more specifically Kaleckians) developed their own typologies, based on the notion of demand regimes. The origin of this approach goes back to attempts to establish Marx–Keynes synthesis models (Bhaduri and Marglin 1990; Marglin and Bhaduri 1990). At the centre of these models was the role of income distribution. Marxists tend to think of the growth process as profit-driven; in contrast, Kaleckians emphasise (as does Keynes 1936 [1973], ch. 19) that workers have higher marginal propensities to consume than capitalists (the so-called consumption differential) and that consumption is thus wage-driven. The Bhaduri–Marglin model synthesises these two by allowing for wage-led as well as for profit-led aggregate-demand regimes, depending on the relative size of the consumption differential between wages and profits, as well as the profit- (as opposed to demand-) sensitivity of investment. This gave rise to a substantial empirical literature that econometrically identifies the relevant regimes (see Blecker 2016 for a survey). According to these studies, the effect of net exports is often substantial (and profit-led), which may give rise to a fallacy of composition problem: for individual countries, wage restraint may stimulate the economy via exports, but if all countries pursue such a policy at the same time, world demand will contract, as countries trade with each other (see, for example, Stockhammer et al. 2009; Onaran and Galanis 2014).

The Kaleckian debates were then generalised in an attempt to apply them to the Neoliberal growth experience (see the contributions in Lavoie and Stockhammer 2013a; and in particular the synthesis in Lavoie and Stockhammer 2013b). Firstly, supply-side considerations were added. Productivity growth can be wage-led or profit-led too (Storm and Naastepad 2013). Secondly, financialisation was incorporated and household debt identified as a potential growth driver. Stockhammer and Wildauer (2016) present an econometric test of the PK demand regimes approach that focuses on the role of house prices, share prices and household and corporate debt (for a panel of OECD countries). They estimate the relevant consumption, investment and export equations to identify the marginal effects and then use the actual changes in the explanatory variables (that is, house prices, household debt, etc.) to assess the growth effects of financial factors for the pre-GFC decade. They find that a large part of the growth performance of the Anglophone and Southern European countries can be explained by financial factors, whereas in the Germanic country group these growth drivers are absent (with the exception of the Netherlands). Third, personal (as opposed to functional) income distribution has been added to the model and linked to different sectoral outcomes (Behringer and van Treeck 2019).

Lavoie and Stockhammer (2013b) argue that in the Neoliberal era, demand is still wage-led, but other growth drivers have taken centre stage: debt-driven and export-driven growth. Hein and Mundt (2013) develop a classification of countries and growth models based on GDP growth decompositions (see also Section 5). To identify export-driven growth models they use the respective contributions of net exports to GDP growth, and for debt-driven models they use the growth contribution of private consumption combined with information on the change in borrowing by the household sector.[9] Thus, PKE arrived at a country classification into different 'growth models' independently of and with different theoretical concerns from those of CPE.

It was the contribution of Baccaro and Pontussen (2016) that explicitly made the case for introducing Kaleckian macroeconomic analysis of demand regimes into CPE, building on Lavoie and Stockhammer (2013b). They aim to break away from VoC on multiple levels, while also offering an alternative country classification. Firstly, they want to bring back in class struggle and political conflict. As documented in Baccaro and Howells (2011), the bargaining position of labour has deteriorated across all varieties of capitalism under Neoliberalism; but the reactions of the countries have differed. Secondly, to understand these, they refer to PK demand regimes. They analyse four country cases for the post-1980 period and distinguish between export-led (Germany and Sweden), what they call 'consumption-led' (the UK), and a failed model (Italy). They consider postwar capitalism as wage-led and the post-1980s as different forms of profit-led regimes. That is potentially confusing as Lavoie and Stockhammer analyse Neoliberal growth regimes as having unsustainable growth drivers within (at least internationally) wage-led demand regimes. Thirdly, they add a Gramscian element by analysing the resulting regime as one of hegemony rather than as a (Neo-Institutionalist) optimal competitive strategy based on specific institutional structures.

Figure 2 provides some conceptual clarification of the notion of growth models and its theoretical underpinnings from a PK perspective. Every (temporarily) successful growth model requires both economic and political/institutional foundations. On the economic side, growth models will have underlying demand and supply regimes. These specify the marginal effects of changes in certain variables (for example, wage shares) on aggregate demand and labour productivity, respectively. The demand-and-supply regime thus describes a *structural* property that is relevant for (counter-factual) questions such as: how would growth react to a change in functional income distribution? Importantly, this is a very different question from what the actual driver of growth has been in a certain period. Indeed, a country could exhibit a wage-led demand-and-supply regime, and at the same time undergo a sustained fall in the wage share, dampening economic growth (see also Hein et al. 2020, p. 4).

Growth models thus also require *growth drivers*, which are a broad set of variables that may impact growth, such as property prices, household debt, fiscal spending, and export complexity. In contrast to the notion of demand-and-supply regimes, growth drivers refer to the actual causes of growth in specific countries and periods rather than a structural property. Growth drivers require economically significant marginal effects on growth, but also need to be empirically relevant, that is, they need to change over time or across countries (see Section 3.3).

---

9.   The exact terminology in Hein and Mundt (2013) differs somewhat. They have 'strongly export-led mercantilist' and 'weakly export-led' regimes and use 'debt-led consumption boom'.

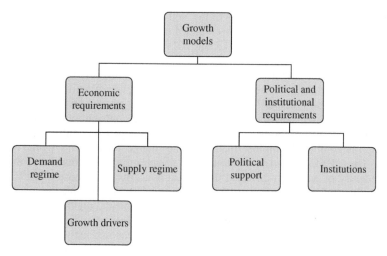

Figure 2   Growth models and their economic, political and institutional requirements

On the political and institutional side, growth models require country-specific institutional settings and social coalitions that support economic growth based on a specific aggregate-demand component (Baccaro and Pontusson 2016; 2019). For example, an export-led growth model will be supported by a social coalition led by the dominant export sector(s), which integrates various sectoral interests and aligns their political interests with those of exporters. The social coalition will seek to align the institutional structure with the growth model and push for corresponding political reforms. For example, labour market institutions may be geared towards containing nominal wage growth and supporting vocational training in favour of high-skilled jobs.

Hope and Soskice (2016) offer a telling reply to Baccaro and Pontusson's Growth Model approach. They reject the need for PKE and explicitly propose to base VoC on the New Keynesian three-equation model, which 'is well placed to shed light on the growth models of advanced economies during the post-Fordist period' (ibid., p. 219). This reasserts that the medium and long-term equilibrium is supply-side-determined. Demand matters, but only in the short run. The inclusion of the financial sector is limited to the central-bank-determined interest rate. There is no household debt, house prices, mortgage securitisation, or financial cycle in their model. Nor is there much reflection on the role of income distribution for demand. This illustrates that CPE can be based on PK as well as on New Keynesian (that is, mainstream) economics.

The Growth Models approach has become widely used in CPE and has inspired various follow-up studies. The forthcoming edited volume by Baccaro, Blyth and Pontusson (2022) contains a state-of-the-art collection of the Growth Models approach.

5   IDENTIFYING GROWTH MODELS

Baccaro and Pontusson's (2016) typology of export-led and consumption-led growth models was developed to describe Western European economies in the decade before the 2008 GFC. Recent contributions have asked what the macroeconomic experience since the GFC implies for the Growth Models perspective. This requires a clarification of how to identify growth models empirically.

Baccaro and Pontusson (2016) used GDP growth decompositions to identify growth models. Growth decompositions measure how much of the growth rate of GDP is due to change in each of its components (consumption, investment, government consumption, exports, and imports).[10] The most dynamic component of aggregate demand would then determine whether a country is consumption- or export-led. Hein and Mundt (2013) and Hein et al. (2020) add a financial dimension to the growth-accounting method. They combine 'growth contributions' of consumption, investment, government consumption, and net exports with the net financial balances of the private, public and external sectors. The addition of financial balances provides insights into how expenditures of different sectors are financed.[11] A major advantage of this approach is its simplicity: the relevant data are readily available from the National Accounts and do not require estimation using a statistical model.

The components of a growth decomposition are often also called 'growth contributions'. However, such terminology can be misleading: growth decompositions simply identify the most dynamic aggregate-demand components, but they do not provide information on why that GDP component grows. In other words, growth decompositions as such do not provide information about the causal drivers of growth and thus are problematic for identifying growth models. For example, a strong contribution of consumption could stem from real wage growth or asset-price inflation, that is, it could be indicative of wage-led as well as of finance-led growth. It could also, if fiscal multipliers are as large as the recent literature suggests, be due to fiscal policy, that is, a form of state-led growth.[12] GDP growth decompositions can thus only give necessary conditions for the identification of a growth model and need to be complemented by additional information.

Kohler and Stockhammer (2021) instead propose the notion of growth drivers, which are economic factors that influence the growth of a demand component without being themselves a part of aggregate income, for example the wage share, real-estate prices, or the fiscal policy stance (see also Stockhammer and Wildauer 2016; Stockhammer and Onaran 2022). In contrast to demand regimes, growth drivers thus refer to the actual causes of growth in specific countries and periods rather than a structural property.[13] To underpin a growth model, growth drivers require relatively stable demand regimes in the sense that their marginal effects on growth should not change substantially over time.

---

10.   More formally, growth decompositions measure the share of a change in aggregate-demand component i in total economic growth $(\widehat{Y})$: $\widehat{Y}_i = \frac{\Delta i_i}{Y_{i-1}}$, where $i = C, I, G, X, -M$ and $Y = C + I + G + X - M$.
11.   Hein et al. (2020) further combine their analysis of demand regimes with a classification of welfare models based on Hay and Wincott (2012).
12.   To illustrate: current fiscal multiplier estimates during recessions are of the order of magnitude of 2.5 (Auerbach and Gorodnichenko 2012, table 1). Assume that the government increases public investment (during a recession) by 1 percentage point of GDP. That would (all things being equal) induce an increase in private consumption by 1.5 percentage points of GDP. A GDP growth decomposition would identify that economy as consumption-led, whereas in fact growth is state-led.
13.   Formally, demand regimes are defined by the marginal effect β of a change in an explanatory variable on economic growth $\beta_j = \frac{\partial \widehat{Y}}{\partial j} \lessgtr 0$, where $j =$ wage share, property prices, ... Growth drivers are represented by actual changes in explanatory variables and their marginal effects on growth: $\widehat{Y}_j = \beta_j \Delta j \lessgtr 0$.

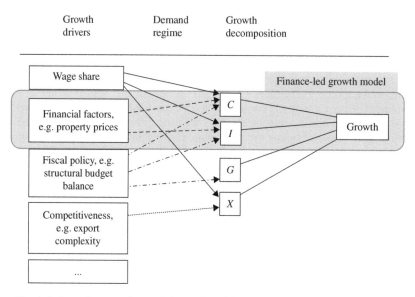

Notes: The shaded area denotes a finance-led growth model as one possible configuration. Other growth models are possible. C = consumption; I = investment; G = government consumption; X = exports.

Figure 3   Growth drivers, demand regime, and growth decomposition

However, the drivers themselves can change in different directions and thereby explain historically specific growth episodes. Figure 3 illustrates the conceptual relationship between growth drivers, demand regimes, and growth decompositions for the case of a finance-led growth model. A growth model can be regarded as a specific configuration of growth drivers that are causally relevant (via the demand regime) and lead to the dominance of certain demand components (reflected in the growth decomposition). In finance-led growth models, real-estate prices are one of the main growth drivers which impact consumption and investment expenditures.

6   CHANGES IN GROWTH MODELS SINCE THE GLOBAL FINANCIAL CRISIS[14]

The way in which growth models are identified empirically has implications for the interpretation of growth models since the GFC. Based on growth decompositions and financial balances, Hein et al. (2020) classify OECD countries into export-led mercantilist, weakly export-led, domestic demand-led, and debt-led private demand boom regimes, for both the pre- (2000–2008) and the post-crisis period (2009–2016). They find that the post-crisis period came with a larger number of countries pursuing export-led regimes as many countries that previously underwent debt-led private demand booms (for example, Southern Europe and the Baltics) switched to positive-growth contributions of net exports. For the Anglo-Saxon countries, they report a shift towards domestic demand-led regimes supported by government deficits.

---

14.   This section states an argument more fully developed in Kohler and Stockhammer (2021).

Kohler and Stockhammer (2021) argue that a classification of growth models that exclusively draws on growth decompositions can yield a misleading picture of macro-economic dynamics in the post-crisis period. They question the shift towards export-led models for most countries and argue that a closer investigation of growth drivers instead of decompositions yields a different picture. While previous work in CPE has indeed considered certain growth drivers, such as real wage growth or price competi-tiveness, a broader and more systematic consideration of growth drivers as well as an appreciation of their cyclical nature is needed to understand economic developments since the GFC.

Firstly, consider financial factors as drivers of private demand. A sizable literature in both PKE and CPE has argued that asset-price inflation, especially in housing mar-kets, is an important driver of consumption and construction (Schwartz 2008; Crouch 2009; Hay 2009; Stockhammer and Wildauer 2016). Baccaro and Pontusson (2016) speak of 'consumption-led' growth, which they consider to be fuelled by credit. However, they implicitly treat household debt as consumer debt and do not offer an explanation as to why household debt has risen. Kohler and Stockhammer (2021) argue that previous country classifications tend to overlook the cyclical nature of this growth model. Drawing on the notion of a 'financial cycle' (Borio 2014) and a Minskyan perspective (Palley 2011; Minsky 2016; Ryoo 2016), debt-led models are expected to exhibit cyclical dynamics where episodes of finance-led growth are fol-lowed by periods of debt-driven stagnation. Against this background, the post-crisis experiences of most countries that were debt-led in the pre-crisis period can be largely understood as a downturn in the financial cycle, in which private deleveraging enforced a contraction in private demand. The resulting collapse in consumption and import demand then led to an improvement in net exports, without a genuine switch to an export-led model as growth decompositions might suggest.

Secondly, fiscal policy constitutes public demand that has been neglected in analyses of the pre-crisis period (for example, Baccaro and Pontusson 2016), but became important with the GFC. From a Keynesian perspective, fiscal policy is espe-cially relevant in times of recession due to higher multiplier effects and can have long-run effects on economic growth through hysteresis (Delong and Summers 2012; Blanchard and Leigh 2014; Gechert and Rannenberg 2018; Gechert et al. 2019). In addition, discretionary fiscal spending can be an important autonomous source of demand that drives long-run growth (Allain 2015; Hein 2018). Based on this, Kohler and Stockhammer (2021) argue that cross-country differences in economic growth since the GFC can partly be attributed to different fiscal policy reactions (Stockhammer et al. 2019). The Southern European countries underwent the double whammy of a downturn of the financial cycle combined with (externally imposed) austerity, whereas the English-speaking countries counteracted the contraction in private demand with a stronger public stimulus.

Thirdly, one can distinguish two sources of competitiveness as drivers of foreign demand. Large parts of the CPE literature on the eurozone crisis focus on nominal wage growth as a determinant of price competitiveness (Hall 2014; Johnston et al. 2014). However, structuralist PKs as well as some of the earlier VoC literature empha-sise the role of non-price competitiveness in the form of knowledge intensity, which is measured as the complexity of exported goods (Sorge and Streeck 1988; Storm and Naastepad 2015; Gräbner et al. 2020). In this view, countries specialising in high value-added goods are better equipped to sustain export demand in times of fierce competition from China and emerging markets. Kohler and Stockhammer (2021) pre-sent evidence that an improvement in price competitiveness, especially in the countries hit by the eurozone crisis, did not come with improved growth or export performance. By contrast, the correlation between export complexity and economic performance has increased in the post-crisis period.

The analysis demonstrates a substantial change in growth drivers between the pre- and the post-crisis period, suggesting that growth models may not be as stable as the extant literature assumes. In particular the prominent dichotomy between export-led and (debt-financed) consumption-led growth has lost some of its usefulness to describe the post-crisis experience. This supports an analysis of growth models based on a broad set of growth drivers, some of which may undergo cyclical changes. The argument leads to a re-conceptualisation of growth processes since the GFC. Weak or negative growth need not signal the end of finance-led growth models but may merely reflect the downturn phase of the financial cycle. It also highlights the possibility of state-led growth models.

Methodologically, identifying growth drivers requires the estimation of one or more behavioural equations to determine the coefficients that govern the growth model. This is more challenging than the calculation of growth decompositions since econometric problems of model specification, endogeneity, and serial correlation need to be dealt with. However, it provides insights into the causal drivers of growth models that growth decompositions do not deliver. We think that the PK literature on growth and demand regimes offers a rich set of potential growth drivers for the analysis of growth models, representing ample scope for further engagement between PKE and CPE.

Given the simplicity and convenience of growth decompositions, they are likely to be used in future research. Unlike the analysis of growth drivers, growth decompositions are themselves insufficient to identify growth models and need to be combined with additional information. Hein and Mundt (2013) and Hein et al. (2020) provide such a procedure for differentiating export-led and debt-led regimes (through sectoral financial balances). What additional measures are used depends on the nature of the hypothesised growth models. For the post-GFC period, information about the relative growth contributions of exports and imports and the fiscal balances are needed to ensure that growth drivers are not misinterpreted.

7   THE IMPORTANCE OF FURTHER ENGAGEMENT BETWEEN POLITICAL ECONOMY AND POST-KEYNESIAN ECONOMICS

The previous section focused on the impact of the Kaleckian stream of PKE on CPE, which has served as the entry point for the dialogue. By way of conclusion, we explore how engaging with political economy raises interesting challenges and opportunities for different streams within PKE. We argue that there is a strategic as well as a theoretical interest for PKE to engage with CPE (and political economy more generally).

Firstly, the strategic case. Arguably the GFC has demonstrated fundamental shortcomings of pre-crisis macroeconomics. In a serious academic discipline, that would have led to some soul-searching and the consideration of a wider set of economic theories. By and large, that has not happened; dynamic stochastic general equilibrium (DSGE) modelling has remained the reference point for mainstream macroeconomics. While there is a very selective reading of some PK authors (notably Minsky), overall the discipline of economics (in the USA) has witnessed a revival of the freshwater–saltwater divide of hard New Classical and New Keynesian approaches. That is very different in the political economy sub-fields, where a more serious engagement with heterodox economics and in particular PKE is taking place. This is not restricted to CPE: Blyth and Matthijs (2017) argue in favour of the (re-)introduction of Kaleckian macroeconomics into IPE. Keynesian and PK arguments have arguably been even more influential in various fields of political economy regarding issues of money creation, financialisation, and international financial regimes (for example, Ingham 2004; van der Zwan 2014; Gabor 2020).

Secondly, on the theoretical side, despite being located in different disciplines, we have argued that PKE and CPE are in fact cousins, in that their joint origin can be traced back to the political economy approach. However, PKE has narrowed its research questions to fit the agenda of the economics discipline. The strength of CPE lies in its systematic and rich study of institutional differences across countries, and CPE has done that for different areas such as industrial relations, welfare states, financial systems and innovation systems. The main achievement is thus to map out differences across countries and insist on the specificity of actually existing capitalisms.

Engagement with CPE raises questions of the mutual determination of the economic and the political spheres. How do economic developments shape political interests and how do these interests feed into policy-making? This brings to the fore an area where its focus on narrow economic issues leads to shortcomings in PKE's own research agenda. PKE tends to treat fiscal and monetary policies as exogenous. In part this is to highlight the potential for different policy choices. However, that is problematic on theoretical as well as on empirical grounds. Theoretically it leaves a key macroeconomic variable underdetermined. Curiously, there are hardly any PK studies that follow up on Kalecki's (1943) famous paper which argues that capitalists may object to full employment policy as it undermines their power vis-à-vis labour. More generally, PKE has had very little to say on why Keynesian policies would be adopted (but see Skocpol 1980; Ferguson 1984; Hall 1989). Empirically, countries will have different institutions and economic policy regimes, and this impacts PKE's ability to explain actual economic performance across countries. In PKE discussions of financialisation, it is clear that financial relations are regarded as power relations that have distributional impacts, but PKE has not so far systematically developed a theory of financial power.

One field where CPE's analysis of institutions and politics can enrich PKE is in growth theory. As discussed in Section 4, PK debates on demand regimes have moved beyond the original Bhaduri–Marglin model's exclusive focus on functional income distribution as a driver of growth. Empirical research has investigated the effects of asset prices and debt (Stockhammer and Wildauer 2016; Blecker et al. 2020; Stockhammer et al. 2021) as well as fiscal policy (Qazizada and Stockhammer 2015; Obst et al. 2020) on aggregate demand. There is a certain convergence of current Kaleckian research and that emerging from the Sraffian supermultiplier (SSM) approach. At the theoretical level, SSM puts forward a theory of demand-led growth that highlights the role of autonomous demand components which do not create capacity (that is, increase the capital stock).[15] Thus far, SSMs have identified autonomous consumption (Freitas and Serrano 2015; Lavoie 2016), exports (Nah and Lavoie 2017), and discretionary government expenditures (Allain 2015) as demand

---

15.   While SSM models are wage-led in the short run in the sense that an increase in the wage share temporarily raises growth, income distribution has no long-run effects on the growth rate. The long-run growth rate of output depends only on the growth rate of autonomous, non-capacity-generating aggregate demand.

components that qualify as autonomous, but without linking this concretely to the growth experience of countries. Empirical research on the SSM has mostly focused on establishing a generic correlation between autonomous demand and GDP or the share of investment in GDP (Girardi and Pariboni 2016; 2020) rather than studying specific growth episodes. However, Fazzari et al. (2020, p. 602) and Dutt (2019, p. 299) note that SSMs 'can be used to understand the logic of the growth process' (ibid., p. 299) of specific countries. While the US housing bubble and fiscal austerity in Europe after the GFC are mentioned as determinants of autonomous demand, a detailed analysis of demand formation is missing.

It is in the study of (autonomous) demand formation in specific countries and periods where the recent PK literature can benefit from the Growth Models approach. For example, export demand is widely regarded as a key driver of the German growth model, but what specific institutional and political settings underpin it? Baccaro and Benassi (2017) argue that a decentralisation of collective bargaining since the mid 1980s and welfare reforms in the 2000s put downward pressure on nominal wages. This improved price competitiveness at a time when exports became more price-sensitive. At the same time, the regressive distributional effects of these policies have depressed consumption demand, making the German model highly dependent on exports.

Baccaro and Pontusson (2019) complement such an Institutionalist analysis with a political theory of sectoral interests.[16] They propose the concept of a 'social bloc', which is a hegemonic coalition dominated by economic sectors that exert a strong influence over key policy decisions. Different sectors will be sensitive to different macroeconomic variables: the manufacturing export industry to nominal wages and the exchange rate, construction to the real interest rate, and finance to consumer prices. These sensitivities translate into different economic policy preferences. An important feature of the social bloc is its ability to project particular sectoral interests as national interests. In the case of Germany, the social bloc is dominated by the manufacturing export industry. After German reunification, the sector pushed for more flexible industrial relations to reduce wage costs. Thanks to the hegemonic character of the social bloc, Neoliberal labour market reforms were eventually enacted by a centre-left government that portrayed the dismantling of collective bargaining and the creation of a workfare regime as policies in the national interest. Baccaro and Pontusson (2019) contrast the German case with Sweden, whose social bloc is broader and also includes public-sector unions. As a result, the Swedish social bloc has a greater interest in policies supporting domestic consumption, rendering the Swedish growth model much more balanced than the German one.

In this way, the Growth Models approach could complement PK growth models by providing an explanation for why certain autonomous-demand components that are treated as exogenous in theoretical models dominate empirically, for example exports in Germany and public and private consumption in Sweden. It also identifies social and economic tensions that come with growth models that are highly unbalanced in their demand composition, which may have implications for the stability of theoretical models and their parameters.

A weakness of the theory of social blocs proposed by Baccaro and Pontusson (2019) is its exclusive focus on sectoral interests. This seems to fit the case of export-oriented

16.   In political economy there are numerous examples where sectoral interests play a major role, for example Frieden (2015), where different sectors have different interests with respect to exchange-rate policy and regimes, or Culpepper (2011), who analyses lobbying of the financial sector.

                    Journal compilation © 2022 Edward Elgar Publishing Ltd

growth models, but is less suited to explaining the political support of other growth models. In particular, in finance-led growth models the political importance of home-ownership cuts across economic sectors. A different strand in CPE flags the social and political impact of housing (Johnston and Kurzer 2020): home-ownership can shape conservative political identities (Schwartz 2008; Watson 2010) and reduce political demand for welfare-state provision (Wiedemann 2021). Home-ownership has also been shown to be of strong predictive value in the voting for Brexit (Ansell and Adler 2019). Housing and home-ownership constitute an interesting intersection between the politics of everyday life as home-ownership (or the absence thereof) impacts large parts of the population (and their sensitivity to monetary policy or credit regulation), but housing finance is at the same time a prime interest of major financial institutions, from mortgage systems to regulation of securitisation. There are massive interests of the financial sector at stake, which have an effective lobbying capacity (Culpepper 2011), but the political support goes beyond those employed in the financial sector. This political economy literature on housing is complementary to a small but growing PK literature on the macroeconomic importance of housing (for example, Ryoo 2016; Kim et al. 2019; Stockhammer and Wolf 2019), which emphasises its centrality for the emergence of endogenous financial cycles in contemporary capitalism.

It is worthwhile recalling that there were earlier attempts to create a more systematic PK analysis where institutions feature prominently. Hodgson (1989) and Arestis (1996) drew heavily on (old) Institutionalism (see Whalen 2020 for an overview). Before that, the French Regulation Theory and the Social Structures of Accumulation approach both made efforts to fuse a historically specific institutional analysis with PKE (Setterfield 2011; Hein et al. 2014); both, however, focused on institutional change over time rather than explaining differences across countries. Similarly many Minskyan analyses have a strong Institutional bent (Whalen 2001; Papdimitriou and Wray 2006; Palley 2011), emphasising that changes in the institutional structure (for example, the rise of securitisation and shadow banking) influence financial stability. Again, these contributions highlight institutional change over time, but do not offer a systematic comparative analysis.

In sum, this article has argued that the recent interest of political economy in PKE is to be welcomed and offers an opportunity for PKE to realise its own research agenda, which is rooted in the political economy approach rather than in the narrow discipline of economics. Past years have already seen a growing engagement between Kaleckian analyses of demand regimes and CPE, which has informed the Growth Models approach. We have argued that the Growth Models approach needs to go beyond the export-led/debt-led dichotomy that has proven useful in the pre-GFC period and consider a richer set of growth drivers. This opens the door for a reinterpretation of existing growth models (allowing for finance-led growth as well as finance-led stagnation) and for considering a broader range of potential growth models (such as state-led growth). Further engagement with the political economy approach has the potential to be useful for other streams, such as Sraffian supermultiplier models and Institutionalist PKs, but it will require PKE to actively engage with a literature outside their usual comfort zone and to address questions of institutions and power more directly than in the past.

ACKNOWLEDGEMENTS

This paper is a part of the Leverhulme grant 'The Political Economy of growth models in an age of stagnation', Leverhulme, RPG-2021-045. The paper has benefited from comments by Guendalina Anzolin, Chiara Benassi, Ian Lovering, Andreas Nölke, Inga Rademacher and Ben Tippet. The usual disclaimers apply.

REFERENCES

Allain, O. (2015), 'Tackling the instability of growth: a Kaleckian–Harrodian model with an autonomous expenditure component', *Cambridge Journal of Economics*, 39(5), 1351–1371, available at: https://doi.org/10.1093/cje/beu039.

Ansell, B. and D. Adler (2019), 'Brexit and the politics of housing in Britain', *Political Quarterly*, 90(S2), 105–116.

Arestis, P. (1996), 'Post-Keynesian economics: towards coherence', *Cambridge Journal of Economics*, 20(1), 111–135.

Auerbach, A. and Y. Gorodnichenko (2012), 'Measuring the output responses to fiscal policy', *American Economic Journal – Economic Policy*, 4, 1–27.

Baccaro, L. and C. Benassi (2017), 'Throwing out the ballast: growth models and the liberalization of German industrial relations', *Socio-Economic Review*, 15(1), 85–115, available at: https://doi.org/10.1093/ser/mww036.

Baccaro, L. and C. Howells (2011), 'A common neoliberal trajectory: the transformation of industrial relations in advanced capitalism', *Politics & Society*, 39(4), 521–563.

Baccaro, L. and J. Pontusson (2016), 'Rethinking Comparative Political Economy: the Growth Model perspective', *Politics & Society*, 44(2), 175–207, available at: https://doi.org/10.1177/0032329216638053.

Baccaro, L. and J. Pontusson (2019), 'Social blocs and growth models: an analytical framework with Germany and Sweden as illustrative cases', Unequal Democracies Working Paper, No 7.

Baccaro, L., M. Blyth and J. Pontusson (eds) (2022), *Diminishing Returns: The New Politics of Growth and Stagnation*, Oxford: Oxford University Press.

Becker, Gary (1957 [1971]), *The Economics of Discrimination*, Chicago: University of Chicago Press.

Behringer, J. and T. van Treeck (2019), 'Income distribution and growth models: a sectoral balances approach', *Politics and Society*, 47(3), 303–332.

Bhaduri, A. and S. Marglin (1990), 'Unemployment and the real wage: the economic basis for contesting political ideologies', *Cambridge Journal of Economics*, 14, 375–393.

Blanchard, O.J. and D. Leigh (2014), 'Learning about fiscal multipliers from growth forecast errors', *IMF Economic Review*, 62(2), 179–212, available at: https://doi.org/10.1057/imfer.2014.17.

Blecker, R. (2016), 'Wage-led versus profit-led demand regimes: the long and the short of it', *Review of Keynesian Economics*, 4(4), 373–390.

Blecker, R., M. Cauvel and Y. Kim (2020), 'Systems estimation of a structural model of distribution and demand in the US economy', PKES Working Paper 2012.

Blyth, M. and M. Matthijs (2017), 'Black swans, lame ducks, and the mystery of IPE's missing macroeconomy', *Review of International Political Economy*, 24(2), 203–231.

Bohle, D. and B. Greskovits (2009), 'Varieties of Capitalism and capitalism "tout court"', *European Journal of Sociology [Archives Européennes de Sociologie]*, 50(3), 355–386.

Borio, C. (2014), 'The financial cycle and macroeconomics: what have we learnt?', *Journal of Banking and Finance*, 45, 182–198, available at: https://doi.org/10.1016/j.jbankfin.2013.07.031.

Clift, B. (2014), *Comparative Political Economy: States, Markets and Global Capitalism*, London: Palgrave Macmillan.

Crouch, C. (2009), 'Privatised Keynesianism: an unacknowledged policy regime', *The British Journal of Politics and International Relations*, 11(3), 382–399, available at: https://doi.org/10.1111/j.1467-856X.2009.00377.x.

Culpepper, Pepper (2011), *Quiet Politics and Business Power*, Cambridge, UK: Cambridge University Press.

Delong, J.B. and L.H. Summers (2012), 'Fiscal policy in a depressed economy', *Brookings Papers on Economic Activity*, 2012(1), 233–297, available at: https://doi.org/10.1353/eca.2012.0000.

Dobusch, L. and J. Kapeller (2012), 'A guide to paradigmatic self-marginalization: lessons for post-Keynesian economists', *Review of Political Economy*, 24(3), 469–487.

Dutt, A.K. (2019), 'Some observations on models of growth and distribution with autonomous demand growth', *Metroeconomica*, 70(2), 288–301, available at: https://doi.org/10.1111/meca.12234.

Fazzari, S.M., P. Ferri and A.M. Variato (2020), 'Demand-led growth and accommodating supply', *Cambridge Journal of Economics*, 44(3), 583–605, available at: https://doi.org/10.1093/cje/bez055.

Ferguson, T. (1984), 'From normalcy to New Deal: industrial structure, party competition, and American public policy in the Great Depression', *International Organization*, 38(1), 41–94.

Frieden, J. (2015), *Currency Politics: The Political Economy of Exchange Rate Policy*, Princeton, NJ: Princeton University Press.

Freitas, F. and F. Serrano (2015), 'Growth rate and level effects, the stability of the adjustment of capacity to demand and the Sraffian supermultiplier', *Review of Political Economy*, 27(3), 258–281, available at: https://doi.org/10.1080/09538259.2015.1067360.

Gabor, D. (2020), 'Critical macro-finance: a theoretical lens', *Finance and Society*, 6(1), 45–55.

Gechert, S. and A. Rannenberg (2018), 'Which fiscal multipliers are regime-dependent? A meta-regression analysis', *Journal of Economic Surveys*, 32(4), 1160–1182, available at: https://doi.org/10.1111/joes.12241.

Gechert, S., G. Horn and C. Paetz (2019), 'Long-term effects of fiscal stimulus and austerity in Europe', *Oxford Bulletin of Economics and Statistics*, 81(3), 647–666, available at: https://doi.org/10.1111/obes.12287.

Girardi, D. and R. Pariboni (2016), 'Long-run effective demand in the US economy: an empirical test of the Sraffian supermultiplier model', *Review of Political Economy*, 28(4), 523–544, available at: https://doi.org/10.1080/09538259.2016.1209893.

Girardi, D. and R. Pariboni (2020), 'Autonomous demand and the investment share', *Review of Keynesian Economics*, 8(3), 428–453, available at: https://doi.org/10.4337/roke.2020.03.07.

Gräbner, C., P. Heimberger, J. Kapeller and B. Schütz (2020), 'Is the Eurozone disintegrating? Macroeconomic divergence, structural polarisation, trade and fragility', *Cambridge Journal of Economics*, 44(3), 647–669, available at: https://doi.org/10.1093/cje/bez059.

Hall, P. (1989), *The Political Power of Economic Ideas: Keynesianism Across Nations*, Princeton, NJ: Princeton University Press.

Hall, P.A. (2014), 'Varieties of capitalism and the euro crisis', *West European Politics*, 37(6), 1223–1243, available at: https://doi.org/10.1080/01402382.2014.929352.

Hall, P.A. and D. Soskice (2001), *Varieties of Capitalism: The Institutional Foundations of Comparative Advantage*, Oxford: Oxford University Press.

Hay, C. (2009), 'Good inflation, bad inflation: the housing boom, economic growth and the disaggregation of inflationary preferences in the UK and Ireland', *The British Journal of Politics and International Relations*, 11(3), 461–478, available at: https://doi.org/10.1111/j.1467-856X.2009.00380.x.

Hay, C. and D. Wincott (2012), *The Political Economy of European Welfare Capitalism*, London: Bloomsbury Publishing.

Hein, E. (2018), 'Autonomous government expenditure growth, deficits, debt, and distribution in a neo-Kaleckian growth model', *Journal of Post Keynesian Economics*, 41(2), 316–338, available at: https://doi.org/10.1080/01603477.2017.1422389.

Hein, E. and M. Mundt (2013), 'Financialization, the financial and economic crisis, and the requirements and potentials for wage-led recovery', in M. Lavoie and E. Stockhammer (eds), *Wage-Led Growth: An Equitable Strategy for Economic Recovery*, London: Palgrave Macmillan, pp. 153–186.

Hein, E., N. Dodig and N. Budyldina (2014), 'Financial, economic and social systems: French Regulation School, Social Structures of Accumulation and Post-Keynesian approaches compared', IPE Working Papers 34/2014.

Hein, E., W.P. Meloni and P. Tridico (2020), 'Welfare models and demand-led growth regimes before and after the financial and economic crisis', *Review of International Political Economy*, 28(5), 1196–1223, available at: https://doi.org/10.1080/09692290.2020.1744178.

Hodgson, G. (1989), 'Post-Keynesianism and institutionalism: the missing link', in J. Pheby (ed.), *New Directions in Post-Keynesian Economics*, Aldershot, UK and Brookfield, VT: Edward Elgar Publishing, pp. 94–123.

Hope, D. and D. Soskice (2016), 'Growth models, Varieties of Capitalism, and macroeconomics', *Politics and Society*, 44(2), 209–226.

Ingham, Geoffrey (2004), *The Nature of Money*, Cambridge, UK: Polity Press.

Jaffe, W. (1956 [1983]), 'Léon Walras and his conception of economics', reprinted in D. Walker (ed.), *William Jaffe's Essays on Walras*, Cambridge, UK: Cambridge University Press, pp. 121–130.

Johnston, A. and P. Kurzer (2020), 'Bricks in the wall: the politics of housing in Europe', *West European Politics*, 43(2), 275–296.

Johnston, A., B. Hancké and S. Pant (2014), 'Comparative institutional advantage in the European sovereign debt crisis', *Comparative Political Studies*, 47(13), 1771–1800, available at: https://doi.org/10.1177/0010414013516917.

Kalecki, Michal (1943), 'Political aspects of full employment', *Political Quarterly*, XIV(4), 322–331.

Keynes, John (1936 [1973]), *The General Theory of Employment, Interest and Money*, in *The Collected Writings of John Maynard Keynes, Volume VII*, London: Macmillan.

Kim, Y.K., G.T. Lima and M. Setterfield (2019), 'Political aspects of household finance: debt, wage bargaining, and macroeconomic (in)stability', *Journal of Post Keynesian Economics*, 42(1), 16–38, available at: https://doi.org/10.1080/01603477.2018.1524263.

Kohler, K. and E. Stockhammer (2021), 'Growing differently? Financial cycles, austerity, and competitiveness in growth models since the Global Financial Crisis', *Review of International Political Economy*, forthcoming, available at: https://doi.org/10.1080/09692290.2021.1899035.

Kregel, Jan (1973), *The Reconstruction of Political Economy: An Introduction to Post-Keynesian Economics*, London: Palgrave Macmillan.

Lavoie, M. (2016), 'Convergence towards the normal rate of capacity utilization in Neo-Kaleckian models: the role of non-capacity creating autonomous expenditures', *Metroeconomica*, 67(1), 172–201, available at: https://doi.org/10.1111/meca.12109.

Lavoie, M. and E. Stockhammer (2013a), *Wage-Led Growth: An Equitable Strategy for Economic Recovery*, London: Palgrave Macmillan.

Lavoie, M. and E. Stockhammer (2013b), 'Wage-led growth: concept, theories and policies', in M. Lavoie and E. Stockhammer (eds), *Wage-Led Growth: An Equitable Strategy for Economic Recovery*, London: Palgrave Macmillan, pp. 13–39.

Marglin, S. and A. Bhaduri (1990), 'Profit squeeze and Keynesian theory', in S. Marglin and J. Schor (eds), *The Golden Age of Capitalism: Reinterpreting the Postwar Experience*, Oxford: Clarendon Press, pp. 153–186.

Minsky, H.P. (2016), 'The financial instability hypothesis: a restatement', in H.P. Minsky, *Can 'It' Happen Again? Essays on Instability and Finance*, New York: Routledge, pp. 59–71.

Nah, W.J. and M. Lavoie (2017), 'Long-run convergence in a neo-Kaleckian open-economy model with autonomous export growth', *Journal of Post Keynesian Economics*, 40(2), 223–238, available at: https://doi.org/10.1080/01603477.2016.1262745.

Obst, T., Ö. Onaran and M. Nikolaidi (2020), 'The effects of income distribution and fiscal policy on aggregate demand, investment and the budget balance: the case of Europe', *Cambridge Journal of Economics*, 44(6), 1221–1243, available at: https://doi.org/10.1093/cje/bez045.

Onaran, Ö. and G. Galanis (2014), 'Income distribution and growth: a global model', *Environment and Planning*, 46(10), 2489–2513.

Palley, T.I. (2011), 'A theory of Minsky super-cycles and financial crises', *Contributions to Political Economy*, 30(1), 31–46.

Papadimitriou D.P. and L.R. Wray (2006), 'The economic contributions of Hyman Minsky: varieties of capitalism and institutional reform', *Review of Political Economy*, 10(2), 199–225.

Qazizada, W. and E. Stockhammer (2015), 'Government spending multipliers in contraction and expansion', *International Review of Applied Economics*, 29(2), 238–258.

Ryoo, S. (2016), 'Household debt and housing bubbles: a Minskian approach to boom–bust cycles', *Journal of Evolutionary Economics*, 26(5), 971–1006, available at: https://doi.org/ 10.1007/s00191-016-0473-5.

Schwartz, H.M. (2008), 'Housing, global finance, and American hegemony: building conservative politics one brick at a time', *Comparative European Politics*, 6(3), 262–284, available at: https://doi.org/10.1057/cep.2008.11.

Schwartz, H. and B. Tranoy (2019), 'Thinking about thinking about Comparative Political Economy: from macro to micro and back', *Politics and Society*, 47(1), 23–54.

Setterfield, Mark (2011), 'Anticipations of the crisis: on the similarities between post-Keynesian economics and regulation theory', *Revue de la Regulation*, 10, available at: https://journals. openedition.org/regulation/9366?&id=9366.

Skocpol, Theda (1980), 'Political response to capitalist crises: neo-Marxist theories of the state and the case of the New Deal', *Politics and Society*, 10(2), 155–201.

Sorge, A. and W. Streeck (1988), 'Industrial relations and technical change: the case for an extended perspective', in W. Streeck and R. Hyman (eds), *New Technology and Industrial Relations*, Oxford: Blackwell, pp. 19–44.

Stockhammer, E. (2022), 'Post-Keynesian macroeconomic foundations for Comparative Political Economy', *Politics and Society*, 50(1), 156–187, available at: https://journals.sagepub. com/doi/full/10.1177/00323292211006562.

Stockhammer, E. and O. Onaran (2022), 'Growth models and post-Keynesian macroeconomics', in L. Baccaro, M. Blyth and J. Pontusson (eds), *Diminishing Returns: The New Politics of Growth and Stagnation*, Cambridge, UK: Cambridge University Press, forthcoming.

Stockhammer, E. and R. Wildauer (2016), 'Debt-driven growth? Wealth, distribution and demand in OECD countries', *Cambridge Journal of Economics*, 40(6), 1609–1634, available at: https://doi.org/10.1093/cje/bev070.

Stockhammer, E. and C. Wolf (2019), 'Building blocks for the macroeconomics and political economy of housing', *Japanese Political Economy*, 45(1–2), 43–67.

Stockhammer, E., Ö. Onaran and S. Ederer (2009), 'Functional income distribution and aggregate demand in the Euro area', *Cambridge Journal of Economics*, 33(1), 139–159.

Stockhammer, E., W. Qazizada and S. Gechert (2019), 'Demand effects of fiscal policy since 2008', *Review of Keynesian Economics*, 7(1), 57–74.

Stockhammer, E., J. Rabinovich and N. Reddy (2021), 'Distribution, wealth and demand regimes in historical perspective: the USA, the UK, France and Germany, 1855–2010', *Review of Keynesian Economics*, 9(3), 337–367.

Storm, S. and C.W.M. Naastepad (2013), 'Wage-led or profit-led supply: wages, productivity and investment', in M. Lavoie and E. Stockhammer (eds), *Wage-Led Growth: An Equitable Strategy for Economic Recovery*, London: Palgrave Macmillan, pp. 100–124.

Storm, S. and C.W.M. Naastepad (2015), 'Europe's hunger games: income distribution, cost competitiveness and crisis', *Cambridge Journal of Economics*, 39(3), 959–986, available at: https://doi.org/10.1093/cje/beu037.

Van der Zwan, N. (2014), 'Making sense of financialisation', *Socio-Economic Review*, 12, 99–129.

Watson, M. (2010), 'House price Keynesianism and the contradictions of the modern investor subject', *Housing Studies*, 25, 413–426.

Whalen, C.J. (2001), 'Integrating Schumpeter and Keynes: Hyman Minsky's theory of capitalist development', *Journal of Economic Issues*, 35(4), 805–823.

Whalen, C. (2020), 'Post-Keynesian institutionalism: past, present, and future', *Evolutionary and Institutional Economics Review*, 17, 71–92.

Wiedemann, Andreas (2021), 'How credit markets substitute for welfare states and influence social policy preferences: evidence from U.S. states', *British Journal of Political Science*, doi: https://doi.org/10.1017/S0007123420000708.

Williamson, O. (2000), 'The new institutional economics: taking stock, looking ahead', *Journal of Economic Literature*, 38(3), 595–613.

Review of Keynesian Economics, Vol. 10 No. 2, Summer 2022, pp. 76–93

The politics of growth models

Lucio Baccaro
Director, Max Planck Institute for the Study of Societies, Cologne, Germany

Jonas Pontusson
Professor of Comparative Politics, University of Geneva, Switzerland

This article develops a framework for studying the politics of growth models. These, the authors posit, are sustained by 'growth coalitions' based in key sectors. Their members are first and foremost firms and employer associations, but fractions of labor are also included, if their interests do not impair the model's functionality. There is no guarantee that a growth coalition and a winning electoral coalition coincide. In normal times, a growth coalition effectively insulates itself from political competition, and mainstream political parties converge on key growth model policies. In moments of crisis, however, the coalition shrinks, favoring the emergence of challengers that fundamentally contest the status quo. The way governing parties respond to electoral pressures can also play an important role in the recalibration of growth models. The authors illustrate the argument by examining the politics of 'export-led growth' in Germany, 'construction-led growth' in Spain, and 'balanced growth' in Sweden.

Keywords: *Comparative Political Economy, politics, Growth Models, macroeconomic management*

JEL codes: *B59, O43, O52, P16*

1 INTRODUCTION

Conceived as a follow-up to our previous work, this article articulates a framework for thinking about the politics of growth models. We argue that stable growth models are sustained by a coalition of organized interests that enjoy privileged access to the policy-making sphere and ensure that government policies, especially macroeconomic policies, reflect its interests and the functional requirements of the growth model. Growth coalitions operate outside the domain of electoral politics, but electoral politics constrain the politics of policy choice, and occasionally generate paradigmatic policy changes that transform the growth model. In the second half of the article, we illustrate some of the analytic leverage provided by this framework through stylized case studies of export-led growth in Germany, construction-led growth Spain, and 'balanced growth' in Sweden.[1]

Our approach builds on the literature on producer coalitions in Comparative and International Political Economy (Gourevitch 1986; Swenson 1991; Frieden and Rogowski 1996, Thelen 2014) while addressing its apparent neglect of electoral politics.

---

1. The ideas presented in this article draw on the introduction to a forthcoming volume, co-authored with Mark Blyth (Baccaro et al. 2022), as well as our previous work (Baccaro and Pontusson 2016; 2019). The case studies on Germany, Spain, and Sweden are syntheses of chapters co-authored with Martin Höpner (Baccaro and Höpner 2022), Fabio Bulfone (Baccaro and Bulfone 2022), and Lennart Erixon (Erixon and Pontusson 2022), respectively. We thank our co-authors for their many direct and indirect contributions.

Journal compilation © 2022 Edward Elgar Publishing Ltd
The Lypiatts, 15 Lansdown Road, Cheltenham, Glos GL50 2JA, UK
and The William Pratt House, 9 Dewey Court, Northampton MA 01060-3815, USA

We conceive a growth coalition as being based in one or more key sectors (for example, export-oriented manufacturing or the nexus of construction and mortgage finance). The members of a growth coalition are first and foremost firms and business associations, but fractions of labor are also included, albeit in a subordinate position, if their interests are in tune with the sectoral profile of the growth model and can be accommodated without impairing the latter's functionality.

Growth coalitions seek to project sectoral interests as coincident with the 'national interest' and to shape public perceptions of 'how the economy works,' but the success of such efforts is by no means a foregone conclusion. Relatedly, growth coalitions and electoral majorities do not necessarily coincide. In normal times, dominant growth coalitions typically succeed in insulating themselves from the electoral arena as mainstream political parties converge on key growth model policies (Hopkin and Voss 2022; Hübscher and Sattler 2022). However, growth coalitions shrink in numerical terms and the ranks of losers swell during economic crises and sustained periods of economic stagnation, favoring the emergence of new parties – or factions within mainstream parties – that challenge existing policy paradigms (Hopkin 2020). Under these conditions, the growth model itself may become politically contested and 'up for grabs.' As illustrated by our Swedish case study, the way governing parties respond to electoral pressures can also play an important role in the recalibration of growth models.

In what follows, we begin in Section 2 by articulating how the Growth Models perspective that we champion differs from the Varieties of Capitalism which has been the dominant paradigm in Comparative Political Economy for several decades. We then set out our conception of the politics of growth models in three steps: in Section 3, by considering the role of key sectors; in Section 4, by bringing in the dimension of class and class power; and, in Section 5, by discussing the role of parties and electoral politics. We illustrate these themes through stylized case studies of Germany, Spain, and Sweden in Sections 6–8. Section 9 provides some concluding remarks.

2   THE COMPARATIVE CAPITALISMS DEBATE

A signature feature of Comparative Political Economy (CPE) is the idea that there are several ways to organize a capitalist economy. CPE scholars have long emphasized the role of institutions that shape the supply side of the economy, enabling as well as incentivizing firms to develop core competences and pursue different production strategies: systems of corporate finance and control, industrial relations, and vocational training. The Varieties of Capitalism (VoC) framework developed by Hall and Soskice (2001) represents the most coherent statement of this broadly shared perspective. To recapitulate very briefly, the VoC framework identifies two fundamentally different types of economies: liberal market economies (LMEs) and coordinated market economies (CMEs). Specializing in economic activities that involve general skills, high-tech as well as low-end services, LMEs are distinguished by institutional arrangements that allow for rapid redeployment of human capital as well other assets. By contrast, CMEs specialize in economic activities that involve industry- and firm-specific skills and depend on institutions that solve the problems of credible commitment associated with the production of such skills. As the institutional ecosystem provides key firms with unique institutional capacities, each regime is efficient in its own way: LMEs excel in radical (product) innovation while CMEs excel in incremental (process) innovation.

Like earlier CPE scholarship, the VoC literature challenges the idea that globalization generates convergence between varieties of capitalism. In the VoC framework,

    Journal compilation © 2022 Edward Elgar Publishing Ltd

globalization instead serves to crystallize differences between regimes. Thus VoC scholars suggested, in the late 1990s, that Sweden, exemplifying the social democratic variant of coordinated capitalism, was becoming more like Germany, while the UK was becoming more like the US, but Germany and the US were becoming more – rather than less – distinct from each other as each economy capitalized on its distinctive advantages, and organized business rallied in defense of existing institutions (Soskice 1999; Iversen and Pontusson 2000).

The alternative perspective sketched by Baccaro and Pontusson (2016) conceives capitalist diversity as the result of different demand drivers of growth. From this perspective, institutional endowments and associated institutional complementarities (or the lack thereof) are of secondary importance in explaining the divergent trajectories among advanced capitalist countries. Instead, our approach starts with the channels through which aggregate demand expands (or fails to expand). The Growth Models perspective remains within the CPE tradition in that it seeks to understand cross-national diversity, but 'growth models' are not only demand-driven as opposed to supply-side driven: they are also more unstable than the types of capitalism identified by Zysman (1983) and Katzenstein (1985) as well as Hall and Soskice (2001).

Inspired by the Neo-Kaleckian tradition in macroeconomics (Palley 2012; Lavoie and Stockhammer 2013; Lavoie 2014) and the French Regulation school (Boyer 2004; 2015), the Growth Models perspective takes common trends as well as country-specific trajectories into consideration. A key theme of the Regulationist literature was the generalized crisis of 'wage-led' or 'Fordist' growth (Boyer and Saillard 2002; Boyer 2004). As commonly recognized, this growth model was premised on real wages growing in line with productivity increases, stimulating both domestic consumption and investment. The indexation of real wages to productivity was institutionally mediated by the presence of strong unions, and multi-employer wage-bargaining systems and the weakening of these institutions, along with global capital mobility and financialization, render the wage-led growth model, at best, very precarious.

Real wages falling behind productivity growth produces a tendency for aggregate demand to stagnate through various mechanisms, notably the greater propensity to consume out of labor income than out of profit income and the demand sensitivity of investment (Lavoie and Stockhammer 2013). Whether countries are able to escape this common stagnationist tendency hinges on their ability to find viable alternatives to wage-led growth (Stockhammer 2015). One alternative, exemplified by the UK prior to the global financial crisis of 2007–2008, consists of stimulating consumption by easing the access to credit. Another alternative is the export-led model that Germany has successfully pursued since the 1990s. The Swedish case represents, we think, a third model, which combines growth driven by credit-financed consumption as well as exports. And yet other models – for instance, Ireland's foreign direct investment (FDI)-led growth, which stimulates investment and exports while boosting the innovative capacities of the economy by attracting foreign capital (Bohle and Regan 2021) – can readily be added to this typology.[2]

---

2.   To clarify, we do not use the term 'growth models' in the same way as Post-Keynesian economists use it. In the Post-Keynesian literature, a 'demand regime' refers to the short-term response of demand/output to a shift in the functional distribution of income (Bhaduri and Marglin 1990) while a 'growth regime' takes into account the long-term implications of the distributional shift (through its impact on the investment function and/or on productivity). Both 'demand' and 'growth' regimes are counterfactual entities: they depend on some structural parameters of the economy (for example, propensities to consume, sensitivity of investment to demand and profit

                        Journal compilation © 2022 Edward Elgar Publishing Ltd

Crucially, our approach to growth models hinges on the claim that the ability to combine different demand drivers of growth differs across countries. For example, domestic consumption growth may be complementary to export growth (Sweden in the pre-crisis period) or there may be a trade-off between them (Germany), such that policies that expand wage growth and domestic consumption lead to a decline of export-led growth. Also, there is no guarantee that countries will find a viable growth driver. For example, economic stagnation has been the dominant tendency of Italy since the mid 1990s (Baccaro and Pontusson 2016).

3   SECTORAL INTERESTS IN MACROECONOMIC POLICY

Our framework for understanding the political foundations of the growth model posits, in a first step, that sectors have distinct 'policy requirements' and, as a corollary, that macroeconomic policies have sector-specific implications. Most obviously, sectors that cater primarily to domestic demand and sectors that cater primarily to foreign demand have very different needs with regard to wage growth. For the former, Keynes's classic fallacy of composition applies: each company would like to reduce costs by paying lower wages than its competitors, but the aggregation of individual choices reduces demand for all companies. The same logic does not apply to an industry relying on foreign demand: in this case, individual and collective rationality are better aligned in that, all else being equal, a reduction of wages relative to international competitors leads to an increase in competitiveness and greater demand for the industry as a whole as well as for individual firms.

In brief, policies promoting wage repression are detrimental for sectors relying on domestic demand and more acceptable, even beneficial, for sectors relying on foreign demand. Two qualifications must immediately be noted: first, the detrimental consequence of wage repression for sectors catering to domestic demand might be offset if domestic demand is stimulated by credit expansion, and, secondly, wage repression may have negative effects for export-oriented sectors too if it undermines the loyalty and commitment of their core workforce. For the latter reason, sectors producing high value-added exports tend to favor wage-repression policies that target the wages of workers engaged in the production of goods and services consumed by their employees rather than the wages of their own core employees (Günther and Höpner 2022).

Another important distinction, partially overlapping with the distinction between sheltered and exposed sectors, is the distinction between sectors whose demand is especially sensitive to the real interest rate and those that are sensitive to the real exchange rate. The two variables are linked by the behavior of prices. Keeping the nominal interest rate fixed, higher domestic inflation reduces the real interest rate. By the same token, if foreign prices do not change and the nominal exchange rate does not adjust (due to fixed exchange rates or a currency union), higher domestic inflation leads to real exchange-rate appreciation.

share, real exchange rate, and demand sensitivity of imports and exports). Actual growth in turn depends on whether public policy is consistent or inconsistent with the underlying growth model (Lavoie and Stockhammer 2012). By contrast, our growth models are purely descriptive entities and are operationalized through growth decomposition exercises – for example, we refer to Germany as 'export-led' because German growth in the period between 1995 and 2015 is largely attributable to (import-corrected) export growth.

Construction is the most obvious example of an interest-rate-sensitive sector. Low real interest rates stimulate demand for housing, and simultaneously make it cheaper for households and firms (both financial and non-financial) to borrow, thus stimulating loan generation by banks. However, the financial sector dislikes inflation intensely because it erodes the real value of liquid financial assets (Mosley 2003). The distinct interests of construction and finance become compatible when inflation is contained within the housing sector, that is, house prices rise while wage and general price inflation remains subdued. The latter condition is likely to hold when the labor market is weakly regulated, and in particular when precarious employment conditions curtail unionization or otherwise keep worker power in check. House prices rising faster than other prices creates opportunities for capital gains that strengthen the balance sheet of households and also produce a wealth effect that stimulates household expenditures to the benefit of other sectors of the economy (Boyer 2000).[3]

By contrast, export-oriented manufacturing is an exchange-rate-sensitive sector, especially if the price sensitivity of exports (or of import-competing domestic producers) is high. A key requirement in this case is a fixed exchange-rate regime, or ideally a single currency, which prevents the nominal exchange rate from adjusting to differences between domestic and foreign inflation. Domestic prices are a function of unit labor costs, that is, nominal wages divided by labor productivity. Keeping labor productivity constant, persistent wage moderation will lead to a depreciation of the real exchange rate and this will stimulate external demand (Höpner and Lutter 2017). External demand, in turn, will generate income and spur investment, with knock-on effects for the domestic economy as well. Crucially, export-led growth is a feasible growth strategy if the export sector is sufficiently large to overcome the depressive effect of wage moderation (Bowles and Boyer 1995).

In sum, macroeconomic policies favor certain sectors and penalize others. It stands to reason, then, that sectoral actors have conflicting preferences about the monetary, fiscal, exchange-rate, and wage-formation policies that influence real exchange rates and interest rates. As emphasized by the supply-side-oriented CPE literature (for example, Thelen 2019), they also have conflicting preferences with respect to the design of social insurance, spending on education, and R&D policy, but there is arguably more space for package deals that simultaneously satisfy multiple constituencies ('logrolling') in these other policy domains. In many instances, policy choices in these other domains might be interpreted, we think, as side payments to sectors whose interests would be better served by different macroeconomic policies.[4]

4   SOCIAL CLASS AND POWER RESOURCES

As indicated at the outset, our approach to the politics of growth models draws on earlier work in Comparative and International Political Economy that conceives politics in terms of coalitions of 'producer groups' defined by class as well as sectoral or, in other words, 'cross-class alliances' (Gourevitch 1986; Swenson 1991; Frieden and Rogowski 1996; Thelen 2014). Much of this literature might be faulted for using a

---

3.   Under conditions of stable wage inflation, inflation-targeting central banks will keep nominal interest rates low even though asset prices increase (Carlin and Soskice 2015).
4.   See Hassel and Palier (2021) for an ambitious framework that bridges the divide between supply-side and demand-side policies and focuses attention on linkages between growth strategies and welfare-state reforms.

simple dichotomy between 'labor' and 'business,' with the former category apparently referring to all 'wage earners.' In our view, more fine-grained class distinctions need to be deployed and more attention should be paid to the question of how people's position in the class structure conditions the salience of sectoral interests.

Following Iversen and Soskice (2001), a reasonable working hypothesis is that the skills of manual workers without university education tend to be sector-specific. Thus, the interests of skilled workers are more closely tied to the prosperity and prospects of the firm and the sector in which they work than the interests of 'routine workers.' The latter care more about macroeconomic conditions and, in particular, about the level of unemployment in the economy as a whole.

Within the middle class, broadly conceived, there are certainly occupations (for example, medical doctors) whose skills are very sector-specific, but the skills of individuals with tertiary education tend to be portable across sectors. For example, high-level managers frequently move, not only between firms but also between sectors. In addition, ownership of financial assets is constitutive of being in the 'upper middle class' and income from financial assets reduces the salience of sectoral interests relative to class interests even if the skills that generate labor income are sector-specific. In short, we posit that sectoral interests are most salient to skilled manual workers and that sectoral interests divide the working class to a greater extent than the middle class.

The concept of sector specificity can also be applied to capital. As documented by Krippner (2011) for the US, the distinction between finance and manufacturing has become blurred as financial activities have become an increasingly important source of profits for large manufacturing corporations since the early 1990s. Still, it remains meaningful, we think, to distinguish between capitalists who own and manage diversified portfolios of financial assets and capitalists who own controlling shares in one or several corporations, whatever the activities of those corporations might be. We posit that large stakeholders as well as executive managers share in the sectoral interests of the corporations that they control, but these interests may be ambiguous in the case of corporations whose economic activities are spread across several sectors.

We now have the basic elements necessary to map the contours of growth coalitions, defined as an enduring cross-class coalition of sectoral interests, first and foremost groups of corporate owners and executive managers but also workers with sector-specific skills. The groups that constitute such a coalition share similar preferences with regard to macroeconomic and sectoral policies. The inclusion of different sectoral and class interests depends on the specific features of the growth model. For reasons to be discussed, the Swedish growth model provides for the accommodation of a wider range of organized interests than either the German or the Spanish growth model.

Haffert and Mertens (2019) provide an interesting illustration of the way growth coalitions operate. Through a time-series cross-sectional analysis, they show that tax policies are shaped by the underlying growth model: the more the growth model is consumption- and debt-led, the lower taxes on consumption are (vice versa for export-led growth). Through a case study of Germany, they also show that the German government used the proceeds of a value-added tax increase to finance a decrease in social security contributions, reducing export prices (through reduced labor costs) while boosting domestic prices. This 'fiscal devaluation' was adamantly opposed by both labor and capital groups in domestic sectors such as construction and retailing, but business associations representing export-oriented sectors supported it. For cross-pressured unions in exposed unions, sectoral interests prevailed over class interests.

Are unskilled workers without strong sectoral attachments ever part of a growth coalition? Iversen and Soskice (2019) argue that technological change has broken 'Fordist' complementarities between semi-skilled and skilled workers, leading to political marginalization of low-skilled workers. In our view, patterns of inclusion and exclusion of low-skilled workers depend on the growth model and on power resources (Korpi 2006). If growth is export-led and export competitiveness depends importantly on keeping the real exchange rate down and the profit share up through nominal and real wage moderation, accommodation of the interests of routine workers becomes difficult. However, routine workers may force policy-makers to accommodate their interests through collective organization, operationalized in the first instance through unionization. Everything else being equal, unionization provides workers with bargaining power and this power must somehow be appeased through policy concessions. Accommodation of routine manual workers may push firms to reduce the price sensitivity of demand through innovation and reorganization, and thus rebalance the growth model. Alternatively, it may undermine the viability of the growth model and lead to a crisis.

5   PARTIES AND ELECTORAL POLITICS

Even under very generous assumptions about linkages between core sectors and other parts of the economic structure, the beneficiaries of a growth model are likely to represent a minority of the voting population. How does a growth coalition prevent the emergence of an adverse electoral coalition composed of workers and capitalists from rival sectors or groups with no specific labor market attachments? In other words, how does a growth coalition ensure its electoral viability?

In an influential contribution, Beramendi et al. (2015, p. 62) argue that 'electoral partisan politics ... should drive explanatory accounts of policy choice in political economy' (see also Häusermann and Kriesi 2015; Kitschelt and Rehm 2015). For these authors, the main mechanism of policy selection is voter choice in competitive elections. Voters are seen as having well-defined policy preferences on issues, and every vote carries the same weight. From these premises, it follows that voters select growth-model policies based on alternative proposals made by political parties, leaving little meaningful space for organized interests and 'growth coalitions' in our understanding of this term.[5]

We agree that elections cannot be ignored. There is no guarantee that the dominant *growth coalition* will also be the dominant *electoral* coalition. Nonetheless, we posit that the key policy foundations of a growth model are shielded from electoral competition through various mechanisms. First, the basic planks of macroeconomic policy are heavily institutionalized and not at the direct disposal of electoral majorities. Monetary policy, for example, has been entrusted to independent central banks. In the eurozone, fiscal policy, too, is heavily constrained by European fiscal rules or constitutional provisions such as 'debt brakes.'

---

5.   At the same time, Beramendi et al. (2015) suggest that macroeconomic policy and industrial policy are not salient issues, due to convergence between left and right or delegation to supranational authorities, and that electoral politics primarily concern other issues (welfare provisions, immigration, education, and the environment). In our view, convergence and delegation are part of the *explanandum* and should not be taken for granted.

                    Journal compilation © 2022 Edward Elgar Publishing Ltd

Second, economic policy is a highly technical domain which lends itself more to the 'quiet politics' of technical agencies and committees, in which well-defined sectoral interests are more likely to be heard, than to the 'noisy politics' of electoral competition (Culpepper 2010). In line with this intuition, Hübscher and Sattler (2022) present evidence of a mismatch between voter preferences and the policies of governments with regard to fiscal policies. They find that voters are opposed to austerity *both* in domestic demand-oriented Britain and in export-oriented Germany. Yet countries relying on export-led growth are considerably more likely to pursue austerity than countries relying on domestic demand.

Third, established parties are likely to converge on policies that are key for the growth model, thus limiting the space for electoral competition to non-threatening issues.[6] Hübscher and Sattler (2022) show that left- and right-leaning governments are equally likely to implement austerity in export-led growth models, while they are much less likely to do so in domestic demand-led models. They rationalize this finding by hypothesizing that governments of different political orientations internalize the functional requirements of the respective growth models. However, partisan differences become relevant in countries in which the two growth drivers contribute approximately equally. In these 'balanced' models, left-leaning governments are less likely to implement austerity than right-leaning governments.

Building on the Gramscian notion of hegemony, it is also plausible to argue that stable growth coalitions successfully project their key interests as the 'national interest.' In Gramsci's (1992) core formulation, the success of such 'framing effects' requires material concessions targeted on potentially disruptive subordinate groups (Przeworski 1985, ch. 4). In any case, there is little doubt that the ability to shape perceptions of 'how the economy works' contributes to reducing the electoral vulnerability of the growth model (Blyth 2002; Schmidt 2008).

The above discussion suggests that a growth coalition – composed of groups and sectors that are key to the success of the growth model – has greater influence on public policy formation than other social groups, and that under conditions of 'normal politics,' partisan competition is unlikely to upset it. This state of affairs is not unchangeable, though. When growth withers away – either due to external shocks or to the accumulation of endogenous dysfunctionalities – and the circle of beneficiaries becomes excessively narrow, previously 'quiet' politics becomes progressively more 'noisy.' The media start questioning the received wisdom about how the economy works (Culpepper 2021). Citizens develop distinct preferences over issues they previously took for granted. Anti-system parties and political entrepreneurs inside established parties politicize the newly salient issues and seek to enhance their electoral appeal by reaching out to the 'losers' of the growth model (Hopkin 2020). In these circumstances, it becomes increasingly difficult for the growth coalition to insulate itself from electoral competition and the growth model itself may become implicated in partisan electoral politics.[7]

---

6.   This formulation draws some inspiration from the cartel party thesis, as articulated by Blyth and Katz (2005) and Hopkin and Blyth (2018). For our present purposes, it is not necessary to engage with the question of whether or not 'cartelization' is a necessary condition for parties to converge on key growth-model policies.

7.   Inspired by Amable and Palombarini (2009), Baccaro and Pontusson (2019) used the Gramscian label of 'dominant social blocs' to refer to the coalitional underpinnings of growth models. We now prefer the label of 'growth coalitions' because it brings the potential for tensions between interest-group politics and electoral politics in focus.

6   THE POLITICS OF EXPORT-LED GROWTH IN GERMANY

We now turn to stylized case studies to illustrate and flesh out some of the propositions set out above, starting with Germany as the representative case of the export-led growth model. Between 1995 and 2015, German growth was largely pulled by exports (75 percent), while the growth contribution of domestic demand was small (–4 percent).[8] By comparison, growth was overwhelmingly pulled by domestic demand in the US and the UK in the same period (89 percent and 82 percent, respectively). Furthermore, exports were the most dynamic component of German aggregate demand in every five-year period between 1995 and 2015, including in the post-global-financial-crisis period. Exports accounted for 62 percent of total growth in 2011–2015, but the following years saw a much greater role for domestic demand, which accounted for 81 percent of total growth in 2016–2018. Thus, there was a rebalancing towards the end of the 2010s. It remains to be seen if it will continue in the post-pandemic phase.

Germany's export-led growth model is underpinned by *institutions* and therefore not easily modifiable through changes in government policy. An inflexible exchange-rate regime (the euro) prevents the correction of competitiveness imbalances, an industrial-relations regime facilitates competitive disinflation, and a system of fiscal federalism severely constrains the fiscal capacity of local governments. These institutions jointly undergird Germany's *undervaluation* regime (Höpner 2018).

Historically, Germany has had lower wage and price inflation than other European countries. This trend should lead to nominal exchange-rate appreciation. However, the euro has made such adjustment impossible. Within the euro, every percentage point of German nominal disinflation translates into real devaluation vis-à-vis other members of the eurozone. In the pre-crisis period this led to a yawning gap in real exchange rates between the periphery of the eurozone and Germany, and correspondingly to account imbalances (Scharpf 2011). Furthermore, as a single currency that encompasses 'strong' and 'weak' countries, the exchange rate of the euro vis-à-vis the rest of the world is in all likelihood lower than the exchange rate of a Deutsche Mark would be.

The wage-bargaining system provides the second plank of the undervaluation regime. The German industrial relations system is no longer as 'coordinated' as it once was, having undergone significant liberalization since the 1990s (Hassel 2014; Baccaro and Howell 2017). Various factors (for example, German unification, greater competitive pressures in export markets) induced German export-oriented companies to engage in a cost-cutting campaign. This was accomplished through the threat of decentralization, through a wave of concessionary bargaining at the plant level, and through the introduction of OT (*ohne Tarifvertrag*) membership. Parts suppliers started leaving their employer associations in the 1990s because they felt the industry-level standards had become too expensive for them. In turn, employer associations responded by allowing OT membership, that is, by allowing companies to remain

---

8.   The figures in parentheses are based on import-adjusted demand contributions to growth. Differently from standard decomposition exercises (for example, Baccaro and Pontusson 2016), which subtract imports solely from exports, import-adjusted demand contributions decompose imports between the part absorbed by domestic demand (for consumption, investment, government expenditures purposes) and the part absorbed by exports (imported intermediate products that are directly or indirectly incorporated into exports) (Auboin and Borino 2017). See the online appendix to Baccaro and Neimanns (2022) for a presentation of methodology. The data are drawn from the OECD Input-Output and Trade in Value Added databases.

members even though they did not apply the contractual standards. The practice of OT membership originated in the manufacturing sector, but became particularly diffuse in low-wage service sectors such as retailing, which had traditionally relied on extension of collective-bargaining agreements to take wages out of competition. With OT membership, employer associations became less willing to allow for statutory extension, because this threatened their OT members. Furthermore, intersectoral dynamics also played a role. In Germany, intersectoral employer associations can exercise a veto power on the sectoral extension of collective-bargaining agreements even when the sectoral social partners agree to it. Dominated by export-oriented sectors, the intersectoral employer associations frequently used their veto power to block statutory extension in service sectors, thus contributing to decoupling wages in low-skilled service sectors from manufacturing wages. Keeping service-sector wages low was expedient for export-led companies because it shifted the costs of real exchange-rate disinflation onto the domestic sectors (Günther and Höpner 2022).

Public-sector workers are not only more highly unionized than those in other sectors, but also have little to fear from relocation and competitive pressures. Yet wage growth was subdued in the German public sector as well (Di Carlo 2018). Another institution explains this phenomenon: German fiscal federalism. A tax reform, implemented in steps between 2000 and 2005, led to a loss of revenue for Länder and municipalities, which are responsible for 90 percent of public-sector employment. The consequence was that the Länder were forced to cut expenditures, putting downward pressure on public-sector wages.

The combination of an inflexible exchange-rate regime and mechanisms that ensure wage moderation both in the private and in the public sector provides the German export-led growth model with solid institutional foundations, which protect it from changes in government majorities. Furthermore, there is also evidence that the largest German parties converged on key policies undergirding the growth model. Thus a center-left government took the key policy decisions of the early 2000s: fiscal consolidation, pressures to decentralize wage setting and facilitate atypical employment, and a thorough overhaul of unemployment insurance.

As the two main parties saw their electoral support erode to the benefit of challenger parties from the mid 1990s onwards, it was relatively easy for them (compared to Sweden, as discussed later in the paper) to form grand coalitions and keep the fundamental orientation towards export-led growth unchanged. If the German trajectory until the early 2000s can be interpreted as an inevitable response to the external shock of unification, the policy approach taken after 2005 is difficult to make sense of without attributing to policy-makers a deliberate intent to shore up the devaluation regime. After a short-lived fiscal expansion during the global financial crisis and Great Recession of 2008–2009, fiscal policy quickly became 'austerian' again, even though there clearly was room (and arguably need) for fiscal expansion. The introduction of the minimum wage in 2015 increased wages in low-skilled service sectors and slightly strengthened domestic demand (Marx and Starke 2017), but the largest contribution to growth continued to come from exports until the late 2010s.

7   THE POLITICS OF CONSTRUCTION-LED GROWTH IN SPAIN

Spain before the global financial crisis and Great Recession illustrates the *modus operandi* of a very different growth model from that of Germany, one in which domestic demand is the key growth driver and construction is the key sector (together with banking). In the period between 1995 and 2015, Spanish growth was 2.1 percent per year on average, higher than in France, Germany, and Italy, and (import-adjusted) domestic demand accounted for 63.5 percent of total growth. However, there is a big difference between the pre-crisis and the post-crisis period in the case of Spain. In the pre-crisis period, Spanish growth was largely pulled by domestic demand, which accounted for 61.5 percent in 1996–2000 and 97.9 percent in 2001–2005. With the euro crisis destroying domestic demand (and imports), total growth fell to zero in 2011–2015 and the growth contribution of domestic demand became negative (–1 percent per year). In this period, the only stimulus to growth came from exports. It would be incorrect to say there was a shift towards export-led growth in the post-crisis period (Kohler and Stockhammer 2021). In fact, when Spain returned to relatively fast growth in 2015–2018 (2.8 percent per year), domestic demand was again the main contributor, accounting for 65 percent of growth.

Within domestic demand, investments played a key role in Spain, growing from 22 percent of GDP in 1995 to 30 percent in 2006. Specifically, construction investments increased from 14 percent to 21 percent of GDP in this period. The construction sector, already large in comparative perspective (9 percent of value-added in 1995), peaked at 12 percent of value-added in 2006. By comparison, the German construction sector contracted from 7 percent of value-added in 1995 to 4 percent in 2007. Furthermore, Spanish house prices more than tripled between the early 1990s and the mid 2000s, while household debt more than doubled as a percentage of disposable income. In brief, all the elements of a debt-driven construction boom were present in Spain.

Membership of the euro favored the construction boom by creating the opposite macroeconomic configuration to the German one. The spread between Spanish and German long-term nominal interest rates declined from 4.5 percent in 1995 to 0.2 percent in 1999, and continued to decline after Spain joined the euro, reaching 0 percent in 2003. However, inflation remained higher than in Germany (by 1.5 percent on average between 1999 and 2007). The consequence was that Spanish long-term real interest rates fell from 6.1 percent in 1995 to 2.6 percent in 1999 to a low of 0.1 percent in 2005. Low real interest rates and an appreciating real exchange rate produced a loss of competitiveness and the accumulation of large current-account deficits before the global financial crisis and Great Recession, which however did not lead to corrective measures until the euro crisis, when capital inflows suddenly stopped.

Interestingly, the demand boom had little to do with growing real wages, and much more to do with credit expansion (Perez and Matsaganis 2018; Cárdenas et al. 2021). Although the wage bill grew thanks to employment creation and a higher employment intensity of growth, real hourly wages did not increase at all between 1995 and 2007, not only in the economy as a whole but also in the booming construction sector. In this period, Spain had even greater real wage moderation than Germany. By contrast, credit to the private non-financial sector almost quadrupled, reaching a peak of 223 percent of GDP in 2009. Credit to non-financial firms increased the most, from 62 percent of GDP in 1995 to 168 percent in 2009, but credit to households also grew from 31 percent in 1995 to 85 percent in 2009. By contrast, private-sector credit shrank in Germany over the same period. Contrary to a popular argument, which sees foreign banks finance the Spanish demand boom by intermediating foreign savings through capital outflows (for example, Quaglia and Royo 2015; Dellepiane-Avellaneda et al. 2021), the bulk of credit was created by domestic banks. While the stock of foreign loans peaked at 53 percent of GDP in 2007, the stock of domestic banks' loans was almost three times larger. Small local saving banks (*cajas*) played a key role in the financing of local development projects (Ruiz et al. 2015).

Spain's main government parties, the conservative PP and the socialist PSOE, while diverging fundamentally on other issues, such as same-sex marriage, shared the same construction-centric economic model and implemented similar policies. In 1998 the PP passed a 'build anywhere' law, by which virtually any land could be reclassified as 'suitable for development,' except land of special naturalistic significance (and even in such cases, exceptions were frequently made) (Burriel 2011). In Spain, responsibility for zoning regulation rests with municipal authorities. Thus, municipalities started to compete with each other to reclassify as much land as possible as 'suitable for development,' in order to attract large development projects, which would bring higher incomes and tax revenues. In turn, developers financed their investments with loans extended by the local *cajas*. This type of intertwining of local politics, housing development, and regional banks was as much a characteristic of PP-run localities in Murcia and Valencia as of socialist-run Andalusia or autonomist Catalunia (López and Rodríguez 2011). Furthermore, the PP strengthened housing demand by deregulating the mortgage market, which led to the emergence of the second-largest securitization market in Europe after the UK (Dellepiane-Avellaneda et al. 2021). Confirming party convergence on key policies for the growth model, when the PP lost the elections in 2004, the PSOE made no attempt to reverse the decisions of its predecessors, letting the housing bubble balloon until 2007.

The social coalition directly profiting from the housing-based economy included developers, bankers, and middle- and upper-class property owners (who often owned multiple houses). Low-skilled workers benefited from the expansion of employment opportunities brought about by the construction frenzy. Firms and workers in adjoining sectors such as infrastructural development and tourism also had a stake in the growth model. By 2007, 85 percent of Spanish households owned at least one house (López and Rodríguez 2011). Even low-income households could use their appreciating housing assets as collateral for consumption finance.

After the crisis, small construction companies went bankrupt, construction workers lost their jobs, and low-income households lost their homes. The local *cajas* were wiped out by a wave of restructuring and only two out of 45 survived. However, large banks like BBVA and Banco Santander consolidated their position in the domestic market and further expanded their reach into foreign markets (Quaglia and Royo 2015). Similarly, large construction groups like Acciona and the ACS Group also benefited from the disappearance of small firms and expanded their activities abroad. Overall, the core growth coalition shrank but did not fundamentally change.

8   THE POLITICS OF GROWTH-MODEL RECALIBRATION IN SWEDEN

Averaging 2.6 percent, Sweden's annual growth rate between 1995 and 2015 was higher than both Germany's and Spain's, and higher than the OECD average. Decomposing GDP growth in the manner described above suggests that two-thirds of growth were attributable to domestic demand and one-third to import-adjusted exports. In the late 1990s, growth was equally pulled (50–50) by exports and domestic demand. However, the story of the Swedish 'balanced' growth model (Baccaro and Pontusson 2016) is not so much about equal weight of growth drivers; rather, it is about sequence and compatibility of growth drivers. While the German growth model became increasingly reliant on exports from the early 1990s onwards, repressing domestic consumption, in Sweden export-led growth pulled the economy out of the recession of the early 1990s, but then generated consumption growth and boosted the growth of import-competing and sheltered services.

Furthermore, the extent of rebalancing after the global financial crisis was much more extensive in Sweden than in Germany. Like the economic recoveries of the early 1980s and mid 1990s, the Swedish recovery of 2010–2011 followed in the wake of a sharp depreciation of the value of the krona and a restoration of the profit share in manufacturing, but sluggish foreign demand, first and foremost due to the austerity measures of eurozone member states, rendered the export-led growth less robust than in the past. The center-right parties in power at the time responded to this situation by stimulating domestic demand via tax cuts. More importantly over the long run, the central bank (*Riksbanken*) embarked on a sustained campaign to boost economic growth by cutting interest rates and quantitative easing from 2012 onwards.

With exports of goods and services accounting for 45 percent of GDP in 2020 (down from an all-time high of 49.8 percent in 2008), the Swedish economy remains highly export dependent, but the balance shifted towards greater reliance on domestic growth drivers in the 2010s. The manufacturing sector's share of total business value-added declined in the pre-crisis period as well as the post-crisis period. While this decline was more than offset by the expansion of export-oriented services in the pre-crisis period, the share of total value-added attributed to sheltered services has increased steadily and the share of exposed services has remained stable in the post-crisis period. Perhaps most strikingly, real estate and construction increased their combined share of total value-added from 13.0 percent in 2008 to 15.4 percent in 2019.[9]

Moreover, wage growth exceeded labor productivity growth by a considerable margin, stimulating internal demand. At the same time, expansionary monetary policy measures and favorable tax treatment of mortgages have boosted construction and sustained private consumption since the early 2010s. In marked contrast to Germany, household indebtedness rose sharply in Sweden as well as the UK and the US from the mid 1990s until the crisis and, in contrast to the UK and the US, the growth of household indebtedness continued unabated through the 2010s in Sweden. In this respect, the rebalanced Swedish growth model of the 2010s bears some resemblance to the construction-led growth model exemplified by pre-crisis Spain.

The different trajectories followed by Sweden and Germany raise two questions which are important for the politics of growth models. First, why did Sweden not follow Germany to become an export-led growth model in the 1990s? And, second, why did Sweden take a 'domestic turn' in the 2010s? Regarding the first question, it is noteworthy that Volvo and other large, export-oriented engineering firms pushed hard for decentralization of wage bargaining in the mid 1980s (see Pontusson and Swenson 1996). The fundamental objective behind this employer offensive was to decouple wage developments in exposed and sheltered sectors and thus to create the conditions for an export-led growth model akin to the model that Germany adopted a decade later. With the tacit support of the Metalworkers' union, wage formation indeed became more decentralized in the 1980s, but wage growth in sheltered services continued to keep apace with wage growth in export-oriented manufacturing. Two considerations are key for understanding why Swedish engineering employers failed to achieve their fundamental objective. To begin with, social democratic governments in the 1980s were (still) unwilling to let the rate of unemployment rise above 4 percent. Second, Sweden's powerful public-sector unions insisted on the wages of their members keeping up with the wages in exposed sectors as well as wage solidarity within the

---

9.   Based on the OECD STAN Database (ISIC Rev. 4, 2020 Edition).

public sector, putting upward pressure on wages in private services. In other words, partisan politics (a social democratic government with strong ties to the union movement) and the bargaining power of public-sector employees, a well-organized interest group outside the growth coalition, prevented the emergence of a purely export-led growth model in the 1980s.

The failure to decouple wages in the exposed and sheltered sectors in turn put pressure on manufacturing firms to invest in new technologies and incentivized capitalists to diversify their holdings. The manufacturing firms that spearheaded the export-led recovery of the 1990s were firms that had invested heavily in information and communication technologies over the previous decade (Erixon 2011). Beyond traditional manufacturing, business services emerged as a leading export sector in this period and, as documented by Thelen (2019), key groups in the Swedish business community also diversified by taking advantage of opportunities created by the privatization of education and publicly financed care services.

The diversification of the growth coalition in Sweden has facilitated the maintenance of a balanced growth model in that labor costs are less of a concern for the leading export sectors than was the case in the 1970s and 1980s. Organized business did not mobilize against macroeconomic policies that served to boost domestic demand in the 2010s. At the same time, electoral politics must be taken into account in order to explain why Sweden pursued more expansionary macroeconomic policies than Germany in the post-crisis period. In both countries, the Great Recession and the sluggishness of the subsequent recovery reinforced rising political disaffection among many voters, especially low-income voters, and the appeal of populist parties. Differently from the German case, however, the long-standing fragmentation of the center-right rules out the formation of grand-coalition governments in Sweden. Competition among the 'bourgeois' parties makes it difficult for one (or two) of these parties to enter into a formal coalition with the social democrats. Since the entry of the populist Sweden Democrats into parliament in 2010, neither of the center-left bloc nor the center-right has commanded a parliamentary majority in the 2010s. In this new situation, minority coalition governments of the center-right (2010–2014) and the center-left (2014–the present) have eschewed austerity measures that seemed likely to weaken their re-election prospects and the mainstream parties have converged on delegating much of macroeconomic management to the *Riksbank*.

9   CONCLUDING REMARKS

The politics of growth models that we have sketched in this paper brings together two traditions in Comparative Political Economy: the producer-group perspective (Gourevitch 1986; Swenson 1991; Thelen 2014) and the electoral perspective (Beramendi et al. 2015). Each can be individually faulted for neglecting the other dimension, but their combination, we posit, goes a long way towards explaining the diversity of growth models in advanced countries.

Growth models rest on growth coalitions with distinct sectoral profiles. In most times and circumstances, producer-group politics prevails and the key policy planks of the growth model are shielded from electoral competition. Various mechanisms concur to produce this outcome. First, macroeconomic policy rests on institutions which are out of reach for electoral majorities. For example, monetary policy is the prerogative of an independent central bank, which in the eurozone is not even a national institution. Fiscal policy is also strongly constrained by supranational rules (such as the Stability and Growth Pact) or constitutional provisions (for example, regarding 'balanced budgets' or 'debt brakes'). Second, economic policy issues are unlikely to be highly salient for voters, thus 'quiet politics' is the dominant mode (Culpepper 2010). Third, established parties converge on policies which are crucial for the growth model. Our case studies suggest that this happened in Germany, where both the SPD and the CDU shared a commitment to strengthen the competitiveness of the export sector, and in Spain, where both the PP and PSOE shared a commitment to create favorable conditions for the construction industry and associated financial activities.

Growth coalitions might also shape the way voters think about economic relationships. When normative consensus goes beyond elites and affects individual perceptions as well, then a growth coalition is hegemonic in the sense of Gramsci and deserves the appellative of 'dominant.' Whether a growth coalition is 'dominant' in this sense needs to be verified empirically, for example through public opinion surveys.

Electoral competition features most clearly in moments of crisis. When the growth model becomes dysfunctional, either due to the endogenous accumulation of problems or to external shocks, politics shifts from 'quiet' to 'noisy' mode. New political entrepreneurs, within or outside mainstream parties, repoliticize issues previously seen as sacrosanct or taken for granted and reach out to the growing pool of losers. In these circumstances, elections may bring about fundamental change in the growth model. To visualize this scenario, think what could have happened if Sanders had won the American election or the Five Star Movement had obtained an electoral majority in the Italian parliament.

Electoral politics also acts as a constraint on what a growth coalition is able to achieve in normal times. This is brought out by the Swedish case. Swedish manufacturing exporters tried but failed to bring about the same decoupling between export-sector and protected-sector wages that the German employers accomplished. They failed because the Swedish social democrats had strong ties to public-sector unions and the fragmentation of 'bourgeois' parties ruled out a German-style grand coalition. With the German route sealed off, Swedish capital had to look for alternatives and started to diversify into services.

The framework we have sketched opens up several avenues for research at the intersection between political science, Post-Keynesian economics, and sociology. We list just a few of them: What exactly are the mechanisms that produce the shift between normal/quiet and crisis/noisy politics for the growth model? To what extent do parties converge on key macroeconomic policy issues? What is the role of the media, both old and new, in making economic policy issues salient for voters? We hope other researchers will join us in the exploration of these questions.

REFERENCES

Amable, Bruno and Stefano Palombarini (2009), 'A neorealist approach to institutional change and the diversity of modern capitalism,' *Socioeconomic Review*, 7(1), 123–143.

Auboin, Marc and Floriana Borino (2017), 'The falling elasticity of global trade to economic activity: testing the demand channel,' WTO Staff Working Papers ERSD-2017-09.

Baccaro, Lucio and Fabio Bulfone (2022), 'Growth and stagnation in Southern Europe: the Italian and Spanish growth models compared,' in Lucio Baccaro, Mark Blyth, and Jonas Pontusson (eds), *Diminishing Returns: The New Politics of Growth and Stagnation*, Oxford: Oxford University Press, forthcoming.

                                    Journal compilation © 2022 Edward Elgar Publishing Ltd

Baccaro, Lucio and Martin Höpner (2022), 'The political–economic foundations of export-led growth: an analysis of the German case,' in Lucio Baccaro, Mark Blyth, and Jonas Pontusson (eds), *Diminishing Returns: The New Politics of Growth and Stagnation*, Oxford: Oxford University Press, forthcoming.

Baccaro, Lucio and Chris Howell (2017), *Trajectories of Neoliberal Transformation: European Industrial Relations Since the 1970s*, Cambridge, UK: Cambridge University Press.

Baccaro, Lucio and Erik Neimanns (2022), 'Who wants wage moderation? Trade exposure, export-led growth, and the irrelevance of bargaining structure,' *West European Politics*, 1–26, doi: https://doi.org/10.1080/01402382.2021.2024010.

Baccaro, Lucio and Jonas Pontusson (2016), 'Rethinking Comparative Political Economy: the Growth Model perspective,' *Politics & Society*, 44(2), 175–207.

Baccaro, Lucio and Jonas Pontusson (2019), 'Social blocs and growth models: an analytical framework with Germany and Sweden as illustrative cases,' Working Paper, University of Geneva.

Baccaro, Lucio, Mark Blyth, and Jonas Pontusson (2022), 'Rethinking comparative capitalism,' in Lucio Baccaro, Mark Blyth, and Jonas Pontusson (eds), *Diminishing Returns: The New Politics of Growth and Stagnation*, Oxford: Oxford University Press, forthcoming.

Beramendi, Pablo, Silja Häusermann, Herbert Kitschelt, and Hanspeter Kriesi (2015), 'Introduction,' in Pablo Beramendi, Silja Häusermann, Herbert Kitschelt, and Hanspeter Kriesi (eds), *The Politics of Advanced Capitalism*, Cambridge, UK: Cambridge University Press, pp. 1–64.

Bhaduri, Amit and Stephen A. Marglin (1990), 'Unemployment and the real wage: the economic basis for contesting political ideologies,' *Cambridge Journal of Economics*, 14, 375–393.

Blyth, Mark (2002), *Great Transformations: Economic Ideas and Institutional Change in the Twentieth Century*, Cambridge, UK: Cambridge University Press.

Blyth, Mark and Richard Katz (2005), 'From catch-all politics to cartelisation: the political economy of the Cartel Party,' *West European Politics*, 28(1), 33–60.

Bohle, Dorothee and Aidan Regan (2021), 'The Comparative Political Economy of Growth Models: explaining the continuity of FDI-led growth in Ireland and Hungary,' *Politics & Society*, 49(1), 75–106.

Bowles, Samuel and Robert Boyer (1995), 'Wages, aggregate demand, and employment in an open economy: an empirical investigation,' in Gerald Epstein and Herbert Gintis (eds), *Macroeconomic Policy After the Conservative Era: Studies in Investment, Saving and Finance*, Cambridge, UK: Cambridge University Press, pp. 143–171.

Boyer, Robert (2000), 'Is a finance-led growth regime a viable alternative to Fordism? A preliminary analysis,' *Economy and Society*, 29(1), 111–145.

Boyer, Robert (2004), *Théorie de la régulation: Les fondamentaux*, Paris: La Découverte.

Boyer, Robert (2015), *Economie politique des capitalismes*, Paris: La Découverte.

Boyer, Robert and Yves Saillard (eds) (2002), *Regulation Theory: The State of the Art*, London and New York: Routledge.

Burriel, Eugenio L. (2011), 'Subversion of land-use plans and the housing bubble in Spain,' *Urban Research & Practice*, 4(3), 232–249.

Cárdenas, Luis, Paloma Villanueva, Ignacio Álvarez, and Jorge Uxó (2021), 'In the eye of the storm: the "success" of the Spanish growth model,' in Luis Cárdenas and Javier Arribas (eds), *Institutional Change After the Great Recession*, London: Routledge, pp. 202–244.

Carlin, Wendy and David Soskice (2015), *Macroeconomics*, Oxford: Oxford University Press.

Culpepper, Pepper D. (2010), *Quiet Politics and Business Power: Corporate Control in Europe and Japan*, New York: Cambridge University Press.

Culpepper, Pepper D. (2021), 'Quiet politics in tumultuous times: business power, populism, and democracy,' *Politics & Society*, 49(1), 133–143.

Dellepiane-Avellaneda, Sebastian, Niamh Hardiman, and Jon Las Heras (2021), 'Financial resource curse in the Eurozone periphery,' *Review of International Political Economy*, 1–27, doi: https://doi.org/10.1080/09692290.2021.1899960.

Di Carlo, Donato (2018), 'Does pattern bargaining explain wage restraint in the German public sector?' MPIfG Discussion Paper, 18/3.

Erixon, Lennart (2011), 'Under the influence of traumatic events, new ideas, economic experts and the ICT revolution: the economic policy and macroeconomic performance of Sweden in the 1990s and 2000s,' in Lars Mjøset (ed.), *The Nordic Varieties of Capitalism*, vol. 28 of *Comparative Social Research*, Bingley, UK: Emerald Group Publishing, pp. 265–330.

Erixon, Lennart and Jonas Pontusson (2022), 'Rebalancing balanced growth: the evolution of the Swedish growth model since the mid-1990s,' in Lucio Baccaro, Mark Blyth, and Jonas Pontusson (eds), *Diminishing Returns: The New Politics of Growth and Stagnation*, Oxford: Oxford University Press, forthcoming.

Frieden, Jeffry A. and Ronald Rogowski (1996), 'The impact of the international economy on national policies: an analytical overview,' in *Internationalization and Domestic Politics*, Robert O. Keohane and Helen V. Milner (eds), Cambridge, UK: Cambridge University Press, pp. 25–47.

Gourevitch, Peter (1986), *Politics in Hard Times: Comparative Responses to International Economic Crises*, Cornell Studies in Political Economy, Ithaca, NY and London: Cornell University Press.

Gramsci, Antonio (1992), *The Prison Notebooks*, New York: Columbia University Press.

Günther, Wolfgang and Martin Höpner (2022), 'Why does Germany abstain from statutory bargaining extensions? Explaining the exceptional German erosion of collective wage bargaining,' *Economic and Industrial Democracy*, Advanced Access (January).

Haffert, Lukas and Daniel Mertens (2019), 'Between distribution and allocation: growth models, sectoral coalitions and the politics of taxation revisited,' *Socio-Economic Review*, 19(2), 487–510.

Hall, Peter A. and David Soskice (2001), *Varieties of Capitalism: The Institutional Foundations of Comparative Advantage*, Oxford and New York: Oxford University Press.

Hassel, Anke (2014), 'The paradox of liberalization: understanding dualism and the recovery of the German political economy,' *British Journal of Industrial Relations*, 52(1), 57–81.

Hassel, Anke and Bruno Palier (eds) (2021), *Growth and Welfare in Advanced Capitalist Economies: How Have Growth Regimes Evolved?*, Oxford: Oxford University Press.

Häusermann, Silja and Hanspeter Kriesi (2015), 'What do voters want? Dimensions and configurations in individual-level preferences and party choice,' in Hanspeter Kriesi, Herbert Kitschelt, Pablo Beramendi, and Silja Häusermann (eds), *The Politics of Advanced Capitalism*, Cambridge, UK: Cambridge University Press, pp. 202–230.

Hopkin, Jonathan (2020), *Anti-System Politics*, Oxford: Oxford University Press.

Hopkin, Jonathan and Mark Blyth (2018), 'The global economics of European populism: growth regimes and party system change in Europe,' *Government and Opposition*, 54(2), 193–225.

Hopkin, Jonathan and Dustin Voss (2022), 'Political parties and growth models,' in Lucio Baccaro, Mark Blyth, and Jonas Pontusson (eds), *Diminishing Returns: The New Politics of Growth and Stagnation*, Oxford: Oxford University Press, forthcoming.

Höpner, Martin (2018), 'The German undervaluation regime under Bretton Woods, 1950–1973: how Germany became the nightmare of the world economy,' MPIfG Discussion Paper, 19/1.

Höpner, Martin and Mark Lutter (2017), 'The diversity of wage regimes: why the Eurozone is too heterogeneous for the Euro,' *European Political Science Review*, 10(1), 71–96.

Hübscher, Evelyne and Thomas Sattler (2022), 'Growth models under austerity,' in Lucio Baccaro, Mark Blyth, and Jonas Pontusson (eds), *Diminishing Returns: The New Politics of Growth and Stagnation*, Oxford: Oxford University Press, forthcoming.

Iversen, Torben and Jonas Pontusson (2000), 'Comparative Political Economy: a Northern European perspective,' in Torben Iversen, Jonas Pontusson, and David Soskice (eds), *Unions, Employers and Central Banks: Macroeconomic Coordination and Institutional Change in Social Market Economies*, Cambridge, UK: Cambridge University Press, pp. 1–37.

Iversen, Torben and David Soskice (2001), 'An asset theory of social policy preferences,' *American Political Science Review*, 95, 875–895.

Iversen, Torben and David Soskice (2019), *Democracy and Prosperity*, Princeton, NJ: Princeton University Press.

Katzenstein, Peter (1985), *Small States in World Markets: Industrial Policy in Europe*, Ithaca, NY: Cornell Univeristy Press.

Kitschelt, Herbert and Philipp Rehm (2015), 'Party alignments: change and continuity,' in Hanspeter Kriesi, Herbert Kitschelt, Pablo Beramendi, and Silja Häusermann (eds), *The Politics of Advanced Capitalism*, Cambridge, UK: Cambridge University Press, pp. 179–201.

Kohler, Karsten and Engelbert Stockhammer (2021), 'Growing differently? Financial cycles, austerity, and competitiveness in growth models since the Global Financial Crisis,' *Review of International Political Economy*, 1–28, doi: https://doi.org/10.1080/09692290.2021.1899035.

Korpi, Walter (2006), 'Power resources and employer-centered approaches in explanations of welfare states and varieties of capitalism,' *World Politics*, 58(2), 167–206.

Krippner, Greta (2011), *Capitalizing on the Crisis*, Cambridge, MA: Harvard University Press.

Lavoie, Marc (2014), *Post-Keynesian Economics: New Foundations*, Cheltenham, UK and Northampton, MA: Edward Elgar Publishing.

Lavoie, Marc and Engelbert Stockhammer (2012), 'Wage-led growth: concept, theories and policies,' ILO Conditions of Work and Employment Series No 41.

Lavoie, Marc and Engelbert Stockhammer (2013), *Wage-Led Growth*, London: Palgrave.

López, Isidro and Emmanuel Rodríguez (2011), 'The Spanish model,' *New Left Review*, (69), 5–29.

Marx, Paul and Peter Starke (2017), 'Dualization as destiny? The political economy of the German minimum wage reform,' *Politics & Society*, 45(4), 559–584.

Mosley, Layna (2003), 'Room to move: international financial markets and national welfare states,' *International Organization*, 54(4), 737–773.

Palley, Thomas I. (2012), *From Financial Crisis to Stagnation*, Cambridge, UK: Cambridge University Press.

Perez, Sofia A. and Manos Matsaganis (2018), 'The political economy of austerity in Southern Europe,' *New Political Economy*, 23(2), 192–207.

Pontusson, Jonas and Peter Swenson (1996), 'Labor markets, production strategies, and wage bargaining institutions: the Swedish employer offensive in comparative perspective,' *Comparative Political Studies*, 29(2), 223–250.

Przeworski, Adam (1985), *Capitalism and Social Democracy: Studies in Marxism and Social Theory*, Cambridge, UK: Cambridge University Press.

Quaglia, Lucia and Sebastián Royo (2015), 'Banks and the political economy of the sovereign debt crisis in Italy and Spain,' *Review of International Political Economy*, 22(3), 485–507.

Ruiz, Juan Rafael, Patricia Stupariu, and Ángel Vilariño (2015), 'The crisis of Spanish savings banks,' *Cambridge Journal of Economics*, 40(6), 1455–1477.

Scharpf, Fritz (2011), 'Monetary union, fiscal crisis and the preemption of democracy,' Max-Planck-Institute Cologne Working Paper.

Schmidt, Vivien A. (2008), 'Discursive institutionalism: the explanatory power of ideas and discourse,' *Annual Review of Political Science*, 11(1), 303–326.

Soskice, D. (1999), 'Divergent production regimes: coordinated and uncoordinated market economies in the 1980s and 1990s,' in H. Kitschelt, P. Lange, and G. Marks (eds), *Continuity and Change in Contemporary Capitalism*, New York: Cambridge University Press, pp. 101–134.

Stockhammer, Engelbert (2015), 'Rising inequality as a cause of the present crisis,' *Cambridge Journal of Economics*, 39(3), 935–958.

Swenson, Peter (1991), 'Labor and the limits of the welfare state: the politics of intraclass conflict and cross-class alliances in Sweden and West Germany,' *Comparative Politics*, 23(4), 379–399.

Thelen, Kathleen (2014), *Varieties of Liberalization and the New Politics of Social Solidarity*, New York: Cambridge University Press.

Thelen, Kathleen (2019), 'Transitions to the knowledge economy in Germany, Sweden, and the Netherlands,' *Comparative Politics*, 51(2), 295–315.

Zysman, John (1983), *Governments, Markets, and Growth: Financial Systems and the Politics of Industrial Change*, Ithaca, NY: Cornell University Press.

Review of Keynesian Economics, Vol. 10 No. 2, Summer 2022, pp. 94–113

Rethinking Varieties of Capitalism and growth theory in the ICT era*

David Soskice
International Inequalities Institute, London School of Economics, UK

Going beyond the Varieties of Capitalism comparative analysis, a theory of advanced capitalism is developed to explain what has been driving advanced capitalism through the massive creative destruction of the information and communication technologies (ICT) revolution of recent decades. Second, it is argued – reconfiguring Varieties of Capitalism – that the advanced capitalist economies should be seen not just in terms of comparative capitalisms, but as an advanced world innovation system of interacting advanced economies. Critically, the dominant position in that system is the (hegemonic but also fragile, problematic and handicapped) United States as the world driver of radical innovation: this reflects the key role of its top research universities, their diasporas and associated deregulated high-risk-taking venture capitalist and investment banking ecosystems; its decentralised and business-porous political and legal systems; and its dominance ab initio *of digitalisation. Problematic has been the major reduction since the early 1990s in Federal R&D, itself a consequence of the anti-public-expenditure Republican gridlock in Congress, and in turn the result of the political, geographical and socioeconomic polarisation associated with technological creative destruction more dramatically in the US than elsewhere. Third, it addresses the paradox – in the contemporary technologically revolutionary age – of productivity growth falling below that of the Fordist era. It is argued that Schumpeterian growth expectations play a much larger role in R&D investment in the high-sunk-cost and high-risk US-centred ICT era than in the relative stability of Fordism and Chandlerian corporations; the author sets out a simple Keynesian–Kaldorian expectations-based multiple equilibrium productivity growth model, where major crashes shift economies down to lower growth equilibria. The conclusion raises six areas of future work which stem from the approaches outlined above.*

Keywords: *Varieties of Capitalism, Kaldorian multiple equilibrium growth, endogenous expectations, American radical innovation*

JEL codes: *E02, I12, O31, O33, O43, P51*

1 INTRODUCTION

As the political scientist, Peter Hall, has said on various occasions, Minerva's owl flies only at dusk. It is tempting at times to see this as a *Requiem* for the volume we edited in 2001, *Varieties of Capitalism: The Institutional Foundations of Comparative Advantage (VoC)* (Hall and Soskice 2001). And certainly, even if capitalism remains very differently organised across, within and between the advanced economies, as well as China

* Thanks to discussions over a long period with Catherine Boone, Wendy Carlin, Torben Iversen, Nicola Lacey, Ciaran Driver, David Hope and Michael Storper; and excellent editorial assistance from Nick Wilson.

Journal compilation © 2022 Edward Elgar Publishing Ltd
The Lypiatts, 15 Lansdown Road, Cheltenham, Glos GL50 2JA, UK
and The William Pratt House, 9 Dewey Court, Northampton MA 01060-3815, USA

and India, the full force of the information and communication technologies (ICT) revolution has radically transformed advanced capitalism.

Thus the first major issue for a student of advanced capitalism (addressed in Section 2) is that of the forces which have driven this radical transformation. This can then answer Wolfgang Streeck's critique of *VoC* that an overall theory of advanced capitalism is needed, as opposed to (simply) an understanding of its varieties (Streeck 2010). In analysing these forces, Streeck and Rodrik (Rodrik 2011; Streeck 2014) both see capital as footloose, and destructive of the autonomy of advanced capitalist democracies. It is argued here, by contrast, that advanced capital, with much of its value in the co-specific non-codifiable skills of well-educated workforces, is not footloose (unlike financial assets or patents), but geographically embedded: advanced democratic states retain their autonomy. And in this picture, broadly defined progressive and aspirational forces in the advanced democratic economies push the ICT revolution and mass higher education in an electoral conflict with populists and conservatives (Iversen and Soskice 2019).

Next, Section 3 suggests that the US should be seen not simply as a liberal market economy (LME) on a par with the UK, but as the core driver of radical innovation in the ICT revolution (Soskice 2021). This reflects the software core of the radical innovation and comparative advantage of US research and finance institutions in rapid software development and scalability. Problematic has been the Chinese; and more problematic the tax hostility and anti-statist role of Republican populism, the Senate gridlock, and the consequent deep decline in Federal R&D (Arora et al. 2018). Despite these, a central argument in the paper is to see the US at the (fragile and sometimes problematic) centre of the advanced capitalist countries as an interrelated advanced world system and the US as its (digitally based) innovation driver (Bloom et al. 2012; Arora et al. 2013; Branstetter et al. 2019a; 2019b).

Section 4 addresses the core paradox – in the *contemporary technologically revolutionary* age – of productivity growth falling *below that of the Fordist era*. It is argued that Schumpeterian growth expectations play a much larger role in R&D investment in the high-sunk-cost and high-risk ICT era than in the relative stability of Fordism and Chandlerian corporations, with partial Federal withdrawal raising both sunk cost and risk; a simple Keynesian–Kaldorian multiple equilibrium productivity growth model is sketched out, where major crashes shift economies down to lower growth equilibria. This process is centred on the US innovation economy and then extended to the rest of the advanced world.

2   A THEORY OF ADVANCED CAPITALISM

The most useful framework for thinking about advanced contemporary capitalism is in terms of a massive prolonged technological revolution: the ICT revolution. As Tylecote, Perez, Freeman, Dosi and others have argued, the two centuries from the early nineteenth century to the present have consisted of a sequence of such technological/organisational revolutions, periods of decades-long Schumpeterian 'creative destruction', highly productive and deeply painful, psychologically as well as materially, as new techno-economic paradigms slowly replace previous ones (Dosi 1982; Freeman and Louçã 2001; Perez 2010; Tylecote 2013). Polanyi saw (in almost Hegelian terms) three broad phases in these prolonged technological revolutions: (i) A first phase in which – as the technologies are invented – the 'rules' get set which 'enable' them to be adopted, weakening the powers (or culture) of the agents and institutions of those who might oppose them; we can loosely identify this 'rule-setting' phase with

    Journal compilation © 2022 Edward Elgar Publishing Ltd

the adoption, by each of the advanced societies in one form or another, of the *neoliberal framework*. (ii) A second phase, exemplifying creative destruction, in which there is widespread adoption, involving massive risk and speculation as innovating capitalists discover the contours of the new technologies; this is associated with financial crises and prolonged recession (as deleveraging takes place), and it is also a phase in which their destructive effect gradually becomes more widely and sharply felt, materially and psychologically, as pre-existing cultures and ways of life are upended, and with the 'safeguarding' institutions of the pre-existing regime having been weakened. Finally, (iii), in Polanyi's argument there is then a third phase (which he misleadingly calls the *second movement*) in which new safeguards are put in place (Polanyi 1944), and a period of comparative technological stability is entered.

2.1   The first phase: the neoliberal framework and mass higher education

To understand the driver of these technological/organisational transformations requires, as Streeck has pointed out, a *theory of advanced capitalism*, not simply a listing of Varieties of Capitalism. Varieties may be embedded in such a theory, but a core question which we need to be able to answer is what drove the setting-up of the neoliberal framework. Streeck's Marxist answer is that advanced capitalism is the driver, and presumptively orchestrated the neoliberal framework. But at the same time this led to the potential destruction of democratic capitalism. For, under the impact of the adoption of a neoliberal framework in the 1980s and 1990s, capital mobility (footloose capitalism) acted to undermine the sovereignty of the advanced democratic state (Streeck 2013).

(Like Streeck, Piketty sees capital as the driver of change: echoing Marx, the title of his *magnum opus* (Piketty 2014) is *Capital in the Twenty-First Century*. Piketty's goal is to understand – and brilliantly draw attention to – the great rise in inequality from the 1980s, especially in the US. Broadly interpreting Piketty, capital woke up in the 1970s and 1980s to the massively successful egalitarian push by unions and social democracy in the post-World War II decades; and the inegalitarian 'recovery' from the 1980s onwards is interpreted as a counter-push by capital. But it is less clear-cut in terms of mechanisms than Streeck's. Piketty considers, but dismisses, the role of the ICT revolution: the growth of inequality was much greater in the US than in Germany, but, he argues, the ICT revolution affected both nations equally.)

Iversen and I argue (against Streeck and also Rodrik) that advanced capitalism is not footloose (Iversen and Soskice 2019): even in the neoliberal world, knowledge competences and innovation capacities are embedded in clusters in the advanced economies; it is true that company ownership (and financial assets generally), as well as patents, are mobile in the neoliberal world, but innovation skills and competences are tacit and locationally embedded. And, contrary to the view that the internet has made the Earth 'flat' (Friedman 2005), tacit knowledge is typically locationally co-specific (Leamer 2007).

(Thus, while the Rodrik (2011) globalisation trilemma – sovereignty, democracy, and the neoliberal framework cannot all three co-exist – may apply to less advanced economies, it does not apply to advanced economies.)

Nor are advanced capitalist companies (who compete fiercely in technologically innovative markets) easily capable of colluding to pressure the advanced democratic state. (This indeed is foundational to Poulantzas's Marxist argument that capitalist companies, inherently competitive – the nature of capitalism – are politically powerless. We agree, but do not follow his theory of the relative autonomy of the state which 'acts for' the interests of advanced capitalism (Poulantzas 1973). In the language of *The Communist Manifesto*, '[t]he executive of the modern state is but a committee for managing the common affairs of the whole bourgeoisie' (Marx and Engels 1848 [2012], p. 1). But Poulantzas wants the reader to take this on trust, to 'only believe', and this is hardly persuasive. Given the empirical evidence of political ambition, and thus concern to win elections, it is not easy to accept this approach.)

Thus, unable to collude against the state, and unable to relocate without leaving the skilled workforces which create much of their value added, the weakness of advanced capitalist companies does not counter the autonomy of the advanced democratic sovereign state.

And there is a more persuasive argument that the move towards a neoliberal framework did not reflect the power of advanced capitalism: in the US and the UK, advanced capitalism is often seen at its most powerful, most shareholder-oriented and least socially responsible. But the top US and UK companies that had dominated the Fordist era were largely broken up by 2020, mainly by the radical opening of corporate governance markets and the transformation of financial institutions, reflecting the neoliberal framework. They were replaced in the US by the FAANG companies (Facebook, Amazon, Apple, Netflix, Google). To take the UK case more explicitly, the Confederation of British Industry (CBI) and much of the financial establishment had been deeply hostile to prime minister Margaret Thatcher's proposals in the late 1970s and 1980s.

In fact Thatcher was not appealing to the established conglomerates of advanced capitalism in the UK, nor to the established bastions of the City (most of the dominating companies in the FTSE100): on the contrary – and not to put too fine a point on it – she broke them up. But she appealed to a large part of the aspirational electorate who wanted upgraded education and careers for their children, and were worried as industry was gradually collapsing. The Labour Party and some of the unions initially responded to Thatcher by swinging – electorally disastrously – to the left under Michael Foot; but under successive leaders, from Neil Kinnock to Tony Blair, they ended by supporting most of her changes including union legislation. And Blair aimed explicitly at the aspirational electorate Thatcher had captured.

We therefore analyse the situation differently, in terms of electoral conflict as hinted above. We see a continuing political conflict conducted in the electoral battlefield in each of the advanced economies between what had become by the early 2000s progressive and populist electorates. In these prolonged creative destructive periods of technological regime change, we see a conflict between the 'progressive' forces in the electorate and the 'populist' ones (Iversen and Soskice 2019); this is closely related to the contemporary divisions in the electorate Hooghe and Marks (2018) persuasively draw between 'greens' and 'populists'.

(How does advanced capitalism line up in the conflict between 'progressive' and 'populist conservative'? It is clear that advanced capitalism is progressive; and as a 'class' in favour of promoting openness, competition, and public-sector help to R&D and to the research environment more generally; also (at least some) ESG values: BlackRock, the largest assets under management (AUM) institution in the world, takes a strong ESG position through its CEO Larry Fink, who argues that long-termism boosts the long-term rate of return, and also innovation and training. Of course, the individual successful company may well individually want protection (!). This is an under-researched area; but clearly most advanced companies in the US have swung broadly behind Democrats – though not all Democrats! The Koch brothers, on the other hand, are strongly Republican. What is the full logic here?)

                                            Journal compilation © 2022 Edward Elgar Publishing Ltd

To come back to our modern version of Polanyi, in the first phase (the rule-setting phase, when the neoliberal framework as well as the strategy of mass higher education was developed) no significant populist opposition had yet arisen, since the adverse consequences of this strategy were not yet felt.

The move towards neoliberalism in the 1980s and 1990s reflected the perceived need in the advanced Western economies for opening up corporate structures and labour markets in response to lack of competition and risk-taking. The goal of the neoliberal framework was primarily to undermine institutional opposition to the ICT revolution; the need to open major companies to change, and also to weaken unions; and to bring about economic change as the industrial world was seen as declining. A key role was assigned to private-sector competition (Schumpeter). The state was seen as too powerful an actor, with close ties to large established corporations, and politicians were potentially concerned to use the state to support loss-making companies and their workforces. Along with the push for more competition came privatisation. In addition, the belief that innovation required risk-taking and entrepreneurship was seen as implying lower taxation, especially on incomes. This coincided with the perceived need for more disciplined macroeconomic management, and especially the need to control inflation, particularly after the major inflation scare in the 1970s and the start of the 1980s. Thus the neoliberal push coincided with constraints on state action, particularly constraints on public expenditure. Disciplined macroeconomic management led to central-bank independence and the use of interest rates for inflation targeting; it also led (critically, and as it turned out, problematically) to controls on fiscal policy, and since lower taxation was seen as important, that implied constraints on government expenditure and targeting of public-sector deficits and public debt in relation to GDP.

In retrospect, there was a major element of fighting the last war; and a major problem – as we will see below – has been that suspicion of public expenditure got baked into policy-making, as well as the electorate. Indeed, we believe this has had a major impact on innovation and productivity growth in the current century.

2.2   The second phase: creative destruction

The second phase exemplifies creative destruction, and the development of serious electoral conflict between progressives and populists builds up during this prolonged period, which has occupied at least the last three decades; and it has six elements which it is useful to point out:

1. enabled by the neoliberal framework, there is a widespread 'creative' adoption of the new technology as it gradually spreads across more and more sectors, accompanied by 'destruction' of existing sectors and ways of life;
2. mass higher education builds up; at the same time, graduate-intensive city agglomerations grow (with growing inequality), polarising those in 'places that don't matter' (Rodríguez-Pose 2018);
3. risk and speculation develop as innovating capitalists gamble on discovering the contours of the new technologies; governments in turn encourage risk-taking by financial institutions, whose behaviour spreads to mortgage markets; this lays the foundation for financial crises;
4. financial crises which lead to prolonged recessions as deleveraging takes place, and as eventually (*pace* the neoliberal disciplined concern with public debt) states withdraw from reflationary macroeconomic policy;

                    Journal compilation © 2022 Edward Elgar Publishing Ltd

5. it is also a phase in which their destructive effect gradually becomes more widely and sharply felt, materially and psychologically, as pre-existing cultures and ways of life are upended, and with the 'safeguarding' institutions of the pre-existing regime having been weakened; 'destruction' comes about via automation and as a result of globalisation (off-shoring, immigration, import competition) … thus in this second phase, electoral conflict begins to be felt as political entrepreneurs engage in the social construction of 'populism';
6. this gradually switches the electoral system from a centre-left/centre-right system (in one form or another, depending on the electoral system) to one between 'populist' and 'progressive' forces (again in one form or another, depending on the electoral system); anything here involves a major generalisation, but a key element in this conflict (in the context of this paper) is educational levels, with aspirational families and graduates living and/or working or learning in big cities, generally cosmopolitan pro-environment and aware of the limits of unregulated markets being central to the progressive forces; these forces engage the electoral systems in the advanced societies in a prolonged period of conflict.

2.3   The third phase: Polanyi's 'second movement'

The third phase is one in which the progressive forces are broadly dominant (parallel to the *trentes glorieuses* of the Fordist era). What is of particular relevance to the paper is that this phase becomes more plausible the greater is higher-education participation. This operates through some version of the Goldin–Katz growth model linking productivity growth to university participation; and we return to this in Section 5.

3   RETHINKING VARIETIES: THE US AS (PROBLEMATIC AND FRAGILE) CENTRE OF THE ADVANCED WORLD RESEARCH SYSTEM

In this section, the US is shown as the driver of radical innovation in the advanced world, with evidence provided in Section 3.1.

What explains this success? We suggest in Section 3.2 that the particularly decentralised nature of American institutions plays a major explanatory role. And we see as complementary to these institutions the core characterisation of ICT innovations – namely that they are *software-dominated*. Software-dominated innovations, which the US has led, are key to innovations across the advanced world in both industries and services (Bloom et al. 2012; Arora et al. 2013; Brynjolfsson and McAfee 2013; Zysman et al. 2013; Branstetter et al. 2019a; 2019b).

But we also underline, in Section 3.3, a deeply problematic side to the American system: the growing disengagement of Federal R&D. The deep polarisation of US society, a consequence of creative destruction, has translated politically into a Republican gridlock in Congress against public expenditure, *inter alia* against Federal R&D; this has weakened the role of basic science in US innovation in the private setor (Arora et al. 2018), and equally importantly has in turn unplugged a major stabilising factor in the American research and financing system, generating much higher risk-taking and probability of crashes. We return to this in Section 4.

The final part of this section, Section 3.4 – perhaps most important for the focus of the paper in reconfiguring Varieties of Capitalism – suggests that something like an *advanced world innovation system* has developed, *with the US at its centre*. In this system, America is the dominating (though fragile and far from hegemonic) player via its role as world driver of radical innovation (greatly more so than China, which is facing its own contradictions) (Soskice 2021). In this advanced world innovation system, US technology is broadly portrayed as the 'frontier' technology; this uses the language of both Acemoglu (2009) and Aghion et al. (2021), though they do not explicitly describe the frontier as American. And a key argument in the productivity growth section, Section 4, is that productivity growth elsewhere in the advanced world is partially determined by changes in the American-determined frontier.

3.1   America for better: what is the evidence that the US is the driver of radical innovation?

Figures 1–3 and Tables 1–2 show the very great American lead in Nobel prizes, academic citations, highly cited patents, superstar companies, and unicorns. And the linkage between the private sector in the US and research universities is greater (see quotation below).

Next, we quote a short section from a careful study comparing the *involvement* of US science with private US companies with the corresponding involvement of

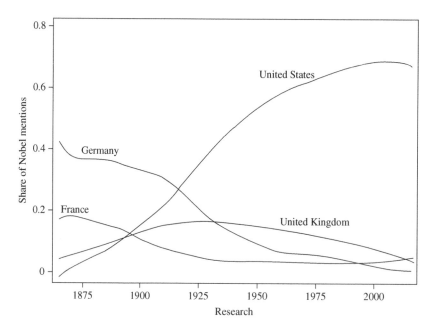

Note: These data are based on a weighted average of university country locations *up to* the Nobel prize award, which captures the contribution of the countries' universities to the research involved in the award, rather than the capacity of universities to hire Nobel prize-winners after the award.
Source: Urquiola (2020, table 1.2).

Figure 1   Share of Nobel prize mentions at pre-Nobel institutions

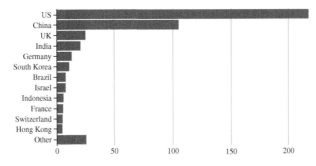

Note: a. Private companies with a valuation over $1b.
Source: CB Insights.

Figure 2   Number of unicorns[a] *by country, 2020*

Superstar firms have become more geographically diverse over the past 20 years, though North American firms still make up the largest share.

Representation of top-decile firms by country or region %

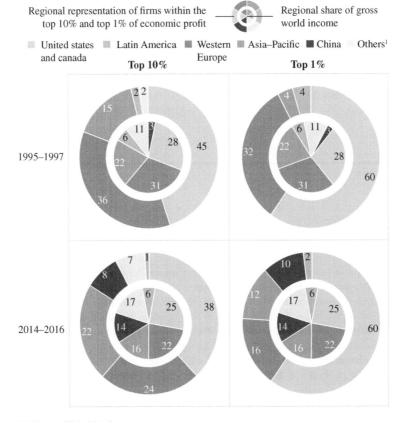

Source: McKinsey Global Institute.

Figure 3   Superstar firms

Table 1   Highly cited researchers by institution

Institutions	Nation	Number HCRs
Harvard University	United States	203
Stanford University	United States	103
Chinese Academy of Sciences	China Mainland	101
Max Planck Society	Germany	73
Broad Institute	United States	60
University of California Berkeley	United States	58
Washington University St Louis	United States	55
Duke University	United States	54
Massachusetts Institute of Technology (MIT)	United States	54
Memorial Sloan Kettering Cancer Center	United States	54
University of California San Diego	United States	54
University of California Los Angeles	United States	52
Yale University	United States	51
University of Cambridge	United Kingdom	50

Source: Clarivate, Highly Cited Scientists 2021 (based on *Web of Science* citations).

Table 2   Patents per country, average 2010–2017

	Patent applications per million inhabitants	Number of top 5% patents per citations	Percentage of top 5% patents per citations
Germany	617.1	170.5	0.4%
Denmark	87.4	0.0	0.0%
United States	1 186.4	32 678.0	71.7%
France	231.1	5.9	0.0%
Norway	316.4	0.3	0.0%
Sweden	129.8	0.3	0.0%

Source: Aghion et al. (2021, p. 323).

European companies, which suggests the much closer link between top American science and the private sector, (Breschi et al. 2006, p. iv):

> The European private companies' contribution to the production of scientific publications highly cited in patents is significantly lower than the contribution of private companies located in other areas, notably the United States. A major weakness of the European systems of research, as compared to other geographical areas, especially the United States, is related to the low degree of involvement of private companies in the conduct of research leading to scientific publications. Whereas the contribution of the public system of scientific research, i.e. universities and public research organisations, is generally comparable to, and often larger than the contribution of the corresponding system in the US, the fraction of scientific publications accounted for by the private system of research is considerably lower. To the extent that the ability of private companies to profit from scientific output generated in the sphere of science depends on the possession of absorptive capabilities and especially on the existence of boundary-spanning individuals, we believe this characteristic represents one of the major obstacles to the effective diffusion of knowledge from the realm of science to that of technology.

            Journal compilation © 2022 Edward Elgar Publishing Ltd

3.2 Explaining US success?

First, we discuss American decentralised institutions, particularly related to research, universities and financing. American 'success' can be understood as the consequence of the extraordinarily decentralised and quasi-deregulated structure of its political economic institutions, especially in the complex of relations between finance, the top research universities, major innovation 'ecosystems' and major city administrations (Soskice 2021). The United States' long dominance of radical innovation (since the late nineteenth century) reflects a particular institutional heritage going back to the (re)foundational period of advanced capitalism by the Republican Ascendancy presidents in the 1880s after the failure of Reconstruction. Although these institutions have evolved over this long period, the institutions that then took shape were unique among the emerging advanced economies, and unusually propitious to radical innovation – four in particular:

1. Highly flexible, decentralised, and competitive systems of research and higher education, largely at university level and in the research diaspora of universities, and/or in the research laboratories of large corporations.
2. Equally flexible and decentralised systems of finance, widely geographically distributed and with a wide variety of institutions, relatively little regulation, and substantial capacity for investment in high-risk ventures as well as ones potentially disruptive to existing corporations (Davis and Neal 2007).
3. Companies capable of scalability, as well as a legal competition system that both ensures reasonably competitive product markets and allows scalability. A key condition for this has been not just a large market (widened, in the late nineteenth century, by external tariffs), but the absence of protection at the state, city or regional level. The weakness of unions (the 'stable' Fordist period from the late 1930s to the 1970s partly excepted) has been an additional element limiting protection (in the wider sense) at the city and state level.
4. Finally, a deep and liquid high-level (professional and technical) labour market in the major research agglomerations that allows easy movement across professions (via professional schools), enables talented individuals to form spin-offs from existing (advanced) companies, and allows individuals to recover status after unsuccessful innovative projects. Flexibility in the high-end labour market has facilitated spin-offs, which has boosted the American capacity for radical innovation over the last century (Klepper 2001; 2007; 2009; 2010; Klepper and Sleeper 2005; Klepper and Thompson 2010).

Highly complementary to and permitted by these factors, Bloom et al. (2012) argue that US management practices have been particularly well-suited to rapid decentralised decision-making in highly ICT-based companies, especially in relation to personnel.

In addition to these decentralised and deregulated 'market institutions' is a second set of factors, 'legal and political institutions' characterising the relation between the political system, the court system, and the business and wealth sectors. This is at the heart of the Hacker–Hertel-Fernandez–Pierson–Thelen understanding of the American political economy (see Hacker et al. 2021; 2022). Their insight is to understand the decentralised business/money porous system, 'multi-venue' so that business could move to different environments. Those multiple venues include counties, cities and states, as well as the federal level, with courts, elections and parties at each level. These 'legal and political institutions' are also decentralised and functionally deregulated. Absent at all these venues is a centralised political authority operating within a clear centralised legal structure. The vacuum is filled not overtly by corruption, but by lobbying and investment by politicians. Thus growing companies can operate in flexible environments (particularly within research-intensive agglomerations).

To summarise all the above: unlike any other advanced economy (with the partial exception of China), the innovative ideas from leading research universities, their academics, and their networked diasporas can be easily financed; teams of able managers, lawyers, research software engineers easily assembled to join (ostensibly) high-risk entrepreneurial teams; scalability (especially initially) within the US is straightforward; and city and county governments pliable through lobby-able political and legal systems. (Paradoxically, the Chinese institutional environment – with the help of ambitious city mayors and regional party secretaries – is comparable to this, while formally quite different; the Chinese environment is more dangerous because of possible and highly unpredictable central interventions. But it suffers from a lack of openness within university communities, in areas such as neurosciences and social sciences which are increasingly important in many areas of innovation – including surveillance.)

3.3   America for worse: creative destruction and Republican gridlock

And the US is torn in a second way, reflecting the deep electoral conflict between progressive and aspirational voters, and populist and conservative forces, as discussed in Section 2. The epicentre of the social and technological disruption is the US.

Carlota Perez, brilliant big-picture analyst of technological regime change, and implicitly echoing Schumpeter's *creative destruction*, emphasises the sharply disruptive impact of the initial decades of the new regime. This impact fell sharply on the erstwhile middle classes (of the Fordist era), who have gone on to form the populist reaction to this creative destruction. To a much greater extent than elsewhere, the US has suffered from a 'hollowing out' of many who in the 1980s were in stable, often unionised employment, in 'routine' jobs vulnerable to automation, typically in manufacturing or clerical white-collar work. Many of these workers ended up in cheaper housing outside large successful cities, where there was limited chance of good jobs, and where many were stuck without the skills to get good jobs in the cities, unable to pay decent city housing and unprepared to live in the poor city areas.

In addition, the very limited American welfare state provided quite limited compensation, in comparison to the advanced economies of Western Europe, as can be seen in Figure 4. This has coincided in the US with a big increase in higher education, and cities have been increasingly populated by graduates on the one hand and the poor on the other. While similar movements have taken place elsewhere (the UK and France particularly), it has not been on the same scale as in the US. While many qualifications should be made, it has at a simplistic level pitted the populists – displaced economically in terms of status, less well-educated, and generally white – against the progressive, the better-educated, those in advanced sectors, those in cities, and aspirational families. It also (in the US) allied the poor with the progressive camp, further reinforcing the hostility of the white, populist camp.

The political polarisation in the US is therefore very strong, as shown in Figure 4. The implication for the argument here is that a central political dividing line is the populist support for low taxes and opposition to public expenditure. That reflects opposition to redistribution (as noted above), with taxes seen by populists as going to the 'undeserving poor'. This reflects in Federal R&D as a percentage of US GDP (see Figure 5).

And here in the US, relative shares of Federal government and business are shown in Figure 6.

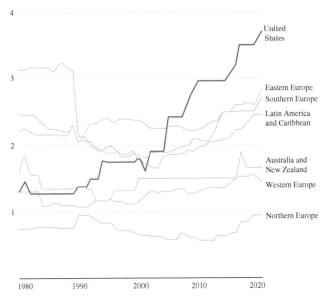

Note: Polarisation ratings are aggregated among countries by region, with not all regions shown. A rating of 0 indicates that opposing political groups tend to interact in a friendly manner, ranging to a rating of 4 that indicates that they tend to be hostile.
Source: Varieties of Democracy Institute - by *The New York Times*.

Figure 4   Political polarisation rating

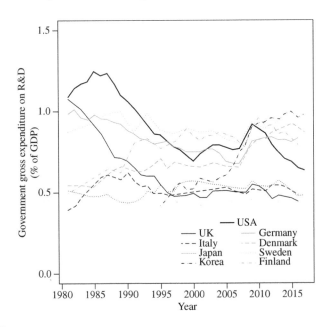

Source: OECD.

Figure 5   Government R&D as a percentage of GDP

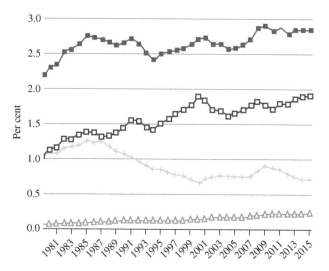

Notes: Top line = share of R&D in US GDP; second line = business R&D percentage; third line = Federal R&D; bottom line = other non-business sources.
Source: National Science Board, *Science and Engineering Indicators* 2018, table 4-3.

Figure 6   US relative shares of Federal government and business

The major implication for the argument of the next section is that the withdrawal of the Federal component of R&D has unplugged a key stabilising element and increased the risk attached to R&D. We see that as raising the importance of the need for strong future expected growth.

3.4   American innovation at the centre of an advanced digital-based world order

Finally, in this sub-section, the US is not just the driver of radical innovation. We suggest here it can usefully be seen as being at the centre of an advanced digital-based world order.

1. The US is widely seen as having dominated software from the 1990s on. It is almost perfectly scalable, hence is at the basis of platform technologies; institutionally it fits well with high-risk venture capital and university diasporas; and it lends itself to deep flexible pools of software engineers, managers, lawyers, and related specialities. Bloom et al. (2012) argue that US management is well suited to it; and Arora et al. (2013) argue that it has quickly developed the relevant labour pools. Software is increasingly core to innovation in services and manufacturing, including IT hardware and research in other frontier areas including the life sciences; and manufacturing is increasingly servitisation-based (Zysman and Breznitz 2012; Zysman et al. 2013). Thus both services and manufacturing in other advanced economies have become dependent on US software technology (Bloom et al. 2012; Arora et al. 2013).
2. In consequence, most big research-oriented non-US multinational enterprises (MNEs) have extensive facilities, research centres, part-ownership of US start-ups,

            Journal compilation © 2022 Edward Elgar Publishing Ltd

and linkages to US research universities; obvious cases are non-US big Pharma corporations, Siemens, Samsung, Daimler, and LG, as well as Ericsson and Nokia, so this can be thought of as the major digital-based research network centred on the US. It is complemented by advanced training (doctorates, post-docs), and then employment in US technology companies, with a subsequent return to a home country. This has gone with setting up research-based networks in the destination country – notably Israel, Taiwan and India – with close links to networks in Silicon Valley (Saxenian 2007; Saxenian and Sabel 2011).

4   IN A TECHNOLOGICAL REVOLUTION, WHY DID PRODUCTIVITY GROWTH DECLINE?

Finally, this section turns to the macroeconomics of growth and innovation. Baccaro and Pontusson have opened up the topic in seminal contributions on the direct demand side of growth (Baccaro and Pontusson 2016; 2019; see also Hope and Soskice 2016). Here we focus on technological change as the supply side of the story; though, as will become clear, the supply side is endogenous. The previous two sections constitute the background to this section; very evidently the leading role of the US is emphasised in driving radical innovation. And in doing so, two other (problematic) factors from Sections 2 and 3 are important: first, that the neoliberal framework was partially fighting the last war against inflation and public-sector deficits (which had traumatised the politicians of the mid 1970s to mid 1980s). Governments and central banks easily turned adverse shocks into recessions as they tried to reduce public-sector debt. Hence, shocks magnified pessimistic expectations. Second, as noted in Section 3.3, this was reinforced by the undemocratic nature of the American Congress generating a tax-cutting anti-public expenditure Republican gridlock over a long period, which in turn unplugged the massive stabilising role the Federal government had played in R&D in the earlier post-war period, and made R&D more sensitive to future expectations.

The basic question to answer is why productivity growth, the pace of innovation, and real wage growth slowed in the early 2000s after the dot-com bubble burst, then slowed more sharply after the global financial crisis? Wendy Carlin and I argue, using a Keynesian–Kaldorian expectations-based multiple growth equilibria framework, that productivity growth equilibrium shifted down first after the dot-com crash in 2000; then even more so after the global financial crisis, reflecting major shifts down in the expected growth rates (Carlin and Soskice 2018), aggravated by the neoliberal framework of deflation-oriented macroeconomic policy rules. Thus the (very simple) Keynesian–Kaldorian model set out by us reflects Palley's approaches in a series of publications in the late 1990s; particular attention is paid to the technical progress function – though here shifting in response to major expectations-based shocks (Palley 1996a; 1996b; 1996c).

And this first question begs an answer to the famous, second, Solow-inspired question: why is productivity growth so low (compared to the post-war Fordist decades), given the omni-present and innovation-oriented digital revolution? In terms of common arguments: we reject the Gordon explanation that the world has run out of innovations (Gordon 2012). We accept that part of the answer is in the market-based way we measure innovations and productivity growth, given the low market price of most of the benefits we get from the ICT revolution, as well as the massive externalities. We also accept the Acemoglu–Restrepo argument that automation moved many of those who lost middle-level productivity employment in manufacturing and clerical work into low measured productivity employment in so-called low-skilled service sectors, damping productivity growth in consequence (Acemoglu and Restrepo 2019).

But the remarkable fact is still the decline in comparison to the growth of labour productivity in the post-WWII decades, when (like Solow) we should have been expecting the opposite to occur given the extraordinary nature of the ICT revolution. And then the subsequent declines in the 2000s after the dot-com crash, and then more sharply after the global financial crisis.

The view which Carlin and I take (as to this 'perverse' difference in productivity and innovation growth performance between the ICT and the Fordist/Chandlerian eras), as well as further declines in the current century, has four basic key components (a more quantitative version is available in Carlin and Soskice 2018):

1. As suggested above, innovation across the advanced 'radical innovation' world order is centred largely on the US (much more than on China). American radical innovation goes to other advanced economies both in Western Europe and East Asia through networks involving research-oriented MNEs (Siemens is an obvious example), with investments in radical innovation sectors in the US. Putting it in a greatly over-simplified way, American radical innovation can be thought of as supplying frontier technologies to the rest of the advanced world (Aghion et al. 2021). In the process, many of the radical uncertainties have been reduced. There is, of course radical innovation elsewhere, such as Israel and arguably Stockholm, but the US seems to be the epicentre. So here the argument focuses on the US.

2. We posit that expectations about future market growth (always important in R&D and innovation-related investment behaviour) are significantly more important in the radical uncertainty of the ICT era than they were under Fordism in the post-WWII world.

   Technology had sufficiently matured in the post-war Fordist world that innovation was for the most part incremental product innovation rather than radical and disruptive. In the post-war decades, corporations had clear knowledge via well-established sales forces of their customer preferences, and the product innovations they would buy. One might say that society (or different components of it) had sufficiently stabilised, in terms of social networks and established consumption patterns.

   Moreover, in the 1960s, research was done in large company research divisions and laboratories, typically on developments needed for agreed products and their modifications. The broad technology was widely known, so risk was relatively low. Expectations about macro growth were not unimportant – but not central. And much research could be 'stored' for a later period when markets picked up (if they had unexpectedly slowed).

   All of that is much less true in today's digital world. Clayton Christensen, at HBS, arguably the leading innovation strategy theorist of the twenty-first century, explained the huge difficulties that successful, established companies had with disruptive products and technologies (Christensen 2013). R&D in the ICT world typically involves high sunk costs and high risks. Thus Christensen's large 'successful' companies either no longer exist or they increasingly buy innovations in products or technology from start-ups. Start-ups (facing huge risks) and venture capitalists are much happier to invest in periods of growth optimism.

   For these reasons, we assume that in the ICT era (potentially) innovating companies place much weight on growth expectations.

3. As Perez argues, in the (prolonged) period of a new (revolutionary) set of technologies, there is huge uncertainty. This is therefore typically a period of financial speculation as many technology and product bets are being made (Perez 2010). This is aggravated in the US. Governments, keen to promote private investment in new technologies, are keen also to promote risk-taking financial institutions. The risk-taking is exaggerated when housing and other assets enter financial markets. Hence bubbles can occur in periods of 'irrational exuberance'; and when they burst, a deflationary period can set in as both households and financial institutions deleverage and reduce debts. If governments are involved as well, and begin to reduce their debt-to-GDP ratios, then there can be a sharp fall in economic activity. This is a consequence of a neoliberal macroeconomic policy. See Carlin and Soskice (2015) for an explanation of the crises in the 2000s.

   Thus, not only are innovating firms (and their financers) in their radically uncertain markets and technological environments much happier to take big risks in when they widely anticipate growing markets, but also in a world of irrational (and therefore rational) speculative exuberance, massive financial crashes are possible with major shifts from pessimism to optimism and vice versa.

4. Particularly interesting work by social psychologists suggests that optimistic (and pessimistic) beliefs can become quickly reinforcing, producing uniformity and conviction. Based on recent work in psychology in financial markets, and the use of conviction narratives, it is argued that major swings in expectations – which become firmly grounded – can thus occur, from optimistic to pessimistic and vice versa (Tuckett 2011; Tuckett and Nikolic 2017; Fenton-O'Creevy and Tuckett 2021): 'this time is different' is a good illustration of an accompaniment to a conviction narrative (Reinhart and Rogoff 2008).

This all suggests a simple model along the following lines. In Figure 7, GDP growth (g) is on the horizontal axis, and technological change (τ) is on the vertical; the growth of the labour force is zero. Equilibrium is on the vertical axis. The technical progress functions are the dashed upward-sloping lines, with *opt* and *pess* standing for optimism and pessimism. The key points are that all actors share the *optimistic* or *pessimistic* state. Basically, increasingly firmly held expectations determine ('anchor') the technical progress function. Growth (g) is determined by aggregate-demand growth. We assume that investment choices, including in R&D, play a part in determining aggregate-demand growth.

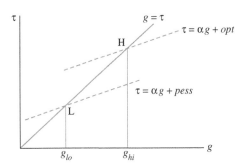

Figure 7   Kaldorian-type growth equilibria, optimistic (H) and pessimistic (L)

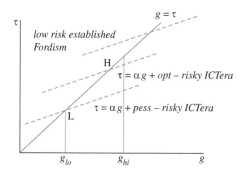

Figure 8   Additional: Fordist low-risk equilibrium

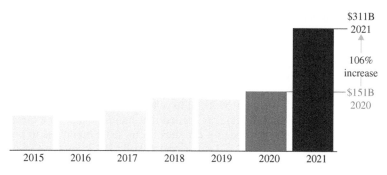

Source: CB Insights.

Figure 9   US venture capital funding, 2015–2021

In any case, if g is greater than g_{hi}, then (with all the necessary qualifications) inflation rises. Then we assume that, via monetary or fiscal policy, g is pulled back to g_{hi}; and vice versa if $g < g_{hi}$.

If we put this in a bigger picture we are thinking of along these lines, then we get something like Figure 8.

We might go one stage further, if more speculatively. The growth model we have proposed only takes steps down from one equilibrium to another.

It is clearly perfectly possible that expectations change in the opposite direction and that a positive expectations climate develops, leading a period of rapid growth in both innovations and innovation funding. Expectations may grow and build up, both about future growth prospects and about innovation waves, and hence innovation funding.

If we take venture-capital funding (measuring risky R&D expenditure) as a measure of expectations, the present moment (2021) might be seen by some commentators as a sign of an *upward* shift in the technical progress function (see Figure 9)!

To summarise the argument so far. This account focuses on the US innovation system, so it is concerned to explain the stepped slowdown in US innovation and productivity growth (and just possibly its current upturn). These shifts in equilibria, however, have occurred not just in the US but across the advanced world. This is the significance of Section 3.4, in which it is argued that the US – as the driver of radical innovation – is at the centre of the advanced world innovation system. This is explained in the Keynesian–Kaldorian growth model here, because the US productivity/innovation

                    Journal compilation © 2022 Edward Elgar Publishing Ltd

slowdowns (or just possibly the current upturn) are then transmitted to the other advanced economies.

5 CONCLUSION

At least six key questions have been posed. Because of space constraints we summarise the questions without answering them!

1. Given the adoption of the neoliberal framework across the advanced world, uniform short-term-oriented capitalism might have been expected, especially in the twenty-first century: why has that not happened at least in Germany and Sweden?
2. Advanced economies have been for the last decade in a double-zero lower bound equilibrium (2ZLBE), with very low real interest and inflation rates, regenerating Keynesian economics and fiscal policy: will that last?
3. What explains global imbalances? And are they a permanent feature of the contemporary advanced world?
4. The Goldin–Katz model predicts increasing participation rates of college participation; that seems one key element in the building of a permanent progressive majority; but has the participation rate growth come to a stop?
5. Why is American inequality so high in comparison with every other advanced economy? Do American decentralised and functionally deregulated institutions which explain radical innovation play a role in explaining poverty and inequality?
6. Finally, what is the future of the Chinese political economy, how secure is Xi, and what is the future of Chinese–US relations?

In answering each of these questions, the major changes in the last two or three decades are stressed, as well as continuing differences in (changed) Varieties of Capitalism, and their developing interrelations.

REFERENCES

Acemoglu, D. (2009), *Introduction to Modern Economic Growth*, Cambridge, MA: MIT Press.
Acemoglu, D. and P. Restrepo (2019), 'Automation and new tasks: how technology displaces and reinstates labor', *Journal of Economic Perspectives*, 33(2), 3–30.
Aghion, P., C. Antonin and S. Bunel (2021), *The Power of Creative Destruction*, Cambridge, MA: Harvard University Press.
Arora, A., L.G. Branstetter and M. Drev (2013), 'Going soft: how the rise of software-based innovation led to the decline of Japan's IT industry and the resurgence of Silicon Valley', *Review of Economics and Statistics*, 95(3), 757–775.
Arora, A., S. Belenzon and A. Patacconi (2018), 'The decline of science in corporate R&D', *Strategic Management Journal*, 39(1), 3–32.
Baccaro, L. and J. Pontusson (2016), 'Rethinking comparative political economy: the growth model perspective', *Politics & Society*, 44(2), 175–207.
Baccaro, L. and H.J. Pontusson (2019), 'Social blocs and growth models: an analytical framework with Germany and Sweden as illustrative cases', Manuscript, Department of Political Economy, University of Geneva.
Bloom, N., R. Sadun and J. Van Reenen (2012), 'Americans do IT better: US multinationals and the productivity miracle', *American Economic Review*, 102(1), 167–201.
Branstetter, L.G., B. Glennon and J.B. Jensen (2019a), 'The rise of global innovation by US multinationals poses risks and opportunities', Peterson Institute of International Economics Policy Brief.

                    Journal compilation © 2022 Edward Elgar Publishing Ltd

Branstetter, L.G., B. Glennon and J.B. Jensen (2019b), 'The IT revolution and the globalization of R&D', *Innovation Policy and the Economy*, 19(1), 1–37.

Breschi, S., G. Tarasconi, C. Catalini, L. Novella, P. Guatta and H. Johnson (2006), 'Highly cited patents, highly cited publications, and research networks', Report for DG Research, European Commission, Bocconi, Milan: CESPRI.

Brynjolfsson, E. and A. McAfee (2013), *Race Against the Machine: How the Digital Revolution is Accelerating Innovation, Driving Productivity, and Irreversibly Transforming Employment and the Economy*, New York: W.W. Norton.

Carlin, W. and D. Soskice (2015), *Macroeconomics: Institutions, Instability and the Financial System*, Oxford: Oxford University Press.

Carlin, W. and D. Soskice (2018), 'Stagnant productivity and low unemployment: stuck in a Keynesian equilibrium', *Oxford Review of Economic Policy*, 34(1–2), 169–194.

Christensen, C.M. (2013), *The Innovator's Dilemma: When New Technologies Cause Great Firms to Fail*, Cambridge, MA: Harvard Business Review Press.

Davis, L.E. and L. Neal (2007), 'Why did finance capitalism and the second industrial revolution arise in the 1890s?', in N.R. Lamoreaux, K.L. Sokoloff and W.H. Janeway (eds), *Financing Innovation in the United States, 1870 to Present*, Cambridge, MA: MIT Press, pp. 129–161.

Dosi, G. (1982), 'Technological paradigms and technological trajectories', *Research Policy*, 2(3), 147–162.

Fenton-O'Creevy, M. and D. Tuckett (2021), 'Selecting futures: the role of conviction, narratives, ambivalence, and constructive doubt', *Futures & Foresight Science*, 121, 1–16, available at: https://doi.org/10.1002/ffo2.111.

Freeman, C. and F. Louçã (2001), *As Time Goes By: From the Industrial Revolutions to the Information Revolution*, Oxford: Oxford University Press.

Friedman, T.L. (2005), *The World is Flat: A Brief History of the Twenty-First Century*, London: Macmillan.

Gordon, R.J. (2012), 'Is US economic growth over? Faltering innovation confronts the six headwinds', National Bureau of Economic Research.

Hacker, J.S., A. Hertel-Fernandez, P. Pierson and K. Thelen (2021), *The American Political Economy: Politics, Markets, and Power*, Cambridge, UK: Cambridge University Press.

Hacker, J.S., A. Hertel-Fernandez, P. Pierson and K. Thelen (2022), 'The American political economy: markets, power, and the meta politics of US economic governance', *Annual Review of Political Science*, 25, forthcoming.

Hall, P.A. and D. Soskice (eds) (2001), *Varieties of Capitalism: The Institutional Foundations of Comparative Advantage*, Oxford: Oxford University Press.

Hooghe, L. and G. Marks (2018), 'Cleavage theory meets Europe's crises: Lipset, Rokkan, and the transnational cleavage', *Journal of European Public Policy*, 25(1), 109–135.

Hope, D. and D. Soskice (2016), 'Growth Models, Varieties of Capitalism, and macroeconomics', *Politics & Society*, 44(2), 209–226.

Iversen, T. and D. Soskice (2019), *Democracy and Prosperity: Reinventing Capitalism in a Turbulent Century*, Princeton, NJ: Princeton University Press.

Klepper, S. (2001), 'Employee startups in high-tech industries', *Industrial and Corporate Change*, 10(3), 639–674.

Klepper, S. (2007), 'Disagreements, spinoffs, and the evolution of Detroit as the capital of the US automobile industry', *Management Science*, 53(4), 616–631.

Klepper, S. (2009), 'Spinoffs: a review and synthesis', *European Management Review*, 6(3), 159–171.

Klepper, S. (2010), 'The origin and growth of industry clusters: the making of Silicon Valley and Detroit', *Journal of Urban Economics*, 67(1), 15–32.

Klepper, S. and S. Sleeper (2005), 'Entry by spinoffs', *Management Science*, 51(8), 1291–1306.

Klepper, S. and P. Thompson (2010), 'Disagreements and intra-industry spinoffs', *International Journal of Industrial Organization*, 28(5), 526–538.

Leamer, E.E. (2007), 'A flat world, a level playing field, a small world after all, or none of the above? A review of Thomas L Friedman's The World is Flat', *Journal of Economic Literature*, 45(1), 83–126.

Marx, K. and F. Engels (1848 [2012]), *The Communist Manifesto*, New Haven, CT: Yale University Press.

Palley, T.I. (1996a), 'Growth theory in a Keynesian mode: some Keynesian foundations for new endogenous growth theory', *Journal of Post Keynesian Economics*, 19(1), 113–135.

Palley, T.I. (1996b), 'Aggregate demand in a reconstruction of growth theory: the macro foundations of economic growth', *Review of Political Economy*, 8(1), 23–36.

Palley, T.I. (1996c), 'Old wine for new bottles: putting old growth theory back in the new', *Australian Economic Papers*, 35(67), 250–262.

Perez, C. (2010), 'Technological revolutions and techno-economic paradigms', *Cambridge Journal of Economics*, 34(1), 185–202.

Piketty, T. (2014), *Capital in the Twenty-First Century*, Cambridge, MA: Harvard University Press.

Polanyi, K. (1944), *The Great Transformation: The Political and Economic Origins of Our Time*, Boston: Beacon Press.

Poulantzas, N. (1973), *Political Power and Social Classes*, London: NLB.

Reinhart, C.M. and K.S. Rogoff (2008), 'This time is different: a panoramic view of eight centuries of financial crises', National Bureau of Economic Research.

Rodríguez-Pose, A. (2018), 'The revenge of the places that don't matter (and what to do about it)', *Cambridge Journal of Regions, Economy and Society*, 11(1), 189–209.

Rodrik, D. (2011), *The Globalization Paradox: Democracy and the Future of the World Economy*, New York: W.W. Norton.

Saxenian, A. (2007), *The New Argonauts: Regional Advantage in a Global Economy*, Cambridge, MA: Harvard University Press.

Saxenian, A. and C.F. Sabel (2011), 'The new Argonauts and the rise of venture capital in the periphery', A. Saxenian and C.F. Sabel, *Handbook of Research on Innovation and Entrepreneurship*, Cheltenham, UK and Northampton, MA: Edward Elgar Publishing, pp. 104–118.

Soskice, D. (2021), 'The US as radical innovation driver: the politics of declining dominance', in J. Hacker, A. Hertel-Fernandez, P. Pierson and K. Thelen (eds), *American Political Economy*, Oxford: Oxford University Press, pp. 321–350.

Streeck, W. (2010), 'E pluribus unum? Varieties and commonalities of capitalism', Discussion Paper, MPIfG 10/12.

Streeck, W. (2013), 'The crisis in context: democratic capitalism and its contradictions', in A. Shaefer and W. Streeck (eds), *Politics in the Age of Austerity*, Cambridge, UK: Polity Press, pp. 262–286.

Streeck, W. (2014), 'How will capitalism end?', *New Left Review*, (87), 35–64.

Tuckett, D. (2011), *Minding the Markets: An Emotional Finance View of Financial Instability*, Berlin: Springer.

Tuckett, D. and M. Nikolic (2017), 'The role of conviction and narrative in decision-making under radical uncertainty', *Theory & Psychology*, 27(4), 501–523.

Tylecote, A. (2013), *The Long Wave in the World Economy: The Current Crisis in Historical Perspective*, Abingdon, UK: Routledge.

Urquiola, M. (2020), *Markets, Minds, and Money: Why America Leads the World in University Research*, Cambridge, MA: Harvard University Press.

Zysman, J. and D. Breznitz (2012), 'Double bind: governing the economy in an ICT era', *Governance*, 25(1), 129–150.

Zysman, J., J. Murray, S. Feldman, N.C. Nielsen and K.E. Kushida (2013), 'Services with everything: the ICT-enabled digital transformation of services', in D. Breznitz and J. Zysman (eds), *The Third Globalization: Can Wealthy Nations Stay Rich in the Twenty-First Century?*, Oxford: Oxford University Press, pp. 99–135.

Review of Keynesian Economics, Vol. 10 No. 2, Summer 2022, pp. 114–135

Varieties of peripheral capitalism: on the institutional foundations of economic backwardness*

Esteban Pérez Caldentey**
Chief, Financing for Development Unit, Economic Development Division, Economic Commission for Latin America and the Caribbean, Santiago, Chile

Matías Vernengo***
Professor, Bucknell University, Lewisburg, PA, USA

This paper critically analyses the literature spawned by Peter Hall and David Soskice's influential book on the varieties of capitalism. It takes as a starting point the critiques within the comparative political economy literature about the supply-side views on economic growth, and the problems with emphasizing the nature of firm behavior as the source of institutional variety. It argues that demand-led growth, as discussed by Post-Keynesian authors, provides an important alternative to the conventional approach to the explanation of varieties of institutional experience. It suggests that understanding the reasons for institutional variety within capitalism requires incorporating the work of Cambridge Keynesians which recovered the work of Classical political economy authors and extended Keynes's ideas on effective demand to explain the process of accumulation. It also requires incorporating the ideas of Prebisch and the Latin American Structuralists, who analysed the limits to accumulation in peripheral countries. The paper also discusses the limitations of Neo-Kaleckian models of demand-led growth used by some authors in the comparative political economy literature, and it suggests a new taxonomy for ordering varieties of capitalism.

Keywords: *heterodox approaches, political economy, comparative economic systems*

JEL codes: *B59, P16, P59*

1 INTRODUCTION

The debates on Comparative Political Economy (CPE) in the period after the collapse of the Berlin Wall and the triumph of Neoliberal Capitalism, as represented by the influential book *Varieties of Capitalism: The Institutional Foundations of Comparative Advantage* by Peter Hall and David Soskice (2001a), referred to as the Varieties of Capitalism (VoC) approach from now on, accepted a great deal of the mainstream Marginalist or Neoclassical approach to economics. Hall and Soskice emphasize the fundamental institutional differences that regulate the functioning of advanced market

---

*   The opinions here expressed are the authors' own and may not coincide with the institutions with which they are affiliated.
**   Email: esteban.perez@cepal.org.
***   Email: m.vernengo@bucknell.edu.

Journal compilation © 2022 Edward Elgar Publishing Ltd
The Lypiatts, 15 Lansdown Road, Cheltenham, Glos GL50 2JA, UK
and The William Pratt House, 9 Dewey Court, Northampton MA 01060-3815, USA

economies, which in their framework are closely related to the work of New Institutionalist authors like Douglas North and Oliver Williamson. Their main distinction is
between what they label liberal market economies (LMEs) and coordinated
market economies (CMEs).[1] Many relevant critiques of what was termed the rational-
ist–functionalist approach in the VoC volume were put forward, even as the authors
tried to broaden their framework (for example, Streeck 2010). Increasingly the spread
of capitalism has led to the establishment of a single global system, even if history has
not ended and ideology still matters. Capitalism is alone, in the words of Milanovic
(2019), and that has led to the perception, at least in some quarters, that the notion
of VoC has outlived its utility (Hay 2020).

Most critiques of the VoC approach fundamentally target the kinds of institutions
that separate the liberal and coordinated forms of capitalism, and in their more sophisticated versions note the theoretical limitations of the essentially Neoclassical framework underlying that initial analysis (for example, Blyth and Matthys 2017). Some
critiques have been explicit about the need to introduce alternative views to the mainstream. Baccaro and Pontusson (2016) suggest that the New Keynesian views of
Soskice and some of his co-authors, regarding the macroeconomics of growth, should
be abandoned in favor of a Post-Keynesian approach, in particular neo-Kaleckian
models that emphasize the ambiguous role of income distribution in the process of
accumulation. They also argue, correctly in our view, that most of the critiques of
the original VoC approach, as well as the fathers of the sub-discipline going back
to the work inspired by Andrew Shonfield's classic *Modern Capitalism* (1965), accept
a narrow definition of CPE, one in which politics is mostly seen through the lens of
partisan electoral politics.

Baccaro and Pontusson (2016; 2018) see the limitations of the conventional CPE
approach in terms of supply and demand, and, more precisely, underscore the inability
to incorporate demand-side perspectives about economic growth. While we agree with
their assessment on the limitations of growth theory within the CPE literature, we go
further and suggest that there are important supply-side limitations to the conventional
CPE approach. Those limitations are ultimately related to the conception of political
economy itself, at an analytical level, and to the very definition of capitalism adopted
by CPE authors, as well as to the role of markets on a historical and institutional level.
In other words, most critiques can be seen as suggesting that there are problems with
the macroeconomic approach utilized by the CPE literature. However, we argue there
are also significant problems with conventional microeconomic analysis and how it is
incorporated in the CPE literature.

Marginalism captured political economy in the late nineteenth century. In our view,
the two most relevant attempts to rethink political economy since then are associated
with the disciples of John Maynard Keynes at Cambridge, UK, and with a group of
Structuralist economists who mostly work out of the Economic Commission for
Latin America and the Caribbean (ECLAC) under the intellectual influence of Raúl
Prebisch. The Cambridge Keynesians can be encompassed under a broad tent definition of Post-Keynesianism as suggested by Lavoie (2014). They emphasized that economic systems are demand-driven, and also rejected the conventional Neoclassical

---

1.   Interestingly, even though they completely ignore the work by VoC and other key CPE
authors, the conceptual basis for Acemoglu and Robinson's (2012) analysis of the reasons for
the relative wealth and poverty of nations is also informed by North and Williamson's New
Institutionalist approach. For a critique of their perspective, see Pérez Caldentey and Vernengo
(2017).

notion that distribution reflects the contributions to the process of production, which necessitates reconsideration of old Classical political economy notions of value and distribution. The Structuralists laid the groundwork for and worked on different aspects of development economics.[2] They emphasized the centrality of geopolitical factors in the development process, including the center-and-periphery distinction and the associated notion of an external constraint as a key barrier to economic development.

Both groups tried to understand the limitations of capitalism during the inter-war crisis. We refer to this alternative view of CPE as Structural Keynesianism, because it highlights a preoccupation with the varieties of capitalism that result from alternative structures of production and insertion in the global economy, and how they interact with alternative demand regimes.[3] The literature on VoC fails to consider that economic activity takes place within a particular system of international relationships characterized by the dichotomy between center and periphery. Center and periphery are analytical categories which bring to light the differences in terms of productive structures, and power relationships between developed and developing economies.

A key distinction between the center and periphery is the stringent limitations faced by the latter to pursue developmental policies through international trade, and monetary and fiscal policies. The crucial distinction between varieties of capitalism is associated with the restrictions imposed on the capabilities of states for coordinating production and managing demand. The notion of the developmental state is brought into the discussion to illuminate the limitations of some countries in the periphery, not just with the center, but also with other peripheral countries. The varieties of peripheral capitalism matter.

The concept of peripheral capitalism, which imitates the production techniques and consumption patterns of advanced economies (Prebisch 1976), was developed by Prebisch in the 1970s and early 1980s after his period at the helm of ECLA – later with the addition of the Caribbean to become ECLAC – and the United Nations Conference on Trade and Development (UNCTAD). However, his understanding of the constraints faced by the periphery to spur economic and social development started during his period as a civil servant in Argentina, in particular as the first director of the central bank in the 1930s. Prebisch's views evolved over time. In his ECLA period during the 1950s and 1960s he emphasized the external constraint (Prebisch 1950). Later, he inclined towards the stagnationist thesis of the 1970s (for example, Prebisch 1981), which is in line with some developments in the heterodox view of demand-driven economic growth, including the Neo-Kaleckian models discussed by Baccaro and Pontusson (2016). In our comparative analysis of Prebisch's views, that turn constituted a regression in his own economic thinking.

To some extent the differences between more liberal, or *laissez-faire*, and more coordinated forms of capitalism are a *mirage*. In the former, very often, the role of

2.   These economists included Celso Furtado, Arthur Lewis, Juan Noyola Vásquez, Aníbal Pinto, Osvaldo Sunkel, and Maria da Conceição Tavares, to name only a few. On Structuralist ideas, see Rodríguez (2006).

3.   In other contexts, the revival of old Classical political economy ideas with the addition of Keynesian demand preoccupations in the long run has been referred to as Classical–Keynesianism (for example, Bortis 1997). Palley (1998) uses the term Structural Keynesian in a sense that is close to the Latin American Structuralist interpretation, perhaps with less emphasis on the importance of old Classical political economy views. For an attempt to integrate the institutional framework with the surplus approach tradition, see Cesaratto and Di Bucchianico (2020).

the state in coordinating economic activities, both to affect the structure of production and to stimulate demand, remains hidden, but is very active. When growth is determined by the autonomous components of demand, government coordination of economic activities is always central. The crucial distinction between varieties of capitalism is about the restrictions imposed on the state's capabilities for coordinating production and managing demand. The failure of the more liberal, or Neoliberal, Latin American peripheral capitalism compared to the more coordinated or political Asian peripheral capitalism, particularly China, exemplifies the importance of the external restriction in understanding the difference between varieties of capitalism not just in the periphery, but also in the center.[4]

The external restriction is essentially a financial constraint. That constraint is to some extent a matter of degree, with a hierarchy of currencies determining the ability to expand demand, and to promote changes in the structure of production at the national level.[5] The current financial and monetary system is anchored around a hierarchical system of reserve currencies, with the United States dollar at the top. The countries that do not issue international reserve currencies, such as the countries of the periphery, need to acquire and have access to the currencies that they cannot issue in order to be able to import essential goods for development. In this sense, the organization of the international monetary system is crucial to understanding the varieties of capitalism, and in that sense, the geopolitical forces behind the shaping and establishment of a hegemonic currency should also be at the center of the CPE literature.

The rest of the paper is divided into four sections. Section 2 analyses the ideas of Prebisch and the development and evolution of the concept of peripheral capitalism. His views are briefly connected with other traditions, and in particular with Post-Keynesian views of the source of economic growth. Section 3 discusses the difficulties of overcoming peripheral capitalism, in particular after the victory of capitalism and the end of the Soviet alternative, and the role of the developmental state in overcoming the external restriction. Section 4 pivots away from that discussion and proposes an alternative taxonomy of the varieties of capitalism, one that compares the VoC literature with the Structural Keynesian approach, among others. Section 5 provides a brief conclusion.

2   PREBISCH AND THE CONCEPT OF PERIPHERAL CAPITALISM

During the 1930s, the difficulties of being directly engaged with managing the Argentine economy forced Raúl Prebisch to think about the peculiar nature of capitalism in

4.   The categories of center and periphery, far from being static, are an evolving concept that changes over time along with the transformation of the world economy. From the mid nineteenth century to the early twentieth, the center *par excellence* was Great Britain, after which it passed to the United States, which Prebisch termed the main dynamic center (that is, Prebisch 1981, p. 230). Arguably, China too is currently acting as a cyclical center, since the country is a source for some of the fluctuations in raw-material prices and the terms of trade that have played a primary role in the dynamism of the economies of Latin America over the last decade.
5.   Following McCombie and Thirlwall (1999, p. 49), we define the external constraint as follows: 'countries face an external constraint when their performance (current and expected) in external markets and the response of the financial markets to this (current and expected) performance delimit and restrict their scope for conducting domestic policies, including fiscal, exchange-rate and monetary policy.' The literature on the external constraint approaches it from the real side of the balance of payments, that is from the side of the balance of trade or current account, but the financial sector might be more relevant in our view.

agrarian-exporting economies. Prebisch (1983) suggested that, before the Great Depression, he firmly believed in the Marginalist or Neoclassical theories he had learnt at the university. However, this should be taken with a grain of salt. His own background was eclectic, and at that point the differences between Classical political economy and the more recent Marginalist economics were poorly understood, and many believed that there was a fundamental continuity, including Alfred Marshall, the most eminent of the Neoclassical authors. Prebisch, for example, was very unclear when he criticized free-trade theories, whether he distinguished between the Ricardian approach and the Neoclassical one, that was incipient at that point, and still being formulated by Eli Heckscher and Bertil Ohlin, and was subsequently formalized and generalized by Paul Samuelson.[6] In fact, it is unlikely that Prebisch had a clear understanding of the main differences in the theory of value and distribution between Classical and Marginalist authors, or that he later followed the capital debates.[7]

Much of his early understanding about the problems of peripheral countries was associated with the management of the balance of payments, and with financial and macroeconomic problems caused by the significant decline in the terms of trade. In other words, his work was based on a critique of the macroeconomic foundations of Neoclassical economics, and its self-adjusting nature, in a similar vein to Keynes's critique of Say's law.[8] Prebisch gave predominance to changes in the flow of money as the main cause of business-cycle fluctuations in the periphery. At first, he placed the emphasis on financial flows, determined on the demand side by Argentina's financing needs and on the supply side by the liquidity stance of developed countries – Great Britain and the United States – as the triggering factor leading to a subsequent expansion of liquidity, prices, and the improvement in business outlook and conditions. Following the dip in agricultural prices provoked by the Great Depression, which led Prebisch to formulate an antecedent of the Prebisch–Singer hypothesis, his attention shifted to export variations as the initiating cause of economic fluctuations.

Even though the perturbations originated in real factors such as the terms of trade and external aggregate-demand shocks, the consequent changes in the flow of money, expenditure, and the circulation velocity of money still played a central role in his

---

6. Prebisch (1992) mentions Ricardo in the first and second volume with regard to his views on monetary issues (Vol. I, pp. 70, 101, 179, 181, and 215; Vol. II, p. 564), in the third volume with regard to Say's law (Vol. III, pp. 464–465) and only in the fourth volume (Prebisch 1993) does he refer to Ricardo in relation to the theory of comparative costs in international trade (Vol. IV, p. 367). Neither Heckscher nor Ohlin are mentioned. However, Prebisch does attribute a strong influence to Taussig's works including his *Economic Principles* and his trade theory, as attested by his continuous references to Williams (a Taussig disciple).

7. Prebisch's analysis and critique of Keynes and the classics is based on the same definition of Classical theory provided by Keynes in *The General Theory* (Prebisch 1992, vol. III, pp. 450–471), which is problematic.

8. His early work was influenced by the reading not just of the dominant Marginalist authors (including Fisher, Hawtrey, Pareto, and Wicksteed, among others), but also from the direct reading of Classical political economists, Marx, and Marxist authors such as Tugan-Baranovsky. He was influenced by Augusto Bunge, and socialist thinkers in Argentina. His views on economic policy were still firmly in the orthodox camp. From 1933 onwards, when he went to the London Economic Conference, and read Keynes's *Means to Prosperity*, published first in *The Times*, and then as the effective manager of the BCRA, he incorporated critically Keynesian ideas about effective demand, and the need for counter-cyclical policy, while being a pioneer in the utilization of capital controls. The same can be said about his work as a money doctor in Paraguay and Santo Domingo during the Triffin missions. See Dosman (2008) and Pérez Caldentey and Vernengo (2019).

explanation of the cycle. His focus on export variations inevitably led Prebisch to develop the other side of the coin: the role of imports and its relationship to exports. More precisely, changes in exports resulted in expenditure variations, some of which then leaked to imports. The extent of the leakage and hence the domestic impact of an export change depended on the size of the propensity to import. By the early 1930s, that led Prebisch to the notion of the coefficient of expansion, which is better known these days as the foreign-trade multiplier.

Prebisch's views on the terms of trade were shaped by his experiences during the 1920s which included his research with Alejandro Bunge, a trip to Australia and the United States, the development of the research department at the Banco Nación, and his work for the Sociedad Rural Argentina. Prebisch came to realize the distinct character of the Great Depression when he became aware of the profound contraction in agricultural prices. The contraction was so sharp that the agricultural price index reached levels that it had not witnessed since the nineteenth century. However, he did not think the fall was merely cyclical. As he put it (Prebisch 1992, vol. II, pp. 346–347 and also p. 135): '[t]he collapse in prices … does not constitute the usual phenomenon of cyclical reaction … rather an intense and pertinent decline to positions each time farther away from the level on which developed the relations of production and credit.' In addition, he argued (ibid., pp. 346–347) that '[i]t [the decline in agricultural prices] is not a simple return to a previous situation, but of an accentuated and progressive contraction of values, that violently upsets the economic structure of the country.' In other words, it was a matter of trend, not cycle, and hence an antecedent of the Prebisch–Singer hypothesis. His thinking already presumed that the differences in the structure of production, in what he would eventually refer to by the 1940s as center and periphery, mattered for understanding the processes of development.[9]

For Prebisch, perhaps the most important elements of the pre-ECLAC development of ideas were the incorporation and understanding of a dynamic version of the multiplier process, and the need for counter-cyclical policies. Additionally, he understood that controls on foreign transactions (such as his well-known proposal for foreign-exchange controls) played a key role in isolating the domestic economy of peripheral countries from the fluctuations of the international business cycles, and were therefore an essential instrument to confront their external constraint (Pérez Caldentey and Vernengo 2016a). After his dismissal from the Central Bank of Argentina in 1943, at the instance of Robert Triffin, Prebisch participated in monetary doctoring activities and in assisting and promoting banking reforms throughout Latin America. Triffin led several Federal Reserve Board missions to the region and considered these to be 'truly revolutionary,' placing the central bank and the financial system at the service of economic and social development (Triffin 1947a; 1947b; 1981; Wallich and Triffin 1953). Prebisch was also the main intellectual force behind the so-called Pinedo Plan, which

---

9.   Toye and Toye (2003) argue that while Prebisch is more well-known in many respects, it was the work of Hans Singer that was essential and original in determining the eponym 'hypothesis.' In their words, 'of the events surrounding the United Nations Economic Commission for Latin America (ECLA) conference in Havana in May 1949 reveals that Prebisch did not discover independently that the terms of trade of primary products were secularly declining, but relied wholly on the previous work of Singer' (ibid., p. 443). Toye and Toye (ibid., p. 443) do not argue that Prebisch was unaware of falling commodity prices, but they do suggest that he thought of this as being merely short-run phenomena. In their words, '[h]e saw it as a feature of depression economics, that is, as a short-run cyclical problem' (ibid., p. 443). This seems incorrect given Prebisch's views in the 1930s.

provided the rationale for industrialization in Argentina. This was all before the 1949 Development Manifesto presented at the Havana conference.

From a general point of view, in ECLA's framework the main limitation of peripheral capitalism was the existence of an external constraint on economic growth. The first initiatives to promote the development of Latin America, through inward state-led industrialization, faced significant external obstacles that were recognized at an early stage.[10] In the late 1950s, the initial concern was the growing import requirement of capital and intermediate goods which exceeded the capacity of exports, thus creating a foreign-exchange gap. ECLA economists understood that to avoid what they termed the external strangulation of Latin American economies, the persistent rise in net imports of capital goods had to be offset by large volumes of financial flows, be it foreign investment or external debt. However, Prebisch was critical of the strategy of industrialization, believing it led to inefficiencies and prevented the generation of economies of scale, which together hindered development prospects.[11]

The inward-oriented development strategy evolved into one that recognized the role played by the external sector in promoting growth. This change in orientation was due in part to the perception that the strategy of state-led industrialization did not provide the required foreign exchange, and that developing countries faced an impending foreign-exchange gap. At a more general level, this change in orientation was a response to the limitations of the industrialization process.[12] Recognition of the limits of the inward industrialization strategy opened the way for a shift towards a new growth-through-trade strategy. That shift was reinforced by the growing importance granted to trade by multilateral organizations, as reflected in the adoption in 1961 of resolution 1707, 'International Trade as the Primary Instrument for Development' by the UN General Assembly.

In this regard, the creation of UNCTAD and the nomination of Raúl Prebisch as its first Director General provided a unique opportunity to articulate the new development strategy. The revised strategy was formulated by UNCTAD for the developing world as a whole (UNCTAD 1964). However, it reflected first and foremost the evolution of Latin American thinking on the relationship between trade and growth. As noted by Love (2005, pp. 170–171): '[t]he original UNCTAD programme ... was that of ECLA *mutatis mutandis* at the global level. Prebisch's reports to the organization in 1964 and 1968 if not fully *cepalismo,* were definitely international adaptations of

---

10.   The most complete formulation of state-led industrialization can be found in Prebisch's Development Manifesto (Prebisch 1949) and subsequently in his *American Economic Review* paper (Prebisch 1959). It rested mainly on a division between the structure and function of countries in the center and those in the periphery. The former countries were self-sustained in their technological progress, which was the dynamic force in the growth process. The countries of the periphery supplied food and raw materials to the countries in the center, but did not manage to benefit equally from the fruits of the technological progress achieved at the center. In fact, the benefits of increased productivity in the periphery were transferred to the center. Countries in the periphery were caught in a poverty trap. The suggested solution was state-led industrialization.

11.   Prebisch (1986, p. 205) states: 'In ECLAC we maintained from the very outset that protection was indispensable as a means of standing up to the centres' technical and economic superiority. Unfortunately, protection as a general rule has been greatly exaggerated if not abusive and has been kept in force for a very long time, affording industries no incentive to reduce their production costs ... .' See Prebisch (1971) and Love (2005, pp. 170–173).

12.   See Arndt (1987, p. 76), who also states that the 'Soviet efforts to neutralise the role of GATT [General Agreements on Tariff and Trade], reinforced by the emerging political muscle of the Third World' was also a factor that influenced this change of orientation.

the regional agency as it had evolved by the early 1960s' (see also Prebisch 1971; 1984). From this new perspective, exports of primary commodities were seen as necessary to finance imports. It also stressed the need for developing countries to export manufactured products.

In this, the work by Prebisch and ECLA authors was moving along the lines of what would eventually be considered Post-Keynesian analysis, emphasizing the importance of demand in the process of economic growth. As such, it should not be a surprise that there was significant cross-fertilization between the ECLA authors and the Cambridge Keynesians, with Nicholas Kaldor and Michał Kalecki serving as consultants and teaching courses organized by the regional UN economic commission. ECLA economists, such as Celso Furtado, also spent time and attended seminars at the University of Cambridge.[13] The historical–structural method of analysis developed at ECLA also incorporated many of the ideas of old Classical political economists, and, in a less explicit manner, the ideas of Marxist authors (Sunkel and Paz 1970). In the same vein, many of the Cambridge Keynesians, in particular Piero Sraffa and his followers, tried to incorporate and extend the ideas of Keynes within a Classical political economy framework.

The notion of center and periphery fell on fertile ground within the so-called Dependency Theory, in particular in the work of Marxists authors like Paul Baran. Those authors followed more closely the radical critiques of Classical political economics, and saw the limits in the process of accumulation as being related to the patterns of consumption of the elites which restricted the size of the surplus, and, hence, the possibilities of further accumulation. By the 1960s, the ideas about stagnationism were widespread in economics.[14] Baran and Sweezy (1966) is, perhaps, the *locus classicus* of these ideas among progressive economists concerned with political economy issues. In Latin America, the work by Celso Furtado (1965) on the causes of stagnation in Brazil is paramount. Palma and Marcel (1989) suggest that among ECLA authors the stagnationist ideas first circulated in a paper written by Nicholas Kaldor during his visit to Chile in 1956.[15]

13.   The works by Joan Robinson on economic growth during this period foreshadow the Neo-Kaleckian growth models discussed by Baccaro and Pontusson (2016), and first formalized by Rowthorn (1981), culminating in the influential work by Marglin and Bhaduri (1990). The work by Kaldor starting in the mid 1960s that emphasized the role of export demand, as formalized by Dixon and Thirlwall (1975), with an emphasis on the supermultiplier and the external constraint, was the other crucial Post-Keynesian contribution to demand-driven economic growth. But in these models the role of the state is limited, and the balance of payments is simply a restriction to economic growth. The notion that autonomous, non-capacity-generating demand is at the heart of economic growth would be developed later by Serrano (1995) and Bortis (1997).
14.   McColloch (2017, p. 561) traces the genealogy of the stagnationist thesis to the work of Paul Sweezy (which incorporated the ideas of Alvin Hansen), and to the work of Joseph Steindl. However, he correctly notes that, for Steindl, stagnation ultimately resulted from policy decisions and not, as it would be eventually in the neo-Kaleckian models, to the effects of a profit squeeze on the process of investment.
15.   Kaldor was closest to Latin American Structuralism and ECLAC, and his work covered a wide spectrum of subjects. At the request of Prebisch, in 1956 Kaldor worked as an ECLAC consultant and prepared the study 'Economic problems of Chile,' which mainly analysed the problem of income inequality and advocated a Structuralist interpretation of inflation. However, Palma and Marcel (1989, p. 246) are essentially correct when they note that Kaldor's views were at odds with the dominant view at ECLA at that time. For them, 'Kaldor's analysis, although connected with the "Structuralist School", did not follow the mainstream of ECLA thought at the time. While the latter located the essence of the LDCs' [less developed countries] economic

                                    Journal compilation © 2022 Edward Elgar Publishing Ltd

During this period, Prebisch's work with ECLA and then UNCTAD remained very much centered on the need for trade liberalization in the center and export diversification in the periphery to avoid the problems of structural heterogeneity, something he had defended at least since 1963. In this UN period, there was little in Prebisch's analysis that could be connected to the stagnationist thesis. It was only in his last book, *Capitalismo Periférico: Crisis y Transformación* (Prebisch 1981), that Prebisch emphasized the patterns of consumption of the Latin American elites, and changed the focus of his analysis to the internal causes for underdevelopment in the region. It was at this point that the concept of surplus became central in Prebisch's writings, even if in some cases the use of it is unclear, and perhaps indistinguishable from Marginalist conceptions of profits.[16] The patterns of consumption in the periphery – imitative of those in the center – and the inability to incorporate surplus labor was at the center of the specificity of peripheral capitalism.[17] Note that the latter had been central in his work since the 1940s, but he had not incorporated the patterns of consumption argument, which had been discussed at ECLA by José Medina Echavarría, who was the main sociologist of the Structuralist school.[18] After ECLA and UNCTAD, Prebisch seems to have embraced the stagnationist thesis that was developed in the 1960s, which was influential to Celso Furtado, along with his ECLA colleagues. In Prebisch's views the external constraint and the external strangulation of Latin American countries lost center-stage and became more of a background characteristic of the workings of peripheral capitalism.

It is important to note that, far from becoming more radical after leaving the United Nations as has been argued (for example, Mallorquín 2007), in some respects his work became more conventional. While it is true that Prebisch seemed to embrace the notion of the surplus, arguably closer to the analytical structure of Classical authors and Marx, he did it in a way that implied the acceptance of Say's law, the notion that profits, or savings, determined accumulation potential, or investment. At the same time, he saw the 1970s/1980s crisis of capitalism as a hegemonic crisis of the United States. In that connection, his contributions were, perhaps, the first to emphasize the importance of

problems outside the LDCs (in the international division of labour and the unequal distribution of gains from trade), Kaldor emphasised that the key problem for Chile's economy did not lie outside the country but inside it – basically, in the absence of a really progressive entrepreneurial class' (ibid., p. 246). For the Structuralist authors at ECLA, there was a similar notion entrenched in Marxist analysis that a national *bourgeoisie* was essential for development. For a critique of these views in the context of some developing countries' experiences in the periphery, see Chibber (2005).

16. Prebisch argued that the production process created an excess demand which was appropriated in the form of surplus by the owners of the means of production (Prebisch 1976, p. 10).

17. Prebisch (1976; 1981) argued that peripheral capitalism had inherent contradictions which included the inefficient accumulation of capital and wasteful investment, the creation of excess growth of labor, and the adverse consequences for development of the inequality of income distribution. Prebisch coined the term 'the dynamic insufficiency' to refer to the incapacity of investment to absorb with improved productivity the continuous increase in the labor force.

18. Prebisch (1981, p. 61) would suggest that '[i]f the surpluses were to be intensively utilized for productive reproduction, then it would be an austere capitalism, where the owners of the means of production, overcoming the temptations emanating from the center, would utilize in full the accumulation potential that they possess in their hands … . There is no such austerity in peripheral capitalism.' Consumption, in particular the consumption of the elites, as determined by the imitative patterns of consumption of the center in a world dominated by mass communication marketing techniques, would be inimical to accumulation and growth.

geopolitics in the process of economic development. Thus, in his famous Development Manifesto he emphasized the shift of hegemonic center from the United Kingdom to the US in the inter-war period.[19]

Prebisch's research on economic dynamics in the 1940s recognized the interrelation between cycle and the growth trend, and emphasized the importance of not simply smoothing out the cycle. He envisaged a global cycle in which the periphery could reduce the downturns and promote rather than curtail the booms, as this would allow the promotion of development, interpreted as closing the gap with the center. In that light, Prebisch was suggesting economic policies could prolong the boom phase of the cycle and also move the trend upwards, thereby allowing the periphery to catch up with the center (Pérez Caldentey and Vernengo 2016b). Although neither of his ideas about the importance of expanding demand in the boom and the external constraint was fully developed into a demand-led model of growth in which consumption and investment dynamics are not inimical – one in which the expansion of mass consumption could lead to growth and adjustment of capacity – those ideas are certainly compatible with such models.[20]

The specificities of Prebisch's peripheral capitalism seem most relevant in the more radical ideas that Prebisch defended in the ECLA/UNCTAD period, but not because of the consumption patterns of the elites or the lack of a national bourgeoisie. Demand expansion depends on exogenous forces. As regards fiscal spending, demand expansion depends on political will and underlying sociopolitical forces allowing for increased government outlays. The expansion of exports depends on the geopolitical arrangements that structure the trade and financial relations between nations, both of which are to a great degree under the control of the hegemonic country that issues the global international reserve currency. In other words, the constraints on economic growth are rooted in domestic and international political factors. Consequently, political economy issues are central for understanding the possibilities of growth in the periphery.

In addition, and contrary to the VoC approach which also introduced the possibility of a range of intermediary positions between the liberal and coordinated varieties, the Structural Keynesian approach views outcomes as being less the result of choice and more the consequence of power.[21] In other words, the varieties of peripheral performance depend not primordially on the institutions that allow for firm interactions and shape how they coordinate their activities, but on the forces that limit the ability of the state to coordinate and affect the structure of production, in particular the diversification of exports, and the expansion of demand. Those constraints are determined at the international level.

---

19.   At this point, the later 1960s early 1970s, Conceição Tavares was moving in the direction of denying the tendency toward stagnation, emphasizing the role of government spending and the geopolitical forces lifting the external constraint in the Brazilian case. Later, by the 1980s, she would emphasize the importance of the persistence of American hegemony – see Vernengo (2022).
20.   The external constraint model to economic growth, hinted at in Prebisch (1959) with a simple numerical example, which prefigured Thirlwall's law, can under certain assumptions be seen as a supermultiplier in which lies the non-capacity-generating autonomous demand that drives the process of accumulation (Vernengo 2015).
21.   See, for example, the work by 'Schneider … [that] in order to accommodate Latin America, add[ed] "hierarchical" to "coordinated" and "liberal" market economies' (Streeck 2010, p. 28).

3   CAPITALISM ALONE AND THE DEVELOPMENTAL STATE

Branko Milanovic's *Capitalism Alone* (2019) brings back Max Weber's definition of capitalism, which – as much as, if not more than Shonfield's views – has been central for the development of the modern CPE literature. The definition of capitalism most economists use, when they use one, rests more on Max Weber than Karl Marx's definition, or on the materialist tradition of the surplus approach upon which the latter was built.[22] Weber defined capitalism very much as the VoC tradition defines the varieties of capitalism, that is, on the basis of the behavior of the firm. For him, 'a rational capitalistic establishment is one with capital accounting, that is, an establishment which determines its income yielding power by calculation according to the methods of modern bookkeeping and the striking of a balance' (Weber 1927 [1981], p. x). Milanovic's (2019) analysis of modern capitalism builds on two archetypes of capitalism that derive from Weber's analysis, which are in a mortal battle for global hegemonic power, namely: Liberal Meritocratic Capitalism, represented by the West and, particularly, by the United States, and Political Capitalism, represented by the rise of the rest, with China at its head. There is a clear analogy in this Weberian tradition with the VoC approach, even if in Milanovic's work the concept is not anchored in the behavior of the firm.

Milanovic (2019, p. 87) uses the Weberian notion of Political Capitalism in order to provide the basis for his argument that China and some other East Asian countries – for example, Malaysia, Singapore, and Vietnam – are in fact capitalist social formations. But he expresses a concern with broader class factors – for example, he underscores how elites maintain control in non-coercive fashion in Liberal Capitalism – and about the need to create an indigenous capitalist class in Political Capitalism. Both point to the issue of class conflict and how surplus is extracted from workers, which tacitly points to an alternative view of capitalism. Somewhat in line with the materialist tradition, Milanovic displays a preoccupation with the role of the bourgeoisie, and gives a nod to Immanuel Wallerstein's notion that there are no capitalists without state support (ibid., p. 116).

To some extent, the final victory of capitalism implies that the literature on the varieties of capitalism took over the place of both the old comparative economic systems field and the research on the so-called transition economies in the post-1989 period.[23] Milanovic's work is central in pointing out this momentous change in which capitalism reigns unchallenged but, because his analysis is based on the Weberian dichotomy between liberal and political capitalism, it ends up being very close to the VoC distinction between liberal and coordinated market economies in which capitalism is reduced to the existence of markets.[24] Though Milanovic puts the state rather than firms at the

22.   Classical political economists were concerned with the process of accumulation. Economic growth was studied in relation to issues of distribution, class relations, and at a lower level of abstraction, taking into consideration historical and institutional factors that affected it. In particular, since distribution was discussed with regard to actual social classes, and those differed according to the ways of organizing society, there was a preoccupation with the historical stages of economic development. These views coalesced into what has been called the four-stage theory of economic development – hunting, pastoral, agricultural, and commercial societies – developed most likely independently by Turgot and Adam Smith (Meek 1971). Marx's development of the concept of the capitalist mode of production builds on that tradition.
23.   Streeck (2010, p. 38) had already noted that the CPE literature would have to start '[c]onceiving of capitalism as a more or less integrated global system.'
24.   Marx was very critical of the naturalization of markets. He said that '[e]ven Adam Smith and Ricardo, the best representatives of the [bourgeois] school, ... treat this mode of production as one eternally fixed by Nature for every state of society' (Marx 1867 [1909], p. 93). That is

center of his distinction between the alternative forms of capitalism, there is little discussion of either the constraints on the state ability to expand demand or the differences between the center and the periphery in that respect, particularly as regards the external constraint. The role of what has been termed the developmental state is absent in the literature on the varieties of capitalism. The secondary role of the state and the absence of a more thorough discussion of the developmental state are the main problems in that literature.

The idea of a developmental state is often associated with the Asian experience in the post-war period, from Japan to China, including in particular South Korea and the other so-called Tigers (that is, Indonesia, Malaysia, Taiwan, Thailand, and, more recently, Vietnam). The theoretical work of Chalmers Johnson and his followers – for example, Alice Amsden, Ha-Joon Chang, Peter Evans, and Robert Wade, to cite the most prominent – was central for the conceptualization of the developmental state (Pérez Caldentey 2008). Their work builds on a tradition that harks back to Friedrich List, but the logic of the developmental state stems from the American experience and the legacy of Alexander Hamilton, who was the inspiration for List, as noted by Cohen and DeLong (2016).

Even that does not quite get to the bottom as England was the ultimate inspiration for Hamilton's *Report on Manufactures*. The origin of the development state concept should be examined in light of what Brewer (1988) calls the British Fiscal-Military State. The central characteristic of the Fiscal-Military State was its ability to borrow in its own currency, more or less without limit, and with relatively low interest rates. At the core of the developmental state is the ability to spend without external restrictions. In other words, a true developmental state must have a hegemonic currency, or it must not have a significant shortfall of it. The ability to spend was evidently central to making war. Satia (2018, p. 27) has shown recently how government procurement policies were central for the creation of what she calls 'not a military-industrial complex, but a steadily expanding military-industrial society.' Charles Tilly's (1975, p. 42) famous *dictum*, according to which 'war made the state, and the state made war,' is correct, or at least Satia seems to agree. She tells us that: 'state institutions drove Britain's industrial revolution in crucial ways … war made the industrial revolution' (Satia 2018, p. 2). What is missing in Tilly's argument about the role of war is the peripheral state, and the relation of the latter to the developmental state. If we take the Asian case as paradigmatic, we could say that the state lost the war, and the loss made the developmental state. The developmental state in the periphery appears in the post-war period with the establishment of American hegemony.

The ability of the United States to spend in its own currency, to impose the dollar as the international currency after the Bretton Woods Agreement, and to expand demand is central for understanding the process of accumulation in the United States. That ability also allowed the United States to promote development in the countries that had lost the war.[25] In other words, the United States allowed and even promoted the

exactly what Max Weber and many Neoclassical economists end up doing. Weber often refers to capitalism when discussing the Middle Ages in Western Europe, ancient China, or the Roman Empire (Weber 1927). This naturalization of capitalism is also typical of VoC authors, who tend to confuse the existence of markets, or the profit motive, with capitalism.

25.   In this sense, the critique by Baccaro and Pontusson (2016) that the VoC needs to account for the expansion of demand is amplified to suggest that the hegemon has an ability to expand demand on a global basis.

industrialization of the countries that lost the war. It did so to prevent the spread of Soviet communism. In the Asian case, the very existence of the developmental state was to some extent tied to the special relation with the United States produced by a geopolitical situation that included not only the Soviet Union, but also communist regimes in China, North Korea, and Vietnam. Additionally, the domino theory held that Asian economies would fall and become communist if a neighboring country also did so. And that is without considering India, Indonesia, and the non-aligned movement which also seemed suspicious to the American establishment.

This generated the conditions for the expansion of American military procurement policy in Asia. Immerwahr (2020) shows that Toyota, the firm famous for 'just-in-time' or flexible production methods that superseded Fordist mass production, was virtually broke at the beginning of the Korean War. The firm was saved by Pentagon purchases which guaranteed demand, and also enforced standards and transferred technology. The United States provided the dollars, lifting the external constraint that precluded development in other parts of the periphery. It also provided the transfer of technology required to master the more advanced methods of production of the time. Immerwahr points out that: '[n]ot only did the contracts provide profits, they offered Japanese firms a chance to master U.S. standards – i.e., the standards that were rapidly spreading out all over the world. The U.S. military was the largest and one of the most exacting standard-setting agencies on the planet' (ibid., p. 361). In other words, the firm-level differences seen in the VoC literature to be central for different types of capitalism derive to a great degree from the behavior of the state.

Immerwahr suggests that the United States' military procurement was central for Japanese economic growth and he refers to the American influence, wherever its military bases appeared, as being necessary but not sufficient for catching up. The broad and vast Baselandia, in Immerwahr's expression – the American version of the military-industrial society – promoted industrialization both at home and abroad. Following the concept used by Wallerstein (1974), it might be referred to as 'promotion by invitation.'[26] China also benefited enormously from the importation of standards – not the military's, but those of giant American retailers like Walmart. The process of learning to meet the demands of Western buyers is what allowed the goods themselves to be reproduced in vast volumes for the increasingly large home market, thereby allowing for a consumer society at home. In other words, the possibilities of expansion of Political Capitalism were firmly tied to its symbiotic relation with the Liberal Meritocratic Western Hegemon.

In the case of Latin America, the legacy of the Monroe Doctrine implied that the benevolent policy of development by invitation was never really a possibility. The limited impact of the developmental state in the region, when compared with the Asian experience, should not be seen as a complete failure. The economies of the region grew relatively fast, and in many ways were able to close the gap with advanced economies before the debt crisis of the 1980s. It was the debt crisis that led the region more decisively into Neoliberalism, even if Neoliberalism had started before in the region, with the Southern Cone at the forefront.

The distinctions between a political capitalism in which the state intervenes in patrimonial ways to maintain the power of the prince in the face of a rising bourgeoisie, are ultimately not so different than the more liberal version in which the bourgeoisie has

---

26.   These ideas have been revived more recently and in line with the notion that demand expansion is central for economic growth by Medeiros and Serrano (1999). Arthur Lewis also discussed the concept of development by invitation (Pérez Caldentey 2007).

free rein and free markets rule. Thus in the United States the developmental state has been somewhat hidden, to use Fred Block's (2008) apt expression. It has been concealed to promote the notion that free markets and democracy guide the functioning of institutions in the United States, and not state or planning which could be confused with socialism, or worse, communism. This was necessary marketing. However, behind the scenes, a strong technobureaucracy connected the visible hand of the state with the large corporations that dominated the economy, and they had moved abroad causing some anxiety about the American challenge, were part of a developmental state, and were best captured in the American marketplace of ideas by John Kenneth Galbraith's (1967) notion of *The New Industrial State*.[27] Arguably, the capabilities of the hidden developmental state in the United States remain intact and continues to work through the military-industrial complex. Although 5 million manufacturing jobs were lost in the first decade of the 2000s, manufacturing output has grown continuously, if somewhat more sluggishly in the decade between the Great Recession and the pandemic.

The disputes between liberal and political or more or less coordinated versions of capitalism conceal the fact that, in both, a significant amount of government intervention and non-market forms of coordination are widespread. It also sidesteps that the crucial differences between states lies in their ability to borrow and spend in their own currencies, creating the conditions for the material reproduction of society without the interference of external agents. As regards the developmental state, the United States' position is unparalleled. Its military power is unmatched, as is the position of the dollar, with the latter being central to its ability to spend more or less without limit. The ability to expand demand is globally uneven and the international monetary institutions associated with the global hegemony of the dollar are at the center of the varieties of peripheral capitalism. Growth is demand-driven and the autonomous components of demand, especially government expenditures, drive the process of economic growth, but also the relative openness of the American economy, both through access to its own market but also through access to dollars via financial institutions, is central to reducing or even eliminating the external constraint, and allowing the process of growth in the periphery.

4   AN ALTERNATIVE TAXONOMY OF INSTITUTIONAL VARIETY

The Structural Keynesian view in which growth is demand-driven and in which the state is constrained in its ability to expand demand, particularly in the periphery, prompts a different explanation of institutional variety in capitalism. Table 1 provides an alternative to Streeck's (2010) classification of models of varieties of capitalism. From a disciplinary perspective it is closer to an economist's understanding of the alternative views regarding institutional varieties of capitalist social formations. The VoC literature builds on the New Institutionalist approach, which in many ways is an extension of the mainstream approach in economics, whereby markets produce

27.   In this sense, Galbraith's (1967) notion of a New Industrial State corresponds in many ways to the discussion of a developmental state in the periphery. Arguably the New Industrial State was just the phase associated with the rise of multinational corporation and reflected the need of a developmental state to promote the interests of American corporations abroad. This is true even if in more recent times the state in the United States seems dysfunctional, and closer to what James K. Galbraith referred to as the Predator State (Galbraith 2008).

Table 1   Models of Varieties of Capitalism

	Neoliberal	New Institutionalist	Corporatist/social embeddedness	Structural Keynesian
Source of variety	Economic/factor endowments/ individual behavior	Institutional/firm behavior	Political/organized labor, corporations, and political parties	Political/power to borrow in its own currency/ class conflict
View of the role of markets	Efficient allocator of resources (government failures are prevalent)	Efficient allocator of resources (transaction costs are prevalent)	Inefficient allocator of resources (market failures are prevalent) and must be embedded in social institutions	Material reproduction of society/markets are instruments for accumulation, not allocation of resources
Source of economic growth	Factor endowment growth, and technical progress (mostly exogenous)	Factor endowment growth, technical progress (mostly endogenous), property rights, and rule of law	Cultural norms and government policies	Demand expansion constrained by political and geopolitical factors

Source: Authors' elaboration.

efficient allocations of resources, and government failures make intervention worse than a *laissez-faire* stance. That view is termed the 'Neoliberal' in the table.[28] Hall and Soskice's (2001) VoC approach is termed New Institutionalist, since that is the main analytical basis for their views. The many alternative critiques raised in the literature in the social sciences are folded into one broad category, referred to here as the corporatist/social-embeddedness view. All are contrasted with the Structural Keynesian view. There are inevitable simplifications in our taxonomy.

Both the Neoliberal and the New Institutionalist approaches emphasize the role of factor endowments and technical progress in economic growth, perhaps with greater emphasis on the possibility of endogenous technical progress in the latter approach. In that connection, an increasing number of economists accept the role of increasing returns in explaining economic growth. According to the Neoliberal view, the free market – or economic freedom in the negative sense of absence of government intervention – is essential for political freedom. Consequently, according to that logic, *laissez-faire* policies should produce both economic convergence and a great deal of institutional convergence too. At the end of the process, when capitalism is alone and countries have converged, Neoclassical economics suggests a version of Fukuyama's end of history, with full convergence to the liberal market model. The source for institutional convergence in the VoC approach is ultimately related to the existence of transaction costs, and the possibilities for alternative forms of firm-level organization and cooperation. Streeck (2010, p. 31), who can be viewed as identifying with a

28.   Here we avoid a discussion of the precise meaning of Neoliberalism. Note that for Mirowski (2020), Neoliberalism is both a school of thought and a political movement, which he refers to as a collectivity or community of thought. In our view all Neoliberal authors tend to accept, knowingly or not, some version of the Neoclassical theory that says that markets are efficient allocators of resources, and that *laissez-faire* policies are needed to avoid inefficiencies.

corporatist/social-embeddedness view of capitalist variety,[29] notes that: 'the inherent economism of the VoC paradigm, as evident in its self-professed "firm-centeredness" and its marginalization of politics in favor of policy' is a limitation of the New Institutionalist approach. However, Streeck misses the point that it is not just a question of economicism, it is also a question of the type of economic assumptions that VoC authors utilize.

Streeck's Neo-Polanyian argument for the limits of the VoC approach seems more to the point. Based on Polanyi's (1957) notion that the economy is an instituted process, he argues that:

> [s]ocial orders … differ in space and change over time. Private property, free markets, wage labor, joint stock companies, and modern finance emerged in or spread to different historical contexts and local traditions, institutions and power structures that could not but imprint themselves on the ways in which capitalism became 'instituted' in different societies. (Streeck 2010, p. 5)

A similar critique of the VoC approach is developed by Hopkin and Blyth (2012, p. 1), who argue that the latter approach 'pays insufficient attention to the ways in which markets can be embedded in stable but apparently dysfunctional institutional arrangements.' Their point is that some forms of regulation might lead to liberal embeddedness that is compatible with the efficiency of markets and the promotion of equality, while other forms of regulation constitute illiberal embeddedness which creates a trade-off favoring strong social groups.[30]

Note that Polanyi (1944) famously argued that a pure market economy is unstable and that free-market policies would lead to a backlash from the losers, requiring a safety net to reduce the negative impact of market outcomes on society. That argument was clearly informed by the inter-war crisis and the end of the so-called 'first globalization.' However, in his analysis it is still true that markets are fundamentally about efficient allocation of resources.[31] The main difference from the New Institutionalist or even the Neoliberal approach seems to be on the question of how markets are embedded. It is worth noticing that, according to Slobodian (2018, p. 18), the Neoliberal movement wanted to embed the market into institutions that would protect it from the redistributive interventions from progressive politicians. In other words, Slobodian (2018, p. 19) suggests that the difference with Polanyi and his concern with the need to

---

29. Streeck (2010) uses both terms to discuss the ideas of two different traditions, and seems to maintain some distance from both, even when he agrees with some of the criticism these authors raise against the VoC approach.
30. Here the discussion of social institutions that promote equality, and interfere with market allocation of resources, differs from Baccaro and Pontusson's (2016) analysis, which emphasizes the role of income distribution in growth regimes. Also, Hopkin and Blyth (2012, p. 26) seem to accept that 'disembedded market liberalism achieves economic efficiency at the expense of equality.'
31. Polanyi tends to think and judge Classical and Neoclassical economics from the point of view of their economic policy prescriptions, and the idea of *laissez-faire*, and sees Classical authors as precursors of the mainstream. He accepts the notion that prices are determined by supply and demand, and that implies that markets produce efficient outcomes in the Marginalist sense of efficient allocation of resources. He explicitly follows the Neoclassical view of prices, suggesting that: '[e]conomic value ensures the usefulness of the goods produced; it must exist prior to the decision to produce them; it is a seal set on the division of labor. Its source is human wants and scarcity' (Polanyi 1944 [2001], p. 267). In other words, relative value depends on demand (human wants) and its limited supply (scarcity).

re-embed markets is fundamentally related to motives. For Polanyi, markets should be embedded to promote social justice, while the Neoliberals wanted to guarantee the freedom of capital.[32] Here it is worth noting that the mobility of capital was one of the fundamental freedoms for the Neoliberal pioneers. As Slobodian (2018, p. 136) says: 'Against Roosevelt's Four Freedoms – of speech, of worship, from fear, from want – neoliberals posed the four freedoms of capital, goods, services, and labor.' By labor freedom, the Neoliberal discourse means labor contracts without the intervention of unions.

The Structural Keynesian approach departs from Neoclassical or Marginalist interpretations of the role of markets and takes an approach that harks back to the work of Classical political economists and Marx. For Classical political economists, markets were an institutional framework for the material reproduction of society, and for the promotion process of accumulation. In the Classical framework, equilibrium prices were not the ones that show the relative scarcity of goods and services as determined by preferences and limited resources. Normal prices – natural prices in Smith and Ricardo, and production prices in Marx – were the ones needed to reproduce the basic needs of society. The overall state of preferences was taken as given, something determined by broad institutional and historical circumstances. That matters because Classical long-term prices require that one distributive variable be determined beforehand. In other words, with real wages set at the subsistence level, something that was seen as historically and institutionally established in their time, the technical conditions of production were sufficient to determine normal prices.[33]

That view is perfectly compatible with Polanyi's notion of the embeddedness of markets. Markets are social constructs, and rules, regulations, and other institutional features are central for the creation of markets. Markets do not just appear out of thin air, in self-organizing fashion.

There is also a commonality between the Neo-Polanyian approach and the Structural Keynesian perspective regarding the importance of demand-led growth for accumulation regimes, which is noted by both Baccaro and Pontusson (2016) and Blyth and Matthijs (2017). However, contrary to the Neo-Kaleckian model, in which income distribution plays a role through its impact on investment, generating either underconsumptionist or exhilarationist regimes, in the Structural Keynesian view income distribution and inequality matter through their indirect political impact on autonomous non-capacity-creating spending.[34]

Structural Keynesians tend to favor the supermultiplier model which allows for a stronger autonomous role for political factors. That fits with the Structural Keynesian approach which is more amenable to emphasizing the importance of the state,

32.   In that Polanyi is closer to John Maynard Keynes and others who suggested the need for state intervention in the economy. Mirowski (2018) explores the often-neglected similarities between Polanyi's work and Friedrich Hayek's analysis, one of the key Neoliberal authors.
33.   This notion is based on Garegnani's (1984) analysis of the analytical core of Classical political economy and Marx's works, and is built on the basis of Piero Sraffa's revival of the surplus approach. In the same vein, see Cesaratto and Di Bucchianico (2020), who provide a more thorough, if somewhat more favorable, discussion of the Polanyian approach.
34.   Note that the quintessential Neo-Kaleckian model, by Bhaduri and Marglin (1990, p. 388, emphasis in the original), was explicitly developed to show that '*models* such as that of "cooperative capitalism" enunciated by the left Keynesian social democrats, the Marxian model of "profit squeeze" or even the conservative model relying on "supply-side" stimulus through high profitability and a low real wage, fit into the more general Keynesian theoretical scheme. They become particular *variants* of the theoretical framework presented here.'

particularly the developmental state and the constraints it faces in creating varieties of capitalism. For example, higher wages alone will lead to higher consumption, given the Kaleckian notion that workers have a higher propensity to consume. However, according to the supermultiplier model it will not affect the rate of economic growth, which depends on autonomous spending.[35] Furthermore, autonomous spending depends less on cultural norms (for example, norms about consumption), and more on the strength of the political and class coalition in power and its ability to pass legislation to expand government expenditures. That makes the idea of the Fiscal-Military State quintessentially relevant.

Growth can be externally constrained, particularly in peripheral capitalism, but less because of the balance-of-payments impacts caused by the conspicuous consumption of the elites. Instead, the more significant cause of the external constraint is the inability of countries to borrow in their own currency and the difficulties in diversifying exports. Alternative growth regimes can result from the lifting of the external constraint by a benevolent hegemon and via the hegemon promoting development by invitation. In other words, growth depends not only on the complex set of domestic political forces that allow for demand expansion at home, but also on the geopolitical factors that impose limitations on the state's ability to spend. Monetary regimes, in which the free mobility of capital is enshrined, something Keynes thought it was paramount to avoid, will tend to impose more significant limitations on countries that do not have the key currency, and will bestow even more power on the hegemonic country.

In sum, in the Structural Keynesian approach growth is quintessentially political. That shares some similarity with the corporatist/social-embeddedness approach's emphasis on the role of political factors in the explanation of capitalist variety. But in the Structural Keynesian approach the source of variety is ultimately the ability of the state to spend in its own currency. At the heart of the varieties of capitalism are two factors. First, the geopolitical factors that explain how the global hegemons exert their powers. Second, the domestic social conflicts, to a great extent class-based, that determine the political ability of certain groups to control the state and use it to promote accumulation.

5   CONCLUDING REMARKS

The Varieties of Capitalism approach has been incredibly influential in the Comparative Political Economy literature. It adopted a New Institutionalist perspective from economics and applied it to understand the emergence of institutional variety within capitalist social formations. Criticism of the VoC approach has pointed out the limited sources of variation, related to firm-level behavior, and the lack of discussion of the role of inequality at the macroeconomic level. It has been rightly noted that the New Institutionalist approach accepts the notion that growth is supply-constrained. To correct that, Neo-Kaleckian models of growth were introduced in the literature, which makes wage and profit-led regimes possible. Furthermore, some authors suggest

35.   The end of the Golden Age of Capitalism, the period of high growth that followed the Bretton Woods Agreement and marked the rise of American Hegemony, can be seen not as the mechanical result of a profit squeeze that reduced the investment of capitalists, but as the outcome of a complex social backlash, which provided political support for more pro-market policies among parts of the working class, in particular those who felt that expansion of civil rights to women and minorities were a threat to their social standing (Vernengo 2021).

that the way that markets are embedded is often neglected by VoC authors, and that the possibility that markets are inefficient, beyond the existence of transaction costs, does not receive significant attention. In our view, all of those criticisms of the original VoC contributions are appropriate.

Using a blend of Post-Keynesian and Latin American Structuralist approaches, referred to as Structural Keynesianism, this paper has argued there are additional deeper problems with the underlying understanding of the sources of economic growth at the macroeconomic level. More importantly, there are significant limitations in the microeconomic understanding of the role of markets. Markets are instruments for the accumulation of capital, but they are neither efficient nor inefficient allocators of resources. Markets provide the basis for the material reproduction of society, and they are not designed to guarantee the full utilization of factors of production. Distribution is conflictive, and plays a parametric role in the process of accumulation which is driven by autonomous spending. At the global level, the hegemonic power has the ability to impose its currency internationally and to spend in its own currency, and how it uses those powers is crucial for understanding the varieties of capitalism. It is hard to disagree with the notion that 'political economy might have to abandon entirely the idea of *national varieties* of capitalism and advance towards a concept of an *internationally variegated* capitalist world system' (Streeck 2010, p. 38, emphases in the original).

REFERENCES

Acemoglu, D. and J. Robinson (2012), *Why Nations Fail: The Origins of Power, Prosperity, and Poverty*, New York: Crown.

Arndt, H.W. (1987), *Economic Development: The History of an Idea*, Chicago: University of Chicago Press.

Baccaro, L. and J. Pontusson (2016), 'Rethinking Comparative Political Economy: the growth model perspective,' *Politics & Society*, 44(2), 175–207.

Baccaro, L. and J. Pontusson (2018), 'Comparative Political Economy and varieties of macroeconomics,' MPIfG Discussion Paper 18/10.

Baran, P. and P. Sweezy (1966), *Monopoly Capital*, New York: Monthly Review Press.

Bhaduri, A. and S. Marglin (1990), 'Unemployment and the real wage: the economic basis for contesting political ideologies,' *Cambridge Journal of Economics*, 14, 375–393.

Block, F. (2008), 'Swimming against the current: the rise of a hidden developmental state in the United States,' *Politics & Society*, 36(2), 169–206.

Blyth, M. and M. Matthys (2017), 'Black swans, lame ducks, and the mystery of IPE's missing macroeconomy,' *Review of International Political Economy*, 24(2), 203–231.

Bortis, H. (1997), *Institutions, Behaviour and Economic Theory: A Contribution to Classical–Keynesian Political Economy*, Cambridge, UK: Cambridge University Press.

Brewer, J. (1988), *The Sinews of Power: War, Money, and the English State, 1688–1783*, Cambridge, MA: Harvard University Press.

Cesaratto, S. and S. Di Bucchianico (2020), 'From the core to the cores: surplus approach, institutions and economic formations,' Centro Sraffa Working Paper, No 45.

Chibber, V. (2005), 'Reviving the developmental state? The myth of the national bourgeoisie,' *Socialist Register*, 41, 144–165.

Cohen, S. and B. DeLong (2016), *Concrete Economics: The Hamilton Approach to Economic Growth and Policy*, Cambridge, MA: Harvard Business Review Press.

Dixon, R. and A. Thirlwall (1975), 'A model of regional growth-rate differences on Kaldorian lines,' *Oxford Economic Papers*, 27(2), 201–214.

Dosman, E. (2008), *The Life and Times of Raúl Prebisch, 1901–1986*, Montreal: McGill–Queens University Press.

Furtado, C. (1965), *Subdesenvolvimento e Estagnação na América Latina*, Rio de Janeiro: Civilização Brasileira.

Galbraith, J.K. (1967 [2007]), *The New Industrial State*, Princeton, NJ: Princeton University Press.

Galbraith, J. (2008), *The Predator State: How Conservatives Abandoned the Free Market and Why Liberals Should Too*, New York: Free Press.

Garegnani, P. (1984), 'Value and distribution in the Classical economists and Marx,' *Oxford Economic Papers*, 36, 291–325.

Hall, J. and D. Soskice (eds) (2001a), *Varieties of Capitalism: The Institutional Foundations of Comparative Advantage*, Oxford: Oxford University Press.

Hall, J. and D. Soskice (2001b), 'An introduction to Varieties of Capitalism,' in J. Hall and D. Soskice (eds), *Varieties of Capitalism: The Institutional Foundations of Comparative Advantage*, Oxford: Oxford University Press, pp. 1–68.

Hay, Colin (2020), 'Does capitalism (still) come in varieties?,' *Review of International Political Economy*, 27(2), 302–319.

Hopkin, J. and M. Blyth (2012), 'What can Okun teach Polanyi? Efficiency, regulation and equality in the OECD,' *Review of International Political Economy*, 19(1), 1–33.

Immerwahr, D. (2020), *How to Hide an Empire: A History of the Greater United States*, New York: Farrar, Straus and Giroux.

Lavoie, M. (2014), *Post-Keynesian Economics: New Foundations*, Cheltenham, UK and Northampton, MA: Edward Elgar Publishing.

Love, J. (2005), 'The rise and fall of Structuralism,' in V. FitzGerald and R. Thorp (eds), *Economic Doctrines in Latin America*, New York: Palgrave Macmillan, pp. 157–181.

Mallorquín, C. (2007), 'The unfamiliar Raúl Prebisch,' in E. Pérez Caldentey and M. Vernengo (eds), *Ideas, Policies and Economic Development in the Americas*, New York: Routledge, pp. 98–122.

Marglin, S. and A. Bhaduri (1990), 'Profit squeeze and Keynesian theory,' in S. Marglin and J.B. Schor (eds), *The Golden Age of Capitalism*, Oxford: Clarendon Press, pp. 153–185.

Marx, K. (1867 [1909]), *Capital: A Critique of Political Economy*, vol. I, Chicago: Charles Kerr & Co.

McColloch, W. (2017), 'Profit-led growth, social democracy, and the left: an accumulation of discontent,' *Review of Radical Political Economics*, 49(4), 559–566.

McCombie, J. and A. Thirlwall (1999), 'Growth in an international context: a post Keynesian view,' in J. Deprez and J. Harvey (eds), *Foundations of International Economics: Post Keynesian Perspectives*, New York: Routledge, pp. 35–90.

Medeiros, C. and F. Serrano (1999), 'Padrões Monetários Internacionais e Crescimento,' in J.L. Fiori (ed.), *Estados e Moedas no Desenvolvimento das Nações*, Petrópolis: Vozes, pp. 119–151.

Meek, R. (1971), 'Smith, Turgot and the "four stages" theory,' *History of Political Economy*, 3, 9–27.

Milanovic, B. (2019), *Capitalism, Alone: The Future of the System That Rules the World*, Cambridge, MA: Harvard University Press.

Mirowski, P. (2018), 'Polanyi vs Hayek?,' *Globalizations*, 15(7), 894–910.

Mirowski, P. (2020), 'Neoliberalism,' in B. Rosser, E. Pérez Caldentey, and M. Vernengo (eds), *The New Palgrave Dictionary of Economics*, London: Palgrave Macmillan.

Palley, T. (1998), *Plenty of Nothing: The Downsizing of the American Dream and the Case for Structural Keynesianism*, Princeton, NJ: Princeton University Press.

Palma, G. and M. Marcel (1989), 'Kaldor on the "discreet charm" of the Chilean bourgeoisie,' *Cambridge Journal of Economics*, 13(1), 245–272.

Pérez Caldentey, E. (2007), 'Strategies of "industrialization by invitation" in the Caribbean,' in E. Pérez Caldentey and M. Vernengo (eds), *Ideas, Policies and Economic Development in the Americas*, New York: Routledge, pp. 183–207.

Pérez Caldentey, E. (2008), 'The concept and evolution of the developmental state,' *International Journal of Political Economy*, 37(3), 27–53.

Pérez Caldentey, E. and M. Vernengo (2016a), 'Reading Keynes in Buenos Aires: Prebisch and the dynamics of capitalism,' *Cambridge Journal of Economics*, 40(6), 1725–1741.

Pérez Caldentey, E. and M. Vernengo (2016b), 'Raúl Prebisch and economic dynamics: cyclical growth and center–periphery interaction,' *ECLAC Review*, (118), 9–24.

Pérez Caldentey, E. and M. Vernengo (2017), 'Institutions, property rights and why nations fail,' in E. Pérez Caldentey and M. Vernengo (eds), *Why Latin American Nations Fail: Development Strategies in the Twenty-First Century*, Berkeley, CA: University of California Press, pp. 1–14.

Pérez Caldentey, E. and M. Vernengo (2019), 'Heterodox central banking in the periphery,' *Research in the History of Economic Thought and Methodology*, 36C, 81–100.

Polanyi, K. (1944 [2001]), *The Great Transformation: The Political and Economic Origins of Our Time*, Boston: Beacon.

Polanyi, K. (1957), 'The economy as instituted process,' in: K. Polanyi, C.M. Arensberg, and H.W. Pearson (eds), *Trade and Market in the Early Empires: Economies in History and Theory*, New York: The Free Press, pp. 243–270.

Prebisch, R. (1949), *Economic Survey of Latin America*, New York: Economic Commission for Latin America, United Nations.

Prebisch, R. (1950), *The Economic Development of Latin America and its Principal Problems*, New York: Economic Commission of Latin America, United Nations.

Prebisch, R. (1959), 'Commercial policy in the underdeveloped countries,' *American Economic Review*, 49(2), 251–273.

Prebisch, R. (1971), *Hacia una Dinámica del Desarrollo Latinoamericano*, Mexico: Fondo de Cultura Económica.

Prebisch, R. (1976), 'Crítica al Capitalismo Periférico,' *Revista de la CEPAL*, 1(1), 7–73.

Prebisch, R. (1981), *Capitalismo Periférico: Crisis y Transformación*, México: Fondo de Cultura Económica.

Prebisch, R. (1983), 'Cinco Etapas de mi Pensamiento sobre el Desarrollo,' *El Trimestre Económico*, 50(2), 1077–1109.

Prebisch, R. (1984), 'Five stages in my thinking on development,' in G. Meier and D. Seers (eds), *Pioneers in Development*, Washington, DC: World Bank, pp. 175–191.

Prebisch, R. (1986), 'Notes on trade from the standpoint of the periphery,' *CEPAL Review*, (28), 203–214.

Prebisch, R. (1992), *Raúl Prebisch: Obras (1919–1948)*, Vols I, II, and III, Buenos Aires: Fundación Raúl Prebisch.

Prebisch, R. (1993), *Raúl Prebisch: Obras 1919–1949*, Vol. IV, Buenos Aires: Fundación Raúl Prebisch.

Rodríguez, O. (2006), *El Estructuralismo Latinoamericano*, México: Siglo XXI.

Rowthorn, B. (1981), 'Demand, real wages and economic growth,' Thames Papers in Political Economy, Autumn.

Satia, P. (2018), *Empire of Guns: The Violent Making of the Industrial Revolution*, New York: Penguin.

Serrano, F. (1995), 'Long period effective demand and the Sraffian supermultiplier,' *Contributions to Political Economy*, 14, 67–90.

Shonfield, A. (1965), *Modern Capitalism*, Oxford: Oxford University Press.

Slobodian, Q. (2018), *Globalists: The End of Empire and the Birth of Neoliberalism*, Cambridge, MA: Harvard University Press.

Streeck, W. (2010), 'E Pluribus Unum? Varieties and commonalities of capitalism,' MPIfG Discussion Paper 10/12.

Sunkel, O. and P. Paz (1970), *El subdesarrollo latinoamericano y la teoría del desarrollo*, México: Siglo XXI.

Tilly, C. (1975), 'Reflections on the history of European state making,' in C. Tilly (ed.), *The Formation of National States in Western Europe*, Princeton, NJ: Princeton University Press, pp. 3–83.

Toye, J. and R. Toye (2003), 'The origin and interpretation of the Prebisch–Singer thesis,' *History of Political Economy*, 35(3), 437–467.

Triffin, R. (1947a), 'Monetary and banking reform in Paraguay,' Washington, DC: Board of Governors of the Federal Reserve System.

Triffin, R. (1947b), 'National central banking and the international economy,' in L. Metzler, R. Triffin, and G. Haberler (eds), *International Monetary Policies*, Post War Economic Studies, Washington, DC: Board of Governors of the Federal Reserve System, pp. 49–76.

Triffin, R. (1981), 'An economist's career: What? Why? How?,' *Banca Nazionale del Lavoro Quarterly Review*, 138(3), 239–259.

UNCTAD (1964), *Proceedings of the United Nations Conference on Trade and Development Geneva, 23 March–16 June 1964, Volume I: Final Act and Report; Volume II: Policy Statements*, UNCTAD.

Vernengo, M. (2015), 'Una lectura crítica de la crítica al modelo de Thirlwall,' *Investigación Económica*, LXXIV(292), 67–80.

Vernengo, M. (2021), 'The consolidation of dollar hegemony after the collapse of Bretton Woods: bringing power back in,' *Review of Political Economy*, 33(4), 529–551.

Vernengo, M. (2022), 'Más Allá de la Economía Vulgar: Maria da Conceição Tavares y la Economía Heterodoxa,' in J. Odísio and M. Rougier (eds), *Pioneros del Desarrollo Económico Latinoamericano*, Bogotá and Santander: Universidad del Rosario and Universidad de Cantabria, forthcoming.

Wallerstein, I. (1974), 'Dependence in an interdependent world: the limited possibilities of transformation within the capitalist world economy,' *African Studies Review*, 17(1), 1–26.

Wallich, H.C. and R. Triffin (1953), 'Monetary and banking legislation of the Dominican Republic 1947 with reports and letter of transmittal,' Federal Reserve Bank of New York.

Weber, M. (1927 [1981]), *General Economic History*, London: Routledge.

                         Journal compilation © 2022 Edward Elgar Publishing Ltd

Review of Keynesian Economics, Vol. 10 No. 2, Summer 2022, pp. 136–162

Varieties and interdependencies of demand and growth regimes in finance-dominated capitalism: a Post-Keynesian two-country stock–flow consistent simulation approach

Franz Prante*
Berlin School of Economics and Law, Institute for International Political Economy (IPE) and Institute for Socio-Economics, University of Duisburg-Essen, Germany

Eckhard Hein
Berlin School of Economics and Law, Institute for International Political Economy (IPE), Germany

Alessandro Bramucci
Berlin School of Economics and Law, Institute for International Political Economy (IPE), Germany

The authors outline and simulate a stylized Post-Keynesian two-country stock–flow consistent model to demonstrate the interconnection of three of the main features/outcomes of finance-dominated capitalism, namely worsening income distribution for the bottom 90 per cent of households, the rise of international imbalances, and the build-up of financial fragility. In the model, two basic regimes emerge, depending on the institutional setting of the respective model economy: the debt-led private demand boom regime and the export-led mercantilist regime. The authors demonstrate the complementarity and interdependence of these two regimes and show how this constellation transformed after a crisis into the domestic demand-led regime stabilized by government deficits, on the one hand, and export-led mercantilist regimes, on the other, depending on the required deleveraging of private household debt, distributional developments and fiscal policy.

Keywords: *Post-Keynesian macroeconomics, financialization, growth regimes, institutions, inequality, debt, stock–flow consistent model*

JEL codes: *B59, E02, E11, E12, E25, E65, F41, O41*

1 INTRODUCTION

Post-Keynesian research has made extensive use of the notion of demand-led macroeconomic regimes. This has been particularly true for Post-Kaleckian distribution and growth models, following the seminal work by Bhaduri and Marglin (1990) and Kurz (1990), which has also recently been introduced into the debate on Varieties of Capitalism in Comparative Political Economy (CPE) (Baccaro and Pontusson 2016; 2018). In contrast to the initial Neo-Kaleckian distribution and growth models of Dutt (1984; 1987) and Rowthorn (1981), Bhaduri and Marglin (1990) and Kurz (1990) showed that in a Kaleckian-based demand-led growth model, wage- as well as profit-led

---

* *Corresponding author:* Franz Prante, University of Duisburg-Essen, Lotharstr. 65, 47057 Duisburg, Germany; email: franz.prante@uni-due.de.

Journal compilation © 2022 Edward Elgar Publishing Ltd
The Lypiatts, 15 Lansdown Road, Cheltenham, Glos GL50 2JA, UK
and The William Pratt House, 9 Dewey Court, Northampton MA 01060-3815, USA

regimes may emerge, depending in particular on the specification of the investment function (see Blecker and Setterfield 2020, ch. 4; Hein 2014, chs 6–7; Lavoie 2014, ch. 6). Previously, Blecker (1989) had also shown that a domestically wage-led demand and growth regime may turn profit-led through the effects of redistribution on net exports. These basic theoretical models have triggered rich econometric work by trying to identify the dominating regime in different countries (and time periods).[1]

To clarify some misunderstandings in the CPE reception of the Post-Kaleckian approach, identifying a country as wage-led or profit-led only provides information on the demand and growth effects of changes in the wage share (and the profit share, of course). It does not imply that in a wage-led demand and growth regime pro-labour distribution policies are necessarily applied, or that in a profit-led demand and growth regime pro-capital policies will dominate (Lavoie and Stockhammer 2013). Therefore, this regime distinction only provides some basic information on the effects of functional redistribution on demand and growth, but no indication yet on the sources and drivers of growth in certain countries during certain periods.

The latter have been the focus of research on the macroeconomics of financialization, or of finance-dominated capitalism, which has generated the notion of macroeconomic regimes in finance-dominated capitalism (Hein 2012; Stockhammer 2015). This was meant to distinguish different ways countries have tried to cope with the depressive macroeconomic effects of financialization and the regressive redistribution of income (that is, falling labour income shares, rising wage dispersion, and rising inequality in the distribution of household income), with negative effects on income-financed consumption, as well as depressed investment in the real capital stock caused by the increasing shareholder value orientation of non-financial corporations' management, in particular. Looking at the growth contributions of the main demand aggregates (private consumption, public consumption, investment, and net exports), as well as the financial balances of the main macroeconomic sectors (external, public, private household, corporations), the focus has been on the sources of GDP growth and the way expenditures have been financed (that is, by income or credit). The two extreme and opposed regimes that have been derived for the period before the global financial crisis (GFC) and the following Great Recession (GR) of 2007–2009, were the 'debt-led private demand boom' (DLPD) regime and the 'export-led mercantilist' (ELM) regime. The former relies on debt-financed private (consumption) demand as the main source of demand and growth and may lead to rising private household debt–income ratios. The latter relies on foreign demand and may lead to rising indebtedness of the foreign sectors (see, for example, Dodig et al. 2016; Hein 2012; 2019).

Linking the research on wage-led vs profit-led demand and growth regimes with the research on macroeconomic regimes in finance-dominated capitalism, it should be clear that certain countries may be wage-led, and may then be dominated by either a DLPD regime or an ELM regime, in order to cope with the depressive demand and growth effects imposed by redistribution at the expense of labour.

Recently, the Post-Keynesian/Kaleckian demand-led regime approaches have resonated in the CPE literature (Baccaro and Pontusson 2016; 2018; Hope and Soskice 2016). In an attempt at overcoming the implications of New Consensus Macroeconomics (NCM)

---

1.   For empirical results, see the general overview in Hein (2014, ch. 7), and in Jimenez (2020) for emerging capitalist economies. For recent multi-country studies, see Hartwig (2014), Onaran and Galanis (2014) and Onaran and Obst (2016). For clarifying discussions on why empirical results generated by different empirical models and methods differ, see Blecker (2016) and Stockhammer (2017).

as the supply-side-dominated macroeconomic backbone of much of the CPE research, in particular of the Varieties of Capitalism approach (Carlin and Soskice 2009; 2015; Hall and Soskice 2001; Hope and Soskice 2016), Baccaro and Pontusson (2016; 2018) have made use of the Post-Keynesian categories of demand-led macroeconomic regimes outlined above. However, they have not properly taken into account the important analytical distinction between wage-led/profit-led regimes on the one hand, and DLPD/ELM regimes on the other (Hein et al. 2021). Post-Keynesians have also provided attempts at linking their demand and growth regime approaches to the CPE literature on institutional varieties of capitalism or on welfare-state models in modern capitalism (Behringer and van Treeck 2018; 2019; Hein et al. 2021; Setterfield and Kim 2020; Stockhammer 2021; Stockhammer and Ali 2018).

Furthermore, a couple of years after the GFC and the GR, 2007–2009, as a result of the contradictory nature of finance-dominated capitalism, several Post-Keynesians started to analyse the shifts of demand and growth regimes (Akcay et al. 2021; Dodig et al. 2016; Dünhaupt and Hein 2019; Hein 2019; Hein and Martschin 2020; Hein et al. 2021). As argued in particular by Hein (2019), Hein and Martschin (2020) and Hein et al. (2021), the type of shift experienced in previous DLPD economies has depended on the requirement of private-sector deleveraging after the GFC, as well as on the ability and willingness to run deficit-financed and stabilizing fiscal policies. The institutional constraints imposed on national fiscal policies in the eurozone, the absence of relevant fiscal policies at the eurozone level, and the turn towards austerity policies when the eurozone crisis started in 2010 therefore explain to a large extent why European DLPD countries in particular turned ELM (or weakly export-led) after the GFC and the GR (Hein and Martschin 2020). Other pre-crisis DLPD countries, in particular the UK and the US, which were able to make use of expansionary deficit-financed fiscal policies, were in a position to compensate private deleveraging by rising public deficits, thus stabilizing aggregate demand in their countries and turning to a domestic demand-led (DDL) regime stabilized by public deficits (Hein 2019).

Kohler and Stockhammer (2021) have recently provided a more systematic cross-country analysis of the underlying growth drivers before and after the 2007–2009 crisis in 30 OECD countries. To explain the emergence of the different post-crisis regimes, they consider the requirements of deleveraging in the context of a financial boom–bust cycle, the role of fiscal policies, and the relevance of price and non-price competitiveness for exports. They find that the former two drivers have had a major role to play, whereas differences and changes in international price competitiveness have been overrated in some of the previous CPE literature on macroeconomic regimes. Furthermore, they abandon the regime distinction that was developed for the pre-crisis period, and rather focus on the distinction of the different growth drivers for the clustering of countries in the post-crisis period. Jungmann (2021) has extended and applied the growth-driver approach by Kohler and Stockhammer (2021) to a set of 19 emerging capitalist economies and has found mixed results.

Hein and Martschin (2021) have kept the typology for macroeconomic regimes in finance-dominated capitalism, based on the examination of growth contributions of demand aggregates and of sectoral financial balances. They link this approach with the Post-Keynesian notion of macroeconomic policy regimes developed and applied in the early 2000s (Fritsche et al. 2005; Herr and Kazandziska 2011; Hein and Truger 2005a; 2005b; 2009). The concept of a 'macroeconomic policy regime' has been used to assess international and intertemporal comparative differences in macroeconomic performances of countries or regions. It describes the set of monetary, fiscal, and wage or income policies, as well as their coordination and interaction, against the

                              Journal compilation © 2022 Edward Elgar Publishing Ltd

institutional background of a specific economy, including the degree of openness and the exchange-rate regime. This concept supposes that macroeconomic policies have not only short-run effects on economic performance, as in the NCM, but also long-run effects on output, income, employment, inflation, distribution and growth. These effects can be derived from Post-Keynesian macroeconomic models generating and considering a full macroeconomic policy mix (Arestis 2013; Hein and Stockhammer 2010; 2011), as an alternative to the one implied by the orthodox NCM. Applying indicators for the stances of monetary and fiscal policies, for wage policies and income distribution, and for price and non-price competitiveness, Hein and Martschin (2021) have shown for the four largest eurozone countries – France, Germany, Italy and Spain – how the country-specific macroeconomic policy regimes have supported the shift (or non-shift) of macroeconomic regimes from the pre- to the post-crisis period.

The remainder of the paper contributes to the literature on macroeconomic regimes in finance-dominated capitalism, focusing in particular on the factors that contributed to the regime shift after the 2007–2009 crisis and the related change in the growth drivers. While the previous analysis has been mainly conceptual and empirical in nature, we will make use of a dynamic equilibrium stock–flow consistent (SFC) macroeconomic simulation model, in which any component of demand can assume the role of the growth driver, depending on the time-specific structural and institutional conditions in the economy. This approach allows us to model the respective drivers of growth for the pre-crisis macroeconomic regimes, as well as the imbalances and instabilities, which have built up within these regimes before the 2007–2009 crisis. Furthermore, we can model the key drivers of regime changes after the crisis, which are related to the financial fragility built up in the pre-crisis period and the required deleveraging and credit restrictions in the course of the crisis and after, to the macroeconomic policy regime, that is, the stances of fiscal policy and income distribution, as well as to the changes in international price and non-price competitiveness.

Our analysis proceeds as follows. In Section 2 we present the structure of our model and the behaviour of the different sectors. In Section 3, we conduct a series of simulation exercises to illustrate stylized versions of the pre-crisis DLPD and ELM regimes. In Section 4, we illustrate post-crisis transitions of these two regimes. Section 5 concludes.

2   THE SFC SIMULATION MODEL

For the simulation, we make use of a stylized Neo-Kaleckian SFC growth model. By adopting an SFC framework in the tradition of Godley and Lavoie (2007), we ensure that our model tracks sectoral financial flows and stocks.[2] The demand and growth regimes emerging from the model will be connected to different patterns of financial balances. For example, in the DLPD regime, the financial sustainability of indebted households will be the focus, once their debt-to-income ratio exceeds a prudency threshold.

---

2.   Our approach is related to the SFC models by Belabed et al. (2017), Detzer (2018) and Kapeller and Schütz (2014), but clearly focuses on the change in growth drivers. The closed-economy model in Kapeller and Schütz (2014) and the three-country model in Belabed et al. (2017) do not address the changes in regimes in the course of and after the GFC and the GR. Detzer's (2018) model for an open economy touches upon this issue, but does not model the foreign economy.

This may then lead to constrained credit access and a disruption of the DLPD regime, with consequences for its trading partner, which will be a stylized ELM economy.

2.1   Aggregate output and income

We develop a two-country model, in which the two countries are linked via their trade relationship and the respective financial flows and emerging stocks. In the following, we only present the behavioural equations for the 'domestic' economy. The behavioural equations of the 'external' economy are defined in analogy to the domestic economy.

With constant prices in the goods market, for the domestic economy, aggregate real output, Y, is the sum of consumption, C, investment, I, government consumption, G, and net export demand, $X - M$.

$$Y = C + I + G + X - M \tag{1}$$

Since we assume constant labour productivity and fully elastic labour supply, with firms adjusting production to demand and with a constant price level, the model is fully demand-determined. Every component of aggregate demand in both countries is composed of an income-autonomous part and an income- or output-induced part, and can thus become a long-run driver of growth. From this it follows that no demand component will be marginalized, even if another demand component is the dominant driver of long-run growth.

The functional distribution of aggregate income between gross wages, W, and gross profits, P, is exogenously given by mark-up pricing, which in turn determines the aggregate wage share, ω. Government income is given by net taxes on wage and profit income, T, assuming a general net tax rate, τ.

$$Y = W + P \tag{2}$$

$$W = \omega Y \tag{3}$$

$$T = \tau Y \tag{4}$$

The balance-sheet matrix of our 'domestic' economy shown in Table 1 displays the internal structure of assets and liabilities for the five sectors, which are the household sector $(_h)$, the corporate sector $(_f)$, the government sector $(_g)$, the banking sector $(_b)$ and the external sector $(_{RoW})$. The external sector is of course the 'external' economy and its own internal accounting structure is completely analogous to the one of the domestic economy.

Following a distinction introduced into Kaleckian models by Dutt (2016), the household sector is divided between top 10 per cent income households, representing the fraction of households which earn manager salaries and distributed profits, and the bottom 90 per cent of the income distribution, which have only marginal (and therefore neglectable) profit incomes.[3]

Deposits of each sector, D_i, held in the domestic banking system are the only financial asset for the non-bank domestic sectors. Firms hold the capital stock and are

---

3.   For differential saving propensities of these groups in the US, see recently Mian et al. (2021).

Table 1   Balance-sheet matrix of domestic economy

	Households		Firms	Government	Banks	RoW	Sum
	Top 10% income	Bottom 90% income					
Deposits	$+D_{h1}$	$+D_{h2}$	$+D_f$	$+D_g$	$-D$		0
Loans	$-L_{h1}$	$-L_{h2}$	$-L_f$	$-L_g$	$+L$	$+NIIP_{RoW}$	0
Fixed capital			$+K$				$+K$
Net worth	$-V_{h1}$	$-V_{h2}$	$-V_f$	$-V_g$	$-V_b$	$-NIIP_{RoW}$	$-K$

themselves – only implicitly – owned by top income capitalist and manager households. The only financial liability for the non-bank domestic sectors are bank loans. Financial claims and liabilities between the domestic and the external economy are captured by the net international investment position of the external sector, $NIIP_{RoW}$, which may be positive if the domestic economy is a (persistent) deficit country, or negative, if the domestic economy is a (persistent) surplus country. Clearance of deposits and domestic and international loans takes place through the domestic banking sector. Each sector may obtain loans from banks, L_i, in order to finance its expenditures if the sector is in deficit. Each sector receives interest payments on its financial assets or pays interest on its outstanding loans. There is only one global interest rate, r, which is set by the monetary authority (we abstract from a banking mark-up). For simplicity, we abstract from aggregate downpayment rates of domestic loans and international credit. Instead, each sector will repay loans when it switches from a deficit to a surplus position.

2.2   The household sector

Capitalist and manager households earn high net wages/salaries, W_{h1}, and receive distributed profits, P_h, from firms. In contrast, worker households receive low net wages, W_{h2}. We take the wage share of the top 10 per cent, ω_{h1}, to be exogenous and determine the distribution of total net wage income between top 10 per cent and bottom 90 per cent households as follows:

$$W_{h1} = \omega_{h1}(1-\tau)W \tag{5}$$

$$W_{h2} = (1-\tau)W - W_{h1} = (1-\tau)(1-\omega_{h1})W. \tag{6}$$

Disposable income of households is therefore given by the sum of their factor incomes and net interest payments/receipts on their net wealth:

$$Y_{d_{h1}} = W_{h1} + P_d + r_{-1}V_{h1-1} \tag{7}$$

$$Y_{d_{h2}} = W_{h2} + r_{-1}V_{h2-1}. \tag{8}$$

Consumption of both household sectors is determined by autonomous consumption demand, $c_{a_{h1}}$, $c_{a_{h2}}$, by consumption from disposable income, with $c_{Y_{d_{h1}}}$ and $c_{Y_{d_{h2}}}$ denoting the respective propensities to spend out of income, and by wealth-based consumption from accumulated deposits, with the propensities $c_{V_{h1}}$, $c_{V_{h2}}$, respectively. Furthermore, the consumption function of the bottom 90 per cent households contains a relative income effect which is proportional to the consumption of top 10 per cent households.

The parameter α can be seen as representing emulation-type behaviours in consumption decisions, a complex phenomenon affected by sociocultural preferences, institutions, the (non-)provision of public goods (especially housing, education and healthcare), and the access to credit. It may thus be viewed as an indicator for the necessity to keep up in an increasingly unequal and competitive society, in which access to credit is easily provided. Changing financial norms and consumption emulation behaviour, including housing, are often linked to inequality and the rise in US household debt observed before the GFC and the GR (Barba and Pivetti 2009; Cynamon and Fazzari 2008; van Treeck 2014; 2015). In this sense, our consumption functions can be interpreted as also covering residential housing expenditures.

$$C_{h1} = c_{a_{h1}} + c_{Y_{d_{h1}}} Y_{d_{h1}} + c_{V_{h1}} D_{h1-1} \tag{9}$$

$$C_{h2} = c_{a_{h2}} + c_{Y_{d_{h2}}} Y_{d_{h2}} + c_{V_{h2}} D_{h2-1} + z\alpha C_{h1} \tag{10}$$

Aggregate consumption is the sum of top 10 per cent and bottom 90 per cent households' consumption:

$$C = C_{h1} + C_{h2}. \tag{11}$$

The propensity to consume from disposable income is assumed to be higher for the bottom 90 per cent households. Without the emulation effect, this means that redistribution in favour of top-income households would have negative effects on consumption demand. However, the relative income effect in the bottom 90 per cent consumption function may mitigate negative distributional effects on consumption, and even overcompensate it, generating what is called a 'seemingly profit-led' demand and growth regime (Hein and Prante 2020; Kapeller and Schütz 2015). If consumption emulation leads to increasing indebtedness, a rising debt–income ratio of bottom 90 per cent households $(L_{h2}/Y_{d_{h2}})$ may exceed the acceptable ratio set by banks (l). Banks then stop lending to bottom 90 per cent households, putting a brake on emulation-driven consumption and triggering an economic downturn. In our simulations below, this constitutes the end of an increasingly fragile DLPD regime.[4]

2.3   The firm sector

Firms' net profits, P_{net}, are given by total profits net of taxes and interest payments/receipts. Net profits are partially saved by firms as retained earnings, P_f, according to the retention rate, s_f, while the rest is distributed to top 10 per cent households as distributed (net) profits, P_d.

$$P_{net} = (1-\tau)P - r_{-1}L_{f-1} + r_{-1}D_{f-1} \tag{12}$$

$$P_d = \begin{cases} P_{net} > 0: (1-s_f)P_{net} \\ \text{otherwise}: 0 \end{cases} \tag{13}$$

$$P_f = P_{net} - P_d \tag{14}$$

4.   The parameter z in the consumption function of bottom 90 per cent households works as a switch parameter. When $L_{h2}/Y_{d_{h2}}$ exceeds l, z assumes the value of zero (one otherwise).

Firms' gross investment, I, into the capital stock, K, in excess of (accumulated) retained earnings can be financed with additional loans provided by the banking sector. We adopt a Neo-Kaleckian investment function (Hein 2014, ch. 6), in which firms' decisions about the rate of gross capital accumulation depend on animal spirits, the rate of economic activity, and the capital scrapping rate.[5] The level of gross investment is determined by two terms: The first term, representing animal spirits and other non-output-induced determinants of investment (for example, innovations, policy-determined investment by state-owned firms, etc.) is the product of the autonomous investment rate, a_a, and the previous period's capital stock, K_{-1}. The second term represents the output-induced component of investment, where a_Y is the propensity to invest and v is the exogenous capital–potential-output ratio, which is technologically determined.

$$I = a_a K_{-1} + a_Y v Y \tag{15}$$

The capital stock is affected by capital scrapping, with δ denoting the capital scrapping rate. The capital stock therefore develops according to the following equation:

$$K = K_{-1} + I - \delta K_{-1}. \tag{16}$$

Full capacity output is determined by the stock of capital and the technologically determined capital–potential-output ratio, v:

$$u = \frac{Y}{Y_{fc}} \tag{17}$$

$$Y_{fc} = \frac{K_{-1}}{v}. \tag{18}$$

2.4   The government sector

Focusing on the role of the government in determining aggregate demand and growth, we assume that the government finances its demand for goods and services, as well as its interest payments on outstanding loans, by net tax revenues, T, and by additional bank loans. Government consumption demand, G, is partially exogenous. We also include an induced component, where σ denotes the government's propensity to demand goods and services from tax revenue.

$$G = G_A + \sigma T \tag{19}$$

This simplistic 'fiscal policy rule' resembles the set-up in Brochier and Macedo e Silva (2019). As in their model, this implies a short-run pro-cyclical fiscal rule. However, different from Brochier and Macedo e Silva (2019), we allow for a growing trend of autonomous and deficit-financed government expenditures. Government expenditures may thus become a deficit-financed growth driver.

---

5.   Instead of using a Post-Kaleckian Bhaduri–Marglin (1990) type of investment function, we deliberately rely on a Neo-Kaleckian investment function which does not allow for profit-led growth through the investment channel. Our aim in the scenarios below is to show how, for principally wage-led economies, negative effects of redistribution have been overcompensated by other growth drivers.

2.5   Trade and the external sector

For the illustration of the simultaneous emergence of the DLPD and the ELM regime, we do need both the domestic and the external economy to be endogenously affected by the developments in their counterparts. Therefore, we assume a two-country model in which the external economy is an exact structural replication of the domestic economy. This modelling choice also ensures that neither the external economy nor the domestic economy is marginalized in size over time when growth in the model is dominated by the growth of one of the domestic or external demand components.

The two economies are linked via the trade equations. For both economies, the import rate (the level of imports normalized by the capital stock) is determined by domestic demand, represented by the rate of capacity utilization, and by a price-competitiveness term, represented by the real exchange rate, e_r, where an increase in e_r implies a real depreciation of the domestic economy and has a negative effect on net exports, provided that the Marshall–Lerner condition holds. Following the trade equations in Rezai (2011) and von Arnim et al. (2014), the levels of imports, exports, and net exports from the perspective of the domestic economy are determined as follows:

$$M = (\phi u - \psi e_r)K_{-1} \tag{20}$$

$$X = \left(\phi_x u_x - \psi_x \frac{1}{e_r} \right)K_{x,-1} \tag{21}$$

$$NX = X - M. \tag{22}$$

Note that the exports of the domestic economy, X, are the imports of the external economy, which carries the index x in all its parameters and variables. Non-price competitiveness affects the parameters of the import equations of both economies. In our simulation exercises below, we will use these parameters to reflect stylized competitiveness shocks.

The trade balances, together with international interest payments/receipts derived from the net international investment position, define the current account for both economies. In the event of a current-account deficit in the domestic economy, the external sector extends new credit to the domestic economy or repays outstanding credit previously extended by the domestic economy. In both cases, the domestic banking sector acts as a clearing system for international transactions.

2.6   The banking sector

The function of the domestic banking sector is to act as a simple clearing mechanism for the credit relations between the two countries. For example, if aggregate demand is persistently higher than aggregate income in the domestic economy, some of the non-bank sectors will start to demand loans from the banking sector, thereby balancing the external claims ($NIIP < 0$) against the domestic banking sector. As mentioned earlier, the banking sector may stop providing consumer credit to bottom 90 per cent households when they have exceeded a certain debt-to-income ratio threshold. Since we do not allow for interest-rate differentials, banks do not make any profits. The real interest rate, r, is set exogenously by an implicit central bank.

The transaction–flow matrix of the domestic economy is shown in Table 2. The financial balance of each sector is determined by the difference between income and

Table 2 Transaction–flow matrix of the domestic economy

| | Households | | Firms | | Government | Banks | RoW | Sum |
	Top 10% income	Bottom 90% income	Current	Capital				
Consumption	$-C_{h1}$	$-C_{h2}$	$+C$					0
Investment			$+I$	$-I$				0
Govt expenditure			$+G$		$-G$			0
Exports			$+X$				$-X$	0
Imports			$-M$				$+M$	0
Wages	$+W_{h1_{gross}}$	$+W_{h2_{gross}}$	$-W$					0
Taxes	$-T_{w_{h1}}$	$-T_{w_{h2}}$	$-T_p$		$+T$			0
Profits	$+P_d$		$-P_{net}$	$+P_f$				0
Int. payments on loans	$-r_{-1}L_{h1-1}$	$-r_{-1}L_{h2-1}$	$-r_{-1}L_{f-1}$		$-r_{-1}L_{g-1}$	$+r_{-1}L_{-1}$	$+r_{-1}NIIP_{RoW-1}$	0
Int. payments on deposits	$+r_{-1}D_{h1-1}$	$+r_{-1}D_{h2-1}$	$+r_{-1}D_{f-1}$		$+r_{-1}D_{g-1}$	$-r_{-1}D_{-1}$		0
Change in loans	$+\Delta L_{h1}$	$+\Delta L_{h2}$		$+\Delta L_f$	$+\Delta L_g$	$+\Delta L$	$-\Delta NIIP_{RoW-1}$	0
Change in deposits	$-\Delta D_{h1}$	$-\Delta D_{h2}$		$-\Delta D_f$	$-\Delta D_g$	$-\Delta D$		0

Journal compilation © 2022 Edward Elgar Publishing Ltd

Table 3   Global balance-sheet matrix with consolidated non-bank sectors

	Domestic economy			External economy			Sum
	Non-banks	Banks	NIIP	NIIP	Banks	Non-banks	
Deposits	$+D$	$-D$			$-D_x$	$+D_x$	0
Loans	$-L_{nb}$	$+L$	$+NIIP$	$+NIIP_x$	$+L_x$	$-L_{nbx}$	0
Fixed capital	$+K$					$+K_x$	$K + K_x$
Net worth	$-V$	0	$-NIIP$	$-NIIP_x$	0	$-V_x$	$-(K + K_x)$

Note: $L = L_{nb} + NIIP$ and $V = V_{h1} + V_{h2} + V_g + V_b + V_{ffin} + K + NIIP$, where V_{ffin} is firms' financial net worth.

expenditure flows and each sector's net worth is the cumulation of past financial balances, except for firms, which also hold the capital stock. To ensure stock–flow consistency, the sectoral flows must sum to zero.

Table 3 displays the balance sheet of the domestic and the external economy and shows the connection in the accounting structure of the two countries. Here we present the balance-sheet matrix of the two-country model with consolidated non-banks for both economies with an additional column for the net international investment positions (*NIIP*). For stock–flow consistency at the global (that is, two-country) level, total net worth must be equal to the overall capital stock.

3   THE EXTREME REGIMES BEFORE THE CRISIS AND ENDOGENOUSLY GENERATED FRAGILITIES

3.1   Simulation approach and baseline scenario

We now present a series of simulations that aim to provide stylized illustrations of some important characteristics of financialization in the pre-crisis period: falling wage shares and rising inequality, less regulated and less prudent credit markets, the simultaneous emergence of DLPD and ELM regimes, and the associated current-account imbalances (Hein 2012). We then illustrate how these regimes may end up in a crisis, and in a second step, we illustrate regime transitions in the post-crisis period.

For all scenarios, we assume an identical initial parameter constellation converging to the same steady-state baseline scenario. To derive the different demand and growth regimes, we impose a series of shocks to the steady-state baseline scenario. These shocks are related to the degree of financialization in the pre-crisis period, the timing of the crisis itself and the post-crisis transition period. Details on numerical parameter values for basesline and shocks, as well as the exact timing of the shocks are presented in Tables A1 and A2 in Appendix 2.[6]

Figure 1 shows the convergence to the baseline steady state with balanced current accounts, balanced government budgets, stable distribution, no emulation, and deficits only in the corporate sectors. Without emulation in the baseline, redistribution at the expense of the bottom 90 per cent would have depressive effects on the domestic and the foreign economy, meaning that both economies show wage-led

6.   Replication code for our simulations is available at https://github.com/franzprante/Prante-Hein-Bramucci-ROKE-2022.

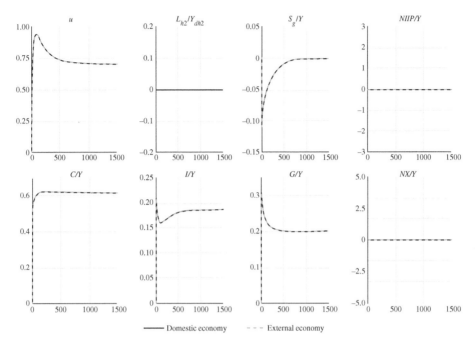

Figure 1   Convergence in the baseline scenario

aggregate demand. The steady-state growth rate of output ($\hat{Y}$) in the baseline converges to 1.63 per cent.

3.2   The DLPD and the ELM regimes in the pre-crisis period

Our first set of shocks then generates a stylized DLPD and ELM regime in a pre-crisis financialization phase. In the domestic economy, we combine a negative distributional shock to the aggregate wage share and a positive shock to the wage share of the top 10 per cent households with a shock to expenditure and financial norms of households and banks by increasing the 'emulation' term (α). At the same time, domestic banks are easing their assessment of the acceptable debt-to-income ratio of households, implying less prudent credit markets. This reflects the strong liberalization of the financial system in the era of financialization witnessed in the period leading up to the GFC, especially in some prominent DLPD economies, like the US. In broad terms, this shock can be interpreted as a consolidated 'financial cycle shock' (Borio 2014; Guttmann 2016; Kapeller and Schütz 2014; Kohler and Stockhammer 2021; Palley 2011), which encompasses the initial phase of the financial cycle, in which more credit becomes available, but also an intermediate phase of the financial cycle, in which Minskyan banks (and households) are lowering their credit standards, due to the perceived stability of high (credit-dependent) growth and seemingly stable economic conditions. Due to rising inequality with easy access to credit and falling saving rates of bottom 90 per cent households, the domestic economy turns to a DLPD regime.

For the external economy, we assume that the aggregate wage share falls while the wage share of top 10 per cent households remains constant. This is in line with the

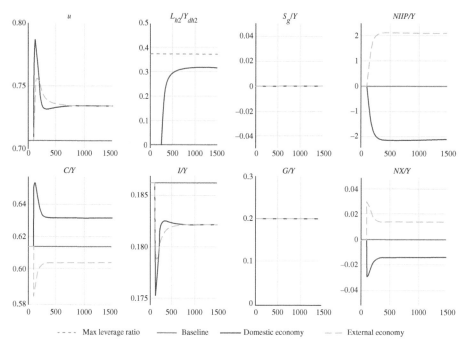

Figure 2   The initial financialization shock and the emergence of the DLPD regime and the ELM regime

more pronounced fall of the aggregate wage share associated with lower personal income inequality in prominent ELM countries, like Germany.[7] In addition, we assume that redistribution at the expense of labour leads to a real depreciation of the external economy's currency. The external economy in our model thus turns into an ELM regime.

Figure 2 shows the adjustment to the initial shocks. In the domestic economy, the share of consumption in output rises. Top 10 per cent households consume more due to the income gains and bottom 90 per cent households partially emulate the expenditures of the rich households, relying on credit finance and increasing their debt-to-income ratio. Capacity utilization in the domestic economy rises and a negative current account and trade balances emerge. The steady-state growth rate increases to 1.67 per cent.

In contrast to the DLPD regime, there is no increase in credit-financed consumption in the (now ELM) external economy which could offset the negative impulse triggered by redistribution.[8] Instead, the external economy needs to rely on the demand and

7.   Germany is a prominent example of an export-led country in the pre-crisis period. However, the export-led regime also arose under other distributional conditions. In China, for example, both the labour income share dropped and personal inequality rose dramatically (Belabed et al. 2017).

8.   In countries like Germany, institutions, financing norms, and more strictly regulated credit markets did not facilitate credit-financed consumption (Behringer and van Treeck 2019, Belabed et al. 2017, Detzer et al. 2017).

growth impulse from the DLPD economy. As a consequence, the external economy's trade and current account turn positive and the net international investment position vis-à-vis the domestic economy rises.

Overall, the financialization-induced increase of domestic spending on consumption has increased utilization in both economies and drives the growth rates of the system above the baseline growth rates. Credit-financed household expenditures in the DLPD economy and rising export demand in the external economy have therefore become the complementary growth drivers in the pre-crisis phase.

3.3 The crisis

In our simulation, the stylized measure of 'financial fragility' is the margin between the debt-to-income ratio of households and banks' acceptable ratio, l. In the course of the emergence of DLPD and ELM regimes, financial fragility in the system has strongly increased. By now, a minimal expansion of the credit-to-income ratio of domestic bottom 90 per cent households can drive the economy into crisis. An additional sequence of marginal distributional shocks to the detriment of the bottom 90 per cent households in the domestic economy (falling ω and rising ω_{h1}) now causes the debt ratio of bottom 90 per cent households to increase further and to eventually exceed the acceptable ratio of banks, which triggers an abrupt end to credit access, plunging the hitherto stable system into crisis (Figure 3). Domestic bottom 90 per cent households can no longer sustain their credit-financed consumption expenditures relative to top 10 per cent households, leading to a sharp decline in capacity utilization and abrupt deleveraging. As a result of the crisis, the financial cycle ends. Here, we assume that the acceptable debt-to-income ratio of banks and the emulation parameter of households both fall to zero, because banks and households become much more prudent.[9] Temporarily, the growth rate of output falls to negative territory and then converges to a lower positive level.

The crisis in the DLPD regime also causes a global decline in growth, exceeding in magnitude the positive growth impulse from the initial financialization shock. Declining domestic demand also leads to declining import demand relative to the external economy's demand for domestic goods and thus to an upward correction in the current-account and trade balances and in international indebtedness.

With the disappearance of credit-financed consumption as a driver of growth, the depressing effects of higher inequality become apparent in both economies. Falling rates of capacity utilization and a lower steady-state growth rate ($\hat{Y} = 1.52$ per cent) indicate the resulting stagnation tendency.

---

9.   Without this 'prudence shock', banks would allow credit access after the debt-to-income ratio drops below their threshold. This would create periodic boom–bust cycles in the model. By setting it to zero, we aim to illustrate a structural shift where the severity of the crisis led to a prolonged credit-supply shock and precautionary saving, similar to the situation after the the GFC and the GR. Of course, credit access and relative income effects could also partially or fully resume after a while, which would also allow for dampened periodic boom–bust cycles in the model. See Kapeller and Schütz (2014) for an elaborate theory of Minsky–Veblen cycles in a closed-economy SFC model.

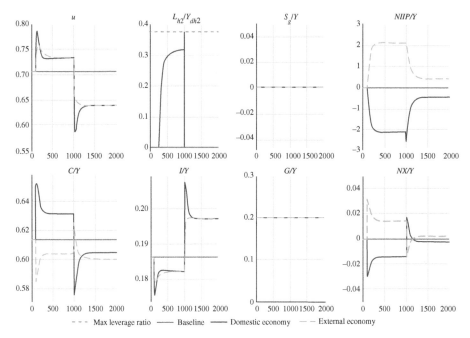

Figure 3 The debt-to-income ratio and utilization: a small additional distributional shock can bring the system to crisis

4 THE REGIMES EMERGING IN THE COURSE OF THE CRISIS AND AFTER, AND THE DRIVERS OF REGIME CHANGE

4.1 Regime changes and their drivers: deleveraging, fiscal policies, income distribution, and open-economy conditions

As pointed out in the introduction, some authors have examined the shift of regimes in the course of the 2007–2009 crisis. Focusing on developed capitalist economies, they have found that some of the DLPD countries have turned DDL stabilized by government deficits, whereas others have become ELM, and that some major ELM countries have maintained their regime.[10] Hein (2019) and Hein and Martschin (2020) have argued that the main drivers behind these regime changes have been the requirements to deleverage in the private household sectors and the ability and willingness to make use of compensatory deficit-financed fiscal policies. Hein et al. (2021) have argued that changes in the welfare models and related changes in income distribution have also played a role, and Hein and Martschin (2021) have insisted that the whole macroeconomic policy mix, including monetary, fiscal and wage/incomes policies, as well as open-economy conditions – that is, openness, price and non-price competitiveness – should be considered in order to explain the changes in regimes. Kohler and Stockhammer (2021) have abandoned the regime classification for the post-crisis period and focused instead on growth drivers, concluding that the post-crisis growth

10. For demand and growth regimes in emerging capitalist economies, the change in regimes, and respective growth drivers, see Akcay et al. (2021) and Jungmann (2021), for example.

                                    Journal compilation © 2022 Edward Elgar Publishing Ltd

performance can be explained by the downswing of the financial cycle – that is, the required deleveraging of the private household sector – and by fiscal policies. Regarding international competitiveness, they claim that it is non-price competitiveness that matters for growth, not price competitiveness.

In order to simulate the transition to the post-crisis regimes, we can now include several factors on which the above-mentioned literature has focused: the required deleveraging of private households related to pre-crisis indebtedness and changing prudential standards of the banking sector, fiscal policy responses, changes in functional and personal income distribution, changes in international price competitiveness related to changes in income distribution, and non-price competitiveness.

4.2   From DLPD to DDL, stabilized by government deficit expenditures

To generate a change from the DLPD to the DDL regime, stabilized by deficit-financed government expenditures, we assume that in the domestic economy, after the crisis and the deleveraging of bottom 90 per cent households, banks and households remain precautionary and prudent, and that both the emulation parameter and banks' accepted debt-to-income ratio remain at zero. A positive fiscal policy shock is employed to generate the regime shift from DLPD to DDL in the domestic economy.[11]

In our policy-shock scenario, fiscal policy in the domestic economy assumes a more expansionary role in response to the crisis. We model this as an increase in the propensity to spend out of tax income, meaning that the parameter σ in equation (19) rises above one. This implies that the government is persistently running fiscal deficits.

The expansionary fiscal policy shock generates a strong rebound of the rate of capacity utilization and steady-state growth ($\hat{Y} = 1.63$ per cent) after the crisis (Figure 4). However, the increase in domestic demand also leads to a renewed expansion of the trade and current-account imbalances, as we have assumed that the counterpart ELM foreign economy does not respond to the crisis with expansionary policies.

4.3   From DLPD to ELM

After the crisis, some DLPD countries moved towards an ELM regime, in particular in the eurozone, mainly because of the constraints imposed on deficit-financed fiscal policies. In such a scenario, domestic demand gets constrained by restrictive fiscal policy. We replace the shock from the previous section with a negative shock to the domestic governments' propensity to spend out of tax income, implying an austere fiscal policy regime. Domestic demand is also further constrained by another worsening of the income distribution with respect to bottom 90 per cent households, which we

---

11.   Monetary policy is not considered. In our simplified modelling framework, we assume only one global interest rate which only affects demand through consumption of households via disposable income. An interest-rate shock in such a setting can easily have counter-intuitive, and hence 'puzzling', macroeconomic effects (Lavoie 1995). After the crisis, both the domestic and the external consolidated household sectors are net creditors with positive interest income. A fall in the interest rate would therefore imply a redistribution of income away from households to firms, which have a much lower average propensity to spend and whose expenditure decisions are also not constrained by interest outlays in our framework.

                    Journal compilation © 2022 Edward Elgar Publishing Ltd

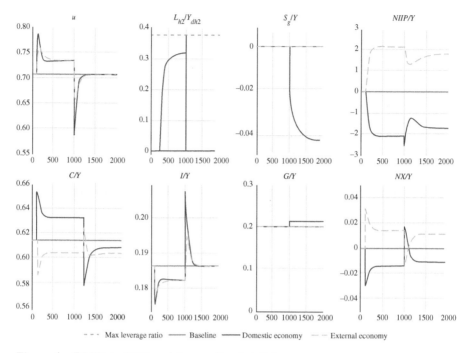

Figure 4   DLPD to DDL: relying on fiscal deficits

model with an additional small negative shock to the aggregate wage share and a small positive shock to the wage share of top 10 per cent households. As in the pre-crisis ELM regime, this distributional shock is paralleled with an improvement in price and non-price competitiveness. Finally, for a transition of the DLPD to an ELM regime, we need to assume that the external economy, a pre-crisis ELM country, now becomes a DDL economy driven by government deficit expenditures (σ_x rises above one). Figure 5 presents this scenario. The signs of the trade and current accounts switch for both economies. Different from all previous scenarios, the external economy now assumes the role of the driver of (low) growth ($\hat{Y} = 1.56$ per cent), imposing on the model the tendency toward stagnation as expected in this type of regime transition (Hein 2019; 2022).

5   CONCLUSIONS

In an attempt to contribute to the recent debate on growth models in the Post-Keynesian and CPE literature, we have outlined and simulated a basic Post-Keynesian two-country SFC model to demonstrate the interconnection of three of the main features/outcomes of finance-dominated capitalism, namely worsening income distribution for the bottom 90 per cent households, the rise of international imbalances, and the build-up of financial fragility. In the model, the baseline simulation has wage-led features. Shocking the model by changing distribution and introducing emulation in consumption, two basic regimes emerge, depending on the institutional setting of the respective model economy, the DLPD and the ELM regimes. We have demonstrated the complementarity and

                    Journal compilation © 2022 Edward Elgar Publishing Ltd

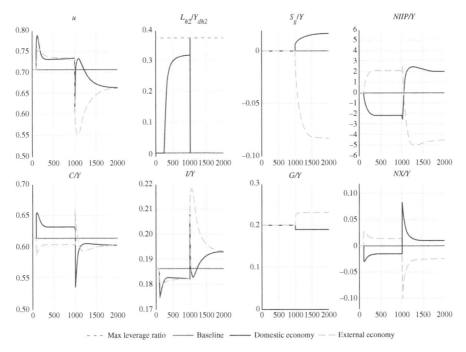

Figure 5   DLPD to ELM: relying on external demand

interdependence of these two regimes. Furthermore, we have shown how this constellation after the crisis transformed into the DDL regime, stabilized by government deficits, on the one hand, and the ELM regimes, on the other, depending on required deleveraging of private household debt, distributional developments, and fiscal policy. Of course, modelling the interconnection of the features of finance-dominated capitalism, as well as the complementarities and interdependencies of the pre- and post- 2007–2009 crisis regimes, some drastic simplifications had to be made to keep the model concise. For example, we have not modelled asset prices, and housing demand has been treated as part of household consumption. The financial cycle has thus been included in a very rudimentary way. And, as is often the case in SFC simulations models, we have to admit that simulation results are quite sensitive to the chosen parameter values. Nonetheless, we hope that this simple two-country model contributes to the understanding of the interconnectedness of the features of finance-dominated capitalism and the varieties, complementarities and interdependencies of the related demand and growth regimes.

ACKNOWLEDGEMENTS

This paper is part of the project 'WIPOSIM: The Economic Policy Online Simulator' funded by the Hans Boeckler Foundation, Düsseldorf, Germany. Previous versions have been presented at the Online Workshop of the Institute for International Political Economy (IPE) on 'Macroeconomic Regimes: Post-Keynesian and Critical Political Economy Perspectives', 25–26 March 2021, and at the WIPOSIM Online Workshop,

16 June 2021. We are most grateful to the participants for their comments. We would also like to thank Clare Hollins for editing assistance. Remaining errors are ours, of course.

REFERENCES

Akcay, Ü., E. Hein and B. Jungmann (2021), 'Financialisation and macroeconomic regimes in emerging capitalist economies before and after the Great Recession', Institute for International Political Economy (IPE), Berlin, IPE Working Paper 158/2021.

Arestis, P. (2013), 'Economic theory and policy: a coherent post-Keynesian approach', *European Journal of Economics and Economic Policies: Intervention*, 10(2), 243–255.

Baccaro, L. and J. Pontusson (2016), 'Rethinking comparative political economy: the growth model perspective', *Politics & Society*, 44(2), 175–207.

Baccaro, L. and J. Pontusson (2018), 'Comparative political economy and varieties of macroeconomics', Max Planck Institute for the Study of Societies, Cologne, MPIfG Discussion Paper 18/10.

Barba, A. and M. Pivetti (2009), 'Rising household debt: its causes and macroeconomic implications: a long-period analysis', *Cambridge Journal of Economics*, 33(1), 113–137.

Behringer, J. and T. van Treeck (2018), 'Varieties of Capitalism and growth regimes: the role of income distribution', Macroeconomic Policy Institute at the Hans-Böckler Foundation, Düsseldorf, IMK Working Paper 194/2018.

Behringer, J. and T. van Treeck (2019), 'Income distribution and growth models: a sectoral balances approach', *Politics & Society*, 47(3), 303–332.

Belabed, C.A., T. Theobald and T. van Treeck (2017), 'Income distribution and current account imbalances', *Cambridge Journal of Economics*, 42(1), 47–94.

Bhaduri, A. and S. Marglin (1990), 'Unemployment and the real wage: the economic basis for contesting political ideologies', *Cambridge Journal of Economics*, 14(4), 375–393.

Blecker, R.A. (1989), 'International competition, income distribution and economic growth', *Cambridge Journal of Economics*, 13(3), 395–412.

Blecker, R.A. (2016), 'Wage-led versus profit-led demand regimes: the long and the short of it', *Review of Keynesian Economics*, 4(3), 373–390.

Blecker, R.A. and M. Setterfield (2020), *Heterodox Macroeconomics: Models of Demand, Distribution and Growth*, Cheltenham, UK and Northampton, MA: Edward Elgar Publishing.

Borio, C. (2014), 'The financial cycle and macroeconomics: what have we learnt?', *Journal of Banking and Finance*, 45, 182–198.

Brochier, L. and A.C. Macedo e Silva (2019), 'A supermultiplier stock–flow consistent model: the "return" of the paradoxes of thrift and costs in the long run?', *Cambridge Journal of Economics*, 43(2), 413–442.

Carlin, W. and D. Soskice (2009), 'Teaching intermediate macroeconomics using the 3-equation model', in G. Fontana and M. Setterfield (eds), *Macroeconomic Theory and Macroeconomic Pedagogy*, London: Palgrave Macmillan, pp. 13–35.

Carlin, W. and D. Soskice (2015), *Macroeconomics: Institutions, Instability, and the Financial System*, Oxford: Oxford University Press.

Cynamon, B.Z. and S.M. Fazzari (2008), 'Household debt in the consumer age: source of growth – risk of collapse', *Capitalism and Society*, 3(2), 1–30.

Detzer, D. (2018), 'Inequality, emulation and debt: the occurrence of different growth regimes in the age of financialisation in a stock-flow consistent model', *Journal of Post Keynesian Economics*, 41(2), 284–315.

Detzer, D., N. Dodig, T. Evans, E. Hein, H. Herr and F.J. Prante (2017), *The German Financial System and the Financial and Economic Crisis*, Cham, Switzerland: Springer International Publishing.

Dodig, N., E. Hein and D. Detzer (2016), 'Financialisation and the financial and economic crises: theoretical framework and empirical analysis for 15 countries', in E. Hein, D. Detzer and N. Dodig (eds), *Financialisation and the Financial and Economic Crises: Country Studies*, Cheltenham, UK and Northampton, MA: Edward Elgar Publishing, pp. 1–41.

Dünhaupt, P. and E. Hein (2019), 'Financialisation, distribution, and macroeconomic regimes before and after the crisis: a post-Keynesian view on Denmark, Estonia, and Latvia', *Journal of Baltic Studies*, 50(4), 435–465.

Dutt, A.K. (1984), 'Stagnation, income distribution and monopoly power', *Cambridge Journal of Economics*, 8(1), 25–40.

Dutt, A.K. (1987), 'Alternative closures again: a comment on "Growth, distribution and inflation"', *Cambridge Journal of Economics*, 11(1), 75–82.

Dutt, A.K. (2016), 'Growth and distribution in heterodox models with managers and financiers', *Metroeconomica*, 67(2), 364–396.

Fritsche, U., M. Heine, H. Herr, G. Horn and C. Kaiser (2005), 'Macroeconomic regime and economic development: the case of the USA', in E. Hein, T. Niechoj, T. Schulten and A. Truger (eds), *Macroeconomic Policy Coordination in Europe and the Role of the Trade Unions*, Brussels: ETUI, pp. 69–107.

Godley, W. and M. Lavoie (2007), *Monetary Economics: An Integrated Approach to Credit, Money, Income, Production and Wealth*, London: Palgrave Macmillan.

Guttmann, R. (2016), *Finance-Led Capitalism: Shadow Banking, Re-Regulation and the Future of Global Markets*, New York: Palgrave Macmillan.

Hall, P.A. and D. Soskice (2001), *Varieties of Capitalism: The Institutional Foundations of Comparative Advantage*, Oxford: Oxford University Press.

Hartwig, J. (2014), 'Testing the Bhaduri–Marglin model with OECD panel data', *International Review of Applied Economics*, 28(4), 419–435.

Hein, E. (2012), *The Macroeconomics of Finance-Dominated Capitalism – And Its Crisis*, Cheltenham, UK and Northampton, MA: Edward Elgar Publishing.

Hein, E. (2014), *Distribution and Growth after Keynes: A Post-Keynesian Guide*, Cheltenham, UK and Northampton, MA: Edward Elgar Publishing.

Hein, E. (2019), 'Financialisation and tendencies towards stagnation: the role of macroeconomic regime changes in the course of and after the financial and economic crisis 2007–09', *Cambridge Journal of Economics*, 43(4), 975–999.

Hein, E. (2022), 'Financialisation and stagnation – a macroeconomic regime perspective', in F. Dantas and L.R. Wray (eds), *The Handbook of Stagnation*, Amsterdam: Elsevier, forthcoming.

Hein, E. and J. Martschin (2020), 'The Eurozone in crisis – a Kaleckian macroeconomic regime and policy perspective', *Review of Political Economy*, 32(4), 563–588.

Hein, E. and J. Martschin (2021), 'Demand and growth regimes in finance-dominated capitalism and the role of the macroeconomic policy regime: a post-Keynesian comparative study on France, Germany, Italy and Spain before and after the Great Financial Crisis and the Great Recession', *Review of Evolutionary Political Economy*, advanced access.

Hein, E. and F. Prante (2020), 'Functional distribution and wage inequality in recent Kaleckian growth models', in H. Bougrine and L.-P. Rochon (eds), *Economic Growth and Macroeconomic Stabilization Policies in Post-Keynesian Economics: Essays in Honour of Marc Lavoie and Mario Seccareccia*, Book Two, Cheltenham, UK and Northampton, MA: Edward Elgar Publishing, pp. 33–49.

Hein, E. and E. Stockhammer (2010), 'Macroeconomic policy mix, employment and inflation in a post-Keynesian alternative to the New Consensus Model', *Review of Political Economy*, 22(3), 317–354.

Hein, E. and E. Stockhammer (2011), 'A post-Keynesian macroeconomic model of inflation, distribution and employment', in E. Hein and E. Stockhammer (eds), *A Modern Guide to Keynesian Macroeconomics and Economic Policies*, Cheltenham, UK and Northampton, MA: Edward Elgar Publishing, pp. 112–136.

Hein, E. and A. Truger (2005a), 'A different view of Germany's stagnation', *Challenge*, 48(6), 64–94.

Hein, E. and A. Truger (2005b), 'What ever happened to Germany? Is the decline of the former European key currency country caused by structural sclerosis or by macroeconomic mismanagement?', *International Review of Applied Economics*, 19(1), 3–28.

Hein, E. and A. Truger (2009), 'How to fight (or not to fight) a slowdown', *Challenge*, 52(2), 52–75.

Hein, E., W. Paternesi-Meloni and P. Tridico (2021), 'Welfare models and demand-led growth regimes before and after the financial and economic crisis', *Review of International Political Economy*, 28(5), 1196–1223.

Herr, H. and M. Kazandziska (2011), *Macroeconomic Policy Regimes in Western Industrial Countries*, London: Routledge.

Hope, D. and D. Soskice (2016), 'Growth models, varieties of capitalism and macroeconomics', *Politics & Society*, 44(2), 209–226.

Jimenez, V. (2020), 'Wage shares and demand regimes in Central America: an empirical analysis for Costa Rica, El Salvador, Honduras, Nicaragua, and Panama, 1970–2016', Institute for International Political Economy (IPE), Berlin, IPE Working Paper 151/2020.

Jungmann, B. (2021), 'Growth drivers in emerging capitalist economies before and after the Global Financial Crisis', Institute for International Political Economy (IPE), Berlin, IPE Working Paper 172/2021.

Kapeller, J. and B. Schütz (2014), 'Debt, boom, bust: a theory of Minsky–Veblen cycles', *Journal of Post Keynesian Economics*, 36(4), 781–814.

Kapeller, J. and B. Schütz (2015), 'Conspicuous consumption, inequality and debt', *Metroeconomica*, 66(1), 51–70.

Kohler, K. and E. Stockhammer (2021), 'Growing differently? Financial cycles, austerity, and competitiveness in growth models since the Global Financial Crisis', *Review of International Political Economy*, advance access.

Kurz, H.D. (1990), 'Technical change, growth and distribution: a steady-state approach to "unsteady" growth', in H.D. Kurz (ed.), *Capital, Distribution and Effective Demand*, Cambridge, UK: Polity Press, pp. 210–239.

Lavoie, M. (1995), 'Interest rates in post-Kaleckian models of growth and distribution', *Metroeconomica*, 46, 146–177.

Lavoie, M. (2014), *Post-Keynesian Economics: New Foundations*, Cheltenham UK and Northampton, MA: Edward Elgar Publishing.

Lavoie, M. and E. Stockhammer (2013), 'Wage-led growth: concept, theories and policies', in M. Lavoie and E. Stockhammer (eds), *Wage-Led Growth: An Equitable Strategy for Economic Recovery*, London: Palgrave Macmillan, pp. 13–39.

Mian, A., L. Straub and A. Sufi (2021), 'What explains the decline in r^*? Rising income inequality versus demographic shifts', Becker Friedman Institute for Economics, University of Chicago, Working Paper No 2021-104.

Onaran, Ö. and G. Galanis (2014), 'Income distribution and growth: a global model', *Environment and Planning*, 46(10), 2489–2513.

Onaran, Ö. and T. Obst (2016), 'Wage-led growth in the EU15 member-states: the effects of income distribution on growth, investment, trade balance and inflation', *Cambridge Journal of Economics*, 40(6), 1517–1551.

Palley, T.I. (2011), 'A theory of Minsky super-cycles and financial crises', *Contributions to Political Economy*, 30(1), 31–46.

Rezai, A. (2011), 'The political economy implications of general equilibrium analysis in open economy macro models', The New School for Social Research, Department of Economics, New York, Working Paper 11/2011.

Rowthorn, R.E. (1981), 'Demand, real wages and economic growth', Thames Papers in Political Economy, Autumn, No TP/PPE/81/3.

Setterfield, M. and Y. Kim (2020), 'Varieties of capitalism, increasing income inequality and the sustainability of long-run growth', *Cambridge Journal of Economics*, 44(3), 559–582.

Stockhammer, E. (2015), 'Rising inequality as a root cause of the present crisis', *Cambridge Journal of Economics*, 39(3), 935–958.

Stockhammer, E. (2017), 'Wage-led versus profit-led demand: what have we learned? A Kaleckian–Minskyan view', *Review of Keynesian Economics*, 5(1), 25–42.

Stockhammer, E. (2021), 'Post-Keynesian macroeconomic foundations for Comparative Poltical Economy', *Politics & Society*, 50(1), 156–187.

Stockhammer, E. and S.M. Ali (2018), 'Varieties of Capitalism and post-Keynesian economics on Euro crisis', *Wirtschaft und Gesellschaft*, 44(3), 349–370.

Van Treeck, T. (2014), 'Did inequality cause the US financial crisis?', *Journal of Economic Surveys*, 28(3), 421–448.

Van Treeck, T. (2015), 'Inequality, the crisis, and stagnation', *European Journal of Economics and Economic Policies: Intervention*, 12(2), 158–169.

Von Arnim, R., D. Tavani and L. Carvalho (2014), 'Redistribution in a Neo-Kaleckian two-country model', *Metroeconomica*, 65(3), 430–459.

APPENDIX 1 EXTENDED LIST OF MODEL EQUATIONS

A1.1 Output domestic economy

$$Y = C + I + G + X - M$$

A1.2 Income domestic economy

$$W = \omega Y$$

$$P = Y - W$$

$$T = \tau Y$$

$$T_{W_{h1}} = \tau W \omega_{h1}$$

$$T_{W_{h2}} = \tau W - T_{W_{h1}}$$

$$W_{h1_{gross}} = \omega_{h1} W$$

$$W_{h2_{gross}} = W - W_{h1_{gross}}$$

$$W_{h1} = (1 - \tau) W \omega_{h1}$$

$$W_{h2} = (1 - \tau) W - W_{h1}$$

$$T_P = \tau P$$

$$P_{net} = (1 - \tau) P - r_{-1} L_{f-1} + r_{-1} D_{f-1}$$

$$P_d = \begin{cases} P_{net} > 0 : (1 - s_f) P_{net} \\ \text{otherwise} : 0 \end{cases}$$

$$Y_{d_{h1}} = W_{h1} + P_d + r_{-1} V_{h1-1}$$

$$Y_{d_{h2}} = W_{h2} + r_{-1} V_{h2-1}$$

$$P_f = P_{net} - P_d$$

A1.3 Households domestic economy

$$C = C_{h1} + C_{h2}$$

$$c_{a_{h1}} = c_{a_{h1-1}} (1 + \widehat{c_{a_{h1}}})$$

$$C_{h1} = c_{a_{h1}} + c_{Y_{d_{h1}}} Y_{d_{h1}} + c_{D_{h1}} D_{h1-1}$$

          Journal compilation © 2022 Edward Elgar Publishing Ltd

$$z = \begin{cases} \dfrac{L_{h2}}{Y_{dh2}} < l: 1 \\ \text{otherwise: } 0 \end{cases}$$

$$c_{ah2} = c_{ah2-1}(1 + \widehat{c_{ah2}})$$

$$C_{h2} = c_{ah2} + c_{Y_{dh2}}Y_{dh2} + c_{D_{h2}}D_{h2-1} + z\alpha C_{h1}$$

$$S_{h1} = Y_{dh1} - C_{h1}$$

$$S_{h2} = Y_{dh2} - C_{h2}$$

$$V_{h1} = V_{h1-1} + S_{h1}$$

$$D_{h_1} = \begin{cases} V_{h1} > 0: V_{h1} \\ \text{otherwise: } 0 \end{cases}$$

$$L_{h_1} = \begin{cases} V_{h1} < 0: -V_{h1} \\ \text{otherwise: } 0 \end{cases}$$

$$V_{h2} = V_{h2-1} + S_{h2}$$

$$D_{h_2} = \begin{cases} V_{h2} > 0: V_{h2} \\ \text{otherwise: } 0 \end{cases}$$

$$L_{h_2} = \begin{cases} V_{h2} < 0: -V_{h2} \\ \text{otherwise: } 0 \end{cases}$$

A1.4   Firms domestic economy

$$I = a_a K_{-1} + a_Y v Y$$

$$S_f = P_f - I$$

$$K = K_{-1} - \delta K_{-1} + I$$

$$u = Y/Y_{fc}$$

$$Y_{fc} = K_{-1}/v$$

$$V_{ffin} = V_{ffin-1} + S_f$$

$$D_f = \begin{cases} V_{ffin} > 0: V_{ffin} \\ \text{otherwise: } 0 \end{cases}$$

$$L_f = \begin{cases} V_{ffin} < 0: -V_{ffin} \\ \text{otherwise: } 0 \end{cases}$$

$$V_f = V_{ffin} + K$$

A1.5   Government domestic economy

$$G_A = G_{A-1}\left(1 + \widehat{G_A}\right)$$

$$G = G_A + \sigma T$$

$$S_g = T - G + r_{-1}V_{g-1}$$

$$V_g = V_{g-1} + S_g$$

$$D_g = \begin{cases} V_g > 0: V_g \\ \text{otherwise: } 0 \end{cases}$$

$$L_g = \begin{cases} V_g < 0: -V_g \\ \text{otherwise: } 0 \end{cases}$$

A1.6   Trade current account and NIIP domestic economy

$$M = (\phi u - \psi e_r)K_{-1}$$

$$X = (\phi^x u^x - \psi^x / e_r)K^x_{-1}$$

$$NX = X - M$$

$$CA = NX + r_{-1}NIIP_{-1}$$

$$R_{CA} = r_{-1}NIIP_{-1}$$

$$NIIP = NIIP_{-1} + CA$$

A1.7   Banks domestic economy

$$L = L_{h1} + L_{h2} + L_f + L_g + NIIP$$

$$R_L = r_{-1}L_{-1}$$

$$D = D_{h1} + D_{h2} + D_f + D_g$$

$$R_D = r_{-1}D_{-1}$$

$$R = R_L - R_D$$

$$V_b = L - D$$

APPENDIX 2   BASELINE PARAMETER CONSTELLATION AND SHOCK SEQUENCES FOR SCENARIOS

Table A1   Baseline parameter constellation

Parameter	Description	Baseline for the domestic and external economy
a_a	Autonomous rate of investment	0.015
a_Y	Propensity to invest	0.016
$c_{a_{h1}}$ in $t = 0$	Autonomous consumption h_1	0.200
$\widehat{c_{a_{h1}}}$	Growth of $c_{a_{h2}}$	0.000
$c_{a_{h2}}$ in $t = 0$	Autonomous consumption h_2	0.200
$\widehat{c_{a_{h2}}}$	Growth of $c_{a_{h2}}$	0.000
$c_{V_{h1}}$	Propensity to consume out of wealth h_1	0.050
$c_{V_{h2}}$	Propensity to consume out of wealth h_2	0.015
$c_{Y_{d_{h1}}}$	Propensity to consume out of disposable income h_1	0.400
$c_{Y_{d_{h2}}}$	Propensity to consume from disposable income h_2	0.700
G_A in $t = 0$	Autonomous government demand	0.500
$\widehat{G_A}$	Growth of G_A	0.010
K in $t = 0$	Fixed capital stock	40.000
l	Banks' maximum acceptable leverage ratio for h_2	0.000
s_f	Firms' retention rate	0.300
V_f in $t = 0$	Firms' net worth	40.000
v	Capital–potential-output ratio	5.000
α	Consumption emulation parameter	0.000
δ	Capital scrapping rate	0.010
σ	Propensity to spend out of tax income	1.000
τ	General net tax rate	0.200
ϕ	Demand effect on imports	0.050
ψ	Price-competitiveness effect on imports	0.010
ω	Aggregate wage share	0.600
ω_{h1}	Wage share of h_1 households	0.200

(continues overleaf)

            Journal compilation © 2022 Edward Elgar Publishing Ltd

Table A1 (continued)

Parameter	Description	Baseline for the domestic and external economy
		Global
e_r	Real exchange rate	1.000
r	Real interest rate	0.010

Table A2   *Shock sequences for scenarios*

Description of shock and timing	Parameter	Domestic economy	External economy
(1) 'Pre-crisis financialization'	l	0.375	
($t = 100$)	α	0.290	
	ω	0.550	0.500
	ω_{h1}	0.300	
	e_r		0.900
(2) Small additional distributional change	ω	0.545	
($t = 1000$)	ω_{h1}	0.305	
(3) Within crisis 'prudence' shocks	l	0.000	
($t = 1009$)	α	0.000	
(4) Post-crisis fiscal deficits in domestic economy ($t = 1010$)	σ	1.080	
(5) DLPD to ELM	σ	0.970	1.150
($t = 1031$)	ϕ	0.040	0.060
	ψ	0.015	
	ω	0.500	
	ω_{h1}	0.250	
	e_r		1.000

Notes:
The table reports only the values of the shocked parameters. Other values remain as in the baseline.
Shock timing: $t = 0$ is the last period of the convergence phase of the baseline.
Combination of shock sequences from table for each scenario:
1. Pre-crisis debt-led and export-led growth (Figure 2): (1)
2. Pre-crisis debt-led and export-led growth with crisis (Figure 3): (1) + (2) + (3)
3. Post-crisis fiscal deficits in domestic economy (Figure 4): (1) + (2) + (3) + (4)
4. DLPD to ELM (Figure 5): (1) + (2) + (3) + (5)

                                    Journal compilation © 2022 Edward Elgar Publishing Ltd